# REENVISIONING
# THEOLOGICAL
# EDUCATION

# REENVISIONING THEOLOGICAL EDUCATION

*Exploring a Missional Alternative to Current Models*

ROBERT BANKS

William B. Eerdmans Publishing Company
Grand Rapids, Michigan / Cambridge, U.K.

© 1999 Wm. B. Eerdmans Publishing Co.
255 Jefferson Ave. S.E., Grand Rapids, Michigan 49503 /
P.O. Box 163, Cambridge CB3 9PU U.K.

Printed in the United States of America

04 03 02 01 00 99      7 6 5 4 3 2 1

**Library of Congress Cataloging-in-Publication Data**

Banks, Robert J.
Reenvisioning theological education: exploring a missional
alternative to current models / Robert Banks
p.      cm.
Includes bibliographical references.
ISBN 0-8028-4620-3 (pbk.: alk. paper)
1. Theology — Study and teaching — United States.   I. Title.
BV4030.B36   1999
230′.071′1 — dc21                              99-32101
CIP

# Contents

## PART ONE
## REASSESSING THEOLOGICAL EDUCATION:
## THE PRESENT STAGE OF DEBATE

CONTENTS

PART TWO
BACKING INTO THE FUTURE:
A BIBLICAL ANGLE OF VISION

# Contents

## PART THREE
## DEVELOPING A MISSIONAL MODEL:
## FROM THE MARGINS TO THE CENTER

CONTENTS

## Contents

## CONCLUSION

# Acknowledgments

I would like to express my thanks to a number of people with whom I had early conversations about this project. In particular I am grateful to Barbara Wheeler and Robert Reber, of Auburn Theological Seminary, during a sabbatical on the East Coast. Also to John Drane, of Stirling University, during his time on the West Coast and at his home in Scotland.

I also appreciate the discussions of various groups who read or heard some of this material. These include a Practical Theology Doctoral Seminar, Restaurant Theology Group, the Ministry Division and School of Theology at Fuller Theological Seminary, a Lilly Endowment–funded Seminar on Evangelical Approaches to Theological Education involving a range of scholars from around the country, and the New Testament Postgraduate Seminar at the Department of Theology in Durham University.

I am also grateful to individuals from my own and other theological institutions who looked at the whole manuscript and commented on it. Thanks here to Ray Anderson, William Dyrness, and Rob Johnston of the School of Theology at Fuller Theological Seminary, to Charles Van Engen of its School of World Mission, and to Linda Cannell and R. Paul Stevens of Trinity Evangelical Divinity School and Regent College, Vancouver, respectively. Thanks also to Dieter Kemmler of the Evangelischer Seminar, Aarau, Switzerland, and to Stephen Barton of the Department of Theology, Durham University, UK, for critiquing the biblical section in detail.

# ACKNOWLEDGMENTS

In addition I would like to thank Chuck Metteer, one of my doctoral students, for creating the index; my research assistant, Simon Holt, who worked carefully through the material detecting and correcting errors; as well as Susan Wood, Terry Larm, and Alex Pak, who turned my inadequate word processing efforts into an excellent manuscript.

*Pasadena*                                                           Robert Banks
*August 1998*

# Introduction

If institutional reality could be remade to heart's desire, what would the ideal theological school look like?

DAVID KELSEY[1]

In my early twenties, shortly after I had graduated from an evangelical Episcopal theological institution, one of the professors asked me whether I had any suggestions for improving what took place there. My experience of seminary was mainly positive. I was introduced to the Bible in a compelling way and came away with a detailed and organic understanding of its contents. At their best, courses were theologically demanding and provocative. Since it was a residential college, there was an emphasis on community, and over my three and a half years' stay I made several lifelong friends, one of whom was on the faculty. Spirituality was important, manifesting itself in daily corporate worship and weekly small groups, as well as in numerous informal settings. Since we had to spend twelve hours each week interning in a local church — leading worship services, teaching and preaching regularly, starting and running groups, doing pastoral visiting and counseling — we gained a wide range of practical experience. I did

1. David Kelsey, *To Understand God Truly: What's Theological About a Theological School?* (Louisville: Westminster/John Knox, 1992), pp. 13-14.

make some minor recommendations in response to the question. Not all the lecturers were of the same standard. Some sermons and classes were better than others at presenting implications for ministry. There were restrictions on how often you could get together with friends and fiancees inside or outside the college. Supervision of our weekend ministries varied in quality. But on the whole there was not much I wanted to change. My sense was that those who taught there had largely gotten it right.

Within a couple of years, however, my view had changed, partly as a result of engaging in pastoral ministry in a large city church, and partly as a result of starting to rethink what church and ministry were all about in the light of biblical perspectives and contemporary challenges. I began to realize that my theological education had required me to learn too much too soon. Its pressurized approach had left too little time to think through and evaluate some of the views our teachers had expressed, or to work out how and where to put them into practice in an effective way. By my early thirties, after more extensive and demanding pastoral experience, as well as serious investigation of authentic ministry and church life, my questions about the best forms of theological education had sharpened and increased. Central to my concern now was a broader approach to theological education that included thoughtful lay people. Around the edges of postdoctoral work and then university teaching, I began to explore more nonformal and informal ways of doing this combined with elements of a more traditional approach. In a sense, I was rediscovering an earlier mode of theological education in which a student spent significant time with a mentor, learning from him or her both theological content and ministry skills.

In my early forties I moved out of academia into a more flexible form of ministry that combined teaching and doing. Although I taught occasionally at a small local seminary, one that was more progressive in its approach to spiritual and vocational formation, and led adult education courses under university auspices for anyone who was religiously open, these were not at the center of my efforts in theological education. On the one hand I initiated a project in nonformal theological education through meeting regularly over several years with marketplace believers in their workplaces as we addressed issues they were facing in a practical theological way. This happened with a number of occupational groups. On the other hand, a few people began to look for an alternative to seminary education, which they regarded as too oriented to pastoral ministry for their lay needs and too focused on cognitive learning at the expense of personal development and practical experience. Out of this grew an experiment involving a group operating largely as a cohort, committing themselves to gaining a basic theological education, and seeking to combine and where possible integrate intellectual, spiritual, and practical formation. In this group we learned together in a highly participatory way, fellowshiped and worshiped together in smaller and larger groups, and undertook ministry as a team in various church, nonprofit, and marketplace settings.

Over the last ten years, somewhat to my surprise, I found myself drawn full-time into a large seminary setting. The ongoing challenge here, in a place that was mostly conducive to flexibility, change, and innovation, was how to translate what I had valued out of these nonformal, sometimes experimental approaches to theological education into a larger, more structured setting. Also, how to help that institution as a whole move more in some of these directions so that it remained on the leading edge of theological education in the face of new circumstances and an increasingly diverse constituency. Everyone who teaches theology has a picture of what theological education ideally should involve. This book contains mine. But I do not set this out idealistically; I talk about concrete ways it can be realized. It is therefore a blend of theory and practice, of theology and strategy, of ideas and recommendations. Indeed it challenges not only the separating of these different modes, but delineates some of the attempts in the debate on theological education to bring them together. For, as someone said years ago, there is nothing more practical than good theory; every effective course of action contains a theoretical dimension. Why write yet another book about theological education when there are more than enough books on the subject already? I have done so for the following reasons.

- Though what I have to say overlaps at points with proposals advanced in the debate, I offer a model that is in some respects different and, I believe, more consistently Christian. The model has its roots in a biblical perspective on formation for ministry, a perspective largely overlooked in the current discussion.
- I also seek to be more practical than most of the contributors to the debate, providing a wide range of recommendations for theo-

logical institutions. Although some of these are challenging, I do take into account the realities of institutional life and in part draw on or extend some proven experiments.

- Though I focus mainly on seminaries, at points I have broadened the discussion to include Bible institutes and mission schools, as well as lay theological centers and programs. This is in keeping with the desire to break out of the standard clerical or professional paradigm of theological education.

## A. The Changing Theological Education Scene Today

Wherever we look today, especially in the West, theological education presents a confusing picture. In part it is a going concern, in part it is going through culture shock, and in part it is undergoing a painful transition. Institutionally we are watching the continued growth of interdenominational and now newer charismatic schools at the expense of mainline and confessional ones. While theological education caters to a wide audience, and the number of lay participants is increasing, so far this has had little impact on its content and pedagogy. As students become older, less mobile, and more part-time, extension centers and distance learning have become more important. Though women and minorities are growing in numbers, they remain underrepresented among faculty, students, and administrators.

### 1. Theological Seminaries and Divinity Schools

In North America more than 275 institutions have affiliated with the Association of Theological Schools.[2] Alongside these, there are several times as many Bible institutes, training schools, and lay theological centers, as well as some substantive parachurch or church-based ventures in theological education. About two-thirds of seminaries are Protestant, one-quarter Catholic, and the remainder Orthodox or

2. On most of what is contained in this and the following paragraph see Barbara G. Wheeler, K. Schuth, and L. W. Raphael, "Theological Education," *Encyclopedia for Educational Research,* ed. M. C. Alkin, 6th ed. (1992), vol. 4, pp. 1422-27, and the more recent survey by Ellis L. Larsen, "A Profile of Contemporary Seminarians Revisited," *Theological Education,* Supplement 1 (1995).

Pentecostal.[3] Five out of six seminaries or divinity schools have a denominational base. While the largest of these institutions has several thousand students, and the smallest only a handful, the average seminary has approximately three hundred students and fifteen faculty. Overall, the number of full-time students is declining, partly because of demographic patterns, partly because of changing student profiles and work patterns, and partly because of the growing number of alternative programs available. In seminaries, more than a third of younger students, and well over half of older students, live off-campus, with higher proportions in some interdenominational seminaries. Though extension centers and distance-learning programs are increasing in numbers, in many places declining enrollments and lower finances are forcing the closure or merger of some older denominational schools.

According to the latest figures, approximately two-thirds of students are male and one-third are female (a figure affected by restriction of the Catholic priesthood to men), though in some mainline theological institutions women make up around 50 percent of the student population. Three quarters of students are white; of the remainder about 9 percent are African-American, nearly 5 percent Asian, and almost 3 percent Hispanic, figures that are not yet fully representative of the population overall. In ATS-affiliated institutions generally, only a fifth of all students now come straight from college: three-fifths are over thirty and this percentage is increasing. About half the student body are married, 40 percent are single, and the remainder are divorced or widowed. Most students work part-time in a church, and many, including some taking a full load of subjects, have an additional part-time job. Overall the proportion of students taking a full load is decreasing in favor of part-time study.

Ecclesiastically, seminaries exhibit many differences. Some belong to mainline or confessional denominations, while others represent evangelical, ethnic, and Pentecostal traditions. There are also many contextual differences. In varying degrees they differ in structure, locale, clientele, curriculum, and ethos, as does their relationship

3. For background on the first of these, globally viewed, see D. G. Hart and R. Albert Mohler, Jr., eds., *Theological Education in the Evangelical Tradition* (Grand Rapids: Baker, 1996); and, for the second, Joseph W. White, *The Diocesan Seminary in the United States: A History from 1980 to the Present* (Notre Dame: University of Notre Dame Press, 1989).

with the church and the academy. This is even more the case with institutions that contain a school of mission, programs for Christian professionals, or an accredited lay ministry curriculum. For all their theological differences, it is as much these contextual factors that distinguish theological institutions from one another.[4] Their main goals may differ — for example, evangelizing and founding churches, providing a basic knowledge of the Christian tradition, seeking personal and social transformation — but seminal figures in their development often affect their ethos more than theological distinctives. Their ideal of community — some view themselves primarily as a form of the church, others more as academic institutions or training centers — has more to do with institutional traditions and reward systems than with explicit theological convictions.

For all their theological differences, seminaries tend to have more in common than appears to be the case.[5] For example, with few exceptions they all recruit formally qualified faculty, use critical methodologies, and value academic accreditation. Most still tend to view pastoral ministry as a profession, and provide training in relevant skills. Only rarely do they question the dominant schooling paradigm by which they fashion their lives. Seminaries have often adopted secular models of education, rather than subject them to rigorous theological or practical evaluation:[6] even where such questioning takes place, it often parallels what is taking place in higher education or training for the

4. On some of this see George Marsden, *The Soul of the American University* (New York: Oxford University Press, 1994); see also Jaroslav Pelikan, *The Idea of the University: A Re-Examination* (New Haven: Yale University Press, 1991), as well as Marsden's review of this, "Christian Schooling: Beyond the Multiversity," *Christian Century* (7 October 1992): 873-75.

5. On much, though not all, of what follows, see David Kelsey, *To Understand God Truly*, pp. 30-61.

6. The foundation for this set of assumptions can be traced back to William Rainey Harper, "Shall the Theological Curriculum Be Modified and How," *The American Journal of Theology* 3 (1) (January 1899): 45-66; Robert Kelly, *Theological Education in America* (New York: George H. Doran, 1924); Williams Adam Brown and Mark A. May et al., *The Education of American Ministers*, 4 vols. (New York: Institute of Social and Religious Research, 1934). It is also found, with some variations, in H. Richard Niebuhr et al., *The Purpose of the Church and Its Ministry: Reflections on the Aims of Theological Education* (New York: Harper and Bros., 1956); H. Richard Niebuhr, Daniel Day Williams, and James M. Gustafson, *The Advancement of Theological Education: The Summary Report of a Mid-Century Study* (New York: Harper & Bros., 1957).

professions generally, not on any distinctive grounds.[7] Even theologically, such institutions often have more in common than they realize, such as certain shared assumptions that exist between liberal and fundamentalist worldviews.[8]

## 2. Bible Institutes and Lay Centers

Turning to Bible institutes, there are now almost one hundred affiliated with the American Association of Bible Colleges, and many others operating without full academic accreditation.[9] Overall, enrollment in the United States is around 25,000, comparable to the number of students attending seminaries and divinity schools. These institutes almost all spring from fundamentalist, evangelical, reformed confessional, and now increasingly charismatic, traditions. Lay education centers, which are still relatively few, are sometimes confessionally and sometimes interdenominationally based. Most Bible institutes give baccalaureate degrees, and the number of those introducing graduate programs is increasing. Some have developed into full-fledged seminaries. This has also happened to one or two institutions that initially majored on graduate-level education for lay people.

The Bible institutes were set up particularly for lay people who wished to train for church-related and missionary work. For many years these were almost the only places where women could undertake formal theological education and enter into "full-time" Christian work. In such institutions today, students tend to be younger, and some go on to graduate theological institutions, though most move into home- or overseas-based work with churches or mission agencies. Though there is less racial diversity, some places have a good representation of students from non-Western countries. Lay theological educa-

7. See further, most recently, Mark R. Schwehn, *Exiles from Eden: Religion and the Academic Vocation in America* (New York: Oxford University Press, 1993).

8. As emerges from Jackson Carroll, Barbara Wheeler, Daniel Aleshire, and Penny Long Marler, eds., *Being There: Culture and Formation in Two Theological Schools* (New York: Oxford University Press, 1997).

9. A very readable history of such institutions may be found in Virginia Liesen Brereton, *Training God's Army: The American Bible School Movement, 1880-1940* (Bloomington, Ind.: Indiana Press, 1990).

tion centers tend to attract women and men in fairly equal numbers, and the age of students tends to be older. In almost all cases, these people continue in their weekday employment, taking courses in and around their working day, week, and year.

Within these institutes and centers, the influence of the schooling approach to theological education is also noticeably present. A significant part of what happens revolves around lectures, classrooms, assignments, and exams. Such places have more of a vocational orientation, and they give more attention inside and outside the classroom to spiritual formation. But they still major on building up students' knowledge of the Christian tradition, and it is this knowledge that they seek to illustrate from experience and to apply in practice. Bible institutes insist on field education alongside studies, and lay centers encourage students to use their workplaces as laboratories for testing what they are learning. Yet in both settings a fully integrated approach to reflection and action is rare. Like seminaries, more holistic approaches occur mainly in courses focusing on ministry and spiritual formation. For the most part, biblical, historical, and theological studies are similar in kind, if different in level and approach, to what takes place in more academic settings. Over the years, in fact, most Bible and missionary colleges have progressively become more academic in character.[10]

## B. The Emergence of a More Wide-Ranging Discussion

Until the eighties, and still in many seminaries today, discussion of theological education revolved around two main sets of issues. First, questions have been raised about its means and ends:

10. On the missionary training movement, see further O. G. Mykleburst, *The Study of Missions in Theological Education* (Oslo: Egrede Instituttet; Vol. I, 1955; Vol. II, 1956); Johannes Verkuyl, *Contemporary Missiology: An Introduction* (Grand Rapids: Eerdmans, 1978), esp. pp. 26-88; and now Andrew F. Walls, "Missiological Education in Historical Perspective," in J. Dudley Woodberry, Charles Van Engen, Edgar J. Elliston, eds., *Missiological Education for the 21st Century: The Book, the Circle, and the Sandals* (Maryknoll, N.Y.: Orbis, 1996), pp. 11-22. On colleges and institutes see S. A. Witmer, *The Bible College Story: Education with Dimension* (Mahasset, N.Y.: Channel, 1962); and Kenneth B. Mulholland, "Missiological Education in the Bible College Tradition," in *Missiological Education for the 21st Century,* pp. 43-53.

- Is it receiving sufficient *resources* for the task? How does it respond to growing financial exigencies, faculty overload, or to the demand for more seminary services?
- Is it receiving proper *governance?* Is leadership being rightly exercised, and do faculty, students, and staff have sufficient involvement in decision-making?
- Is it enabling faculty and students to give *priority* to their main responsibilities, and how much do internal or external demands distract them from these?
- Is adequate attention given to faculty, staff, and trustee *development,* and how much should this focus on enhancing personal or pedagogical skills?

Only intermittently did discussion revolve around the aims and purposes of theological education. Where this has taken place, it has done so only in a limited way. Here are some of the issues that tend to surface:

- Is the seminary attaining its primary *goal?* Does it need to strike a better balance between spiritual formation, professional development, and academic excellence?
- Is it relating adequately to its contemporary *context?* How can it become more aware of its immediate local and wider church setting?
- Is it creating the proper *ethos* for its members? Is there sufficient opportunity for intellectual exchange, experience of community, and inclusion of minorities?
- Is it providing the most appropriate *curriculum?* How well is it managing to integrate theory and practice, and relating theology to significant contemporary issues?

These are not the only issues talked about until the eighties, or in many seminaries today, but these matters turn up most frequently in conversations or meetings. But people treat them primarily as *operational* issues, as aspects of the more general question "How well are we doing?" academically and administratively.

INTRODUCTION

## 1. From Operational to Theological Concerns

Since the mid-eighties a new debate on graduate theological education in North America has gone beyond posing the main issues in this way. It has raised more overt *theological* questions about the aims and purposes of the whole enterprise. Though this is not the first time such concerns have come into view — the debate on theological education in the sixties included some reference to them — these now occupy the fundamental place.[11] At times this has also transposed discussion about means and ends into a new key. Our unwillingness to think theologically about these matters has hindered our ability to resolve some of our ongoing concerns, even after extensive and repeated discussion. Although it is now fifteen years old, this debate shows little sign of diminishing. Initially it took place mainly between mainline scholars, but now has better Catholic and evangelical representation. The debate has managed to establish a relatively new *genre* for reflecting on theological education, raised the *level* of discussion beyond the developing abstract mission statements and mere curriculum changes, and provided an *agenda* applicable to the realities of most theological schools.[12] Unfortunately, it has not yet changed the way most theological institutions operate.

Alongside this academic debate, other voices argue the need for a more radical approach. In the Third World, some have insisted that the prevailing paradigm of theological education, and even current proposals for its reform, exists within a Western frame of reference that is fundamentally flawed. This is one of the reasons why students from such countries who attend Western theological institutions often do not return home or, if they do return, find it hard to operate in a culturally effective way. In any case, since virtually all theological institutions in developing countries have adopted the Western model, they are unable to train their own students for ministry in the most appropriate way. Some of these voices plead for a more indigenous form of theological education. Others have looked to a more culturally sensitive, biblically oriented model.

11. In *The Purpose of the Church and Its Ministry,* pp. 3-4, H. Richard Niebuhr insisted on the importance of thinking theologically, not just pragmatically, educationally, or socio-psychologically about theological education.
12. So Barbara Wheeler in *Shifting Boundaries: Contextual Approaches to the Structure of Theological Education,* ed. Barbara Wheeler and Edward Farley (Louisville: Westminster/John Knox, 1991), pp. 27-31.

10

A different kind of critique comes from within the West itself. Some of this is not new. Many pastors and denominational leaders have asked whether seminaries provide their graduates with the kind of knowledge and expertise that they need to fulfill their ministry responsibilities.[13] There is much talk about the widening gap between the seminary and the church, part of it stemming from the fact that these days less faculty have ministry experience. Concern about this leads to various educational innovations and in-service programs or, on occasion, to struggles for political control between denominational authorities and seminary boards. Similar criticism has come more recently from postdenominational megachurches and house churches. Both of these criticize the way theological institutions take people away from their local settings and fail to give them the practical habits and skills they require for effective ministry. A few of these churches have begun to develop alternative forms of theological education or are seriously considering doing so.[14] Some lay organizations also complain that formal theological education fails to sufficiently prepare people to help them with the vocational and civic concerns they face, and do not present models of spirituality or community that connect with their everyday issues and responsibilities.

## 2. A General Outline of the Book

Where does my contribution fit into these various circles of discussion? While I have oriented it chiefly to the academic debate about

13. Some sweeping criticisms of mainline seminaries may be found in Thomas C. Oden, *Requiem: A Lament in Three Movements* (Nashville: Abingdon, 1995). A not uncritical defense is provided by Donald E. Messer, *Calling Churches and Seminaries into the 21st Century* (Nashville: Abingdon, 1995). See also Lyle E. Shaller, *Confessions of a Contrarian: Second Thoughts on the Pastoral Ministry* (Nashville: Abingdon, 1989); and Carnegie S. Calian, *Where's the Passion for Excellence in the Church?: Shaping Discipleship Through Ministry and Theological Education* (Wilton, CN: Morehouse-Barlow, 1989).

14. See, for example, Leith Anderson, *The Church for the Twenty-first Century* (Minneapolis: Bethany House, 1992); George Barna, *Today's Pastor* (Ventura, Calif.: Regal, 1993); Tony Campolo, *Can Mainline Denominations Make a Comeback?* (Valley Forge: Judson, 1995), pp. 130-31. Generally, see Harry L. Poe, "The Revolution in Ministry Training," *Theological Education* 33 (1) (1996): 25-27.

theological education, I have sought to address the main issues raised by these other discussions.

- In the first section I begin with a concise but comprehensive account of the key positions advanced in the debate over the last fifteen years. This is more exhaustive and up-to-date than any other survey. I have drawn here on David Kelsey's helpful classification of the proposals, but have substituted other terms and extended his typology.[15] I have also discussed some lesser-known proposals to see if they have anything to offer. Throughout, I make some basic criticisms of the debate as a whole, suggesting that it operates with some assumptions that are open to challenge, and within some limits that constrain a proper reenvisioning of theological education.
- The second section lays the groundwork for a more satisfactory model of theological education by examining how ministry formation took place in biblical times. Since this is an unusual way to proceed — even from one, like myself, who is a biblical scholar — I give some time to hermeneutical issues raised by such an approach. Through these issues I seek to distinguish the exercise from a biblicist or anachronistic exercise. I follow with an investigation of the way ministry formation took place in prophetic circles, among Jesus' group of disciples, and within Paul's band of companions. This opens up a largely unexplored model in the debate, what I call a missional model of theological education.
- The third section builds on the new possibilities opened up by this biblical investigation, beginning with some less well-known contributions to the debate that point in the direction I have in mind. After reconsidering some of the key concerns around which discussion has revolved — unity and diversity, pluralism

15. While there is a summary of some of the main contributions to the debate in L. N. Rhodes and N. D. Richardson, *Mending Severed Connections: Theological Education for Communal Transformation* (San Francisco: San Francisco Network Ministries, 1991), pp. 22-45, and a brief account of some of its main features by Barbara Wheeler in her introduction to *Shifting Boundaries*, pp. 7-33, the fullest analysis to date comes from David Kelsey, *Between Athens and Berlin: The Theological Education Debate* (Grand Rapids: Eerdmans, 1993). This builds on the typology formulated in his earlier book, *To Understand God Truly*, cited above.

and contextualization — I explore other vital issues such as the link between reflection and action, and between theory and practice. Lastly, I identify the consequences of this approach for teaching and learning. All this helps to sharpen the missional approach to theological education by applying it to the key areas of knowledge and sets of practices around which theological education revolves.

- The fourth section of the book lays out a range of practical ways in which we can move our present patterns of theological education in a more holistic and practical direction. I discuss these in the context of key changes taking place among students today, the role of spiritual and communal formation in theological education, and the shaping influence of the culture of the seminary, professional guilds, and the church. Finally, and very much in the order it should come, I discuss issues that have to do with the curriculum, both at the graduate and postgraduate levels.

I conclude by asking about the likelihood of theological institutions acting on this proposal, and whether change will come instead through new ventures in theological education on the margins of the church and the academy.

# PART ONE

# REASSESSING THEOLOGICAL EDUCATION: THE PRESENT STAGE OF DEBATE

Frequently . . . theological education in the United States has been conceived not as a theological problem, but as a matter of practical application and technique. Our attention has been focused not on the theological grounds and reasons for doing what we do, but on questions of how to do it effectively. But the authors and discussants who have contributed to discussions during the last decade . . . have treated theological education as a form of Christian practice and thus the question of what should be its nature and purposes as a theological question. The result has been a nascent practical theology of theological education. . . .

BARBARA WHEELER[1]

1. Barbara G. Wheeler in her introduction to *Shifting Boundaries: Contextual Approaches to the Structure of Theological Education,* ed. Barbara Wheeler and Edward Farley (Louisville: Westminster/John Knox, 1991), p. 9.

# 1. Retrieving Aspects of the "Classical" Model

In the current debate on theological education, the pragmatic questions that have mostly preoccupied theological institutions give way to a number of more profound issues, challenging the standard terms in which many traditional concerns have been posed, along with the conventional wisdom that has been applied to them. There is a desire to go behind the operational concern, "How well are we doing?" to the deeper theological one, "What should we be doing anyway?" In asking this, contributors to the current debate all share a sense of crisis concerning the main directions and practices of theological education.

This has altered the content of the questions being asked about each of the areas mentioned beforehand, and brought those concerned with the aims and purposes of theological education into central focus. These questions now primarily take the following form:

- concerning *goals* — How can theological education be developed for both lay and clergy leaders, and what is the proper balance between personal, intellectual, and vocational formation?
- concerning *context* — Is the environment in which we are working merely a diverse one — ethnically, culturally, denominationally, theologically — or is it radically pluralist in character?
- concerning *ethos* — How much should a theological institution view itself as part of the academy and how much as part of the church, and to what extent is it a preparation for ministry or a setting for ministry?

17

- concerning *content* — In what does the unity of theological education basically consist, and how can its main pedagogical fields be better integrated and more life-related?

Though there is continuing interest in the means and ends of theological education, these issues are also viewed in a different way:

- concerning *resources* — How do we move from merely quantitative assessments of growth and efficiency to an assessment that gives more attention to issues of both quality and effectiveness?
- concerning *governance* — Should this not undergo theological as well as organizational reevaluation, and is this reevaluation not also needed for the model and practice of leadership within theological institutions?
- concerning *responsibilities* — For faculty, what is the balance between teaching, research, and training, and how does the institution's reward system provide the proper incentives for discovering this balance?
- concerning *formation* — To what extent should this be formally provided for faculty, staff, and trustees, and how much does it require turning the whole institution into an intentional learning organization?

Reflection on these issues involves a genuine theology of both theological education and theological institutions. The central issue is not just "What's theological about theological *education?*" but "What's theological about a theological *school?*" It also involves reevaluation of what genuine *theological* reflection involves, and on whether the customary move from theory to application in theological education is defensible.

In what follows I examine the main proposals put forward in the ongoing debate on theological education that is taking place in the theological academy. Other voices from outside this mainstream — and until recently largely mainline — debate will come in for consideration at appropriate points in later sections.

In the earliest stages of the debate, two main types of proposals were set forward. These emerged primarily from mainstream Protestant theological institutions that were moving into a postliberal phase. Contributors questioned prevailing university and professional models of theological education, and revisited earlier ones in an attempt to retrieve what had been lost. These proposals largely bypassed continuing Catholic and confessional Protestant approaches that were less attached to the models under question. A helpful classification of these proposals has been provided by David Kelsey, who talks about the "Athens" and "Berlin" approaches to theological education. Although, as I have indicated, I will suggest different labels and consider other proposals, my debt to Kelsey's discussion will be obvious.

I use the broader term "classical" rather than "Athens" here because, although the model has its roots in the capital of ancient Greece, it first came to Christian expression in other centers such as Alexandria, and it became normative throughout Antiquity. Current reformulations of this model contain significant differences as well as similarities.

## A. The Centrality of Theological Wisdom

The main advocate for this approach is Edward Farley, who was chiefly responsible for initiating the current debate.[2] For Farley, theology is neither an academic subject nor a set of beliefs, but a form of divine wisdom accessible to all people as they seek to live out their faith in a concrete way. It is faith's internal process of becoming reflective, and as such is based on our human capacity for intuitive knowledge of divine things. However, full understanding and appropriation of these comes only through divine enlightenment and assistance. *Theologia* is a cognitive activity that is both contemplative and deductive. It has an affective side to it, and helps develop a propensity for action. Though the individual student is central, *paideia* is a corporate affair. It has to do with cultivating a person's spirit, character, and mind so that their faith is deepened and they are better prepared for the practice of ministry. Development of this *habitus* or disposition is a decidedly intuitive

2. See Edward Farley, *Theologia: The Fragmentation and Unity of Theological Education* (Philadelphia: Fortress, 1983), and *The Fragility of Knowledge: Theological Education in the Church and the University* (Philadelphia: Fortress, 1988), as well as articles on "The Reform of Theological Education as a Theological Task," *Theological Education* 17 (2) (1981): 93-117, and "Theology and Practice Outside the Clerical Paradigm," in *Practical Theology: The Emerging Field in Theology, Church and World,* ed. Don S. Browning (San Francisco: Harper & Row, 1983), pp. 21-41.

and speculative affair, and takes place through formal, structured learning as well as through the institutional culture and structure in which this learning is set.

In light of this understanding of *theologia,* Farley argues that theological education is fragmented because the reigning academic model abstracts the objects of knowledge from their concrete settings, and because it equates church leadership with individual clerical functions. Curriculum divisions that resulted from establishing the pervasive fourfold structure of theological education — biblical studies, church history, systematics, and practical theology (and the overlay of their specialized disciplines) — also contribute to the problem. The most sobering feature of the career of theology during the last few hundred years

> . . . is simply the disappearance of theology as wisdom and theology as discipline (science) from the theological school — their disappearance, that is, as the overall unity and rationale. In a very restricted way theology, even in these two ancient senses, persists, but in the form of idiosyncratic aspects of the curriculum, something available for certain kinds of students and certain kinds of ministers. It is not too strong to say that the theological school will make little progress in understanding its present nature and situation if it overlooks the disappearance of the very thing which is supposed to be its essence, agenda, and telos.[3]

This situation can only be overcome if there is movement in two related directions. First, by returning to a less abstract, more intuitive and practical, theological wisdom or *theologia.* This is the true nature of theology, and at its best this is what theology has been principally about. Even research needs to be oriented more concretely in this direction. *Theologia* needs no goal or justification outside itself, but fulfills its objectives in and through its own process or *paideia.* Second, though its unity does not consist in training for a specialized ministerial role, it does require a reenvisioning of what ministry involves. Central to this are certain dispositions or "habits of the intellect," not a set of professional skills and specialized functions. Everything is at stake in placing *theologia* at the heart of the theological education enterprise. As Edward Farley puts it,

3. E. Farley, *Theologia,* p. 44.

. . . significant reform of theological education which addresses its deepest problems must find a way to recover *theologia.* Without that recovery theological education will continue to perpetuate its enslavement to specialties, its lack of subject matter and criteria, its functionalist and technological orientation.[4]

To bring this about, teachers must have expert knowledge of the basic texts and practices of the Christian faith, and should be engaged in a personal quest to know God, themselves, and the world. The resulting wisdom contains several elements. It involves a particular way of thinking, a form of discipline, and it becomes an inbuilt disposition. It exhibits the traditional goals of clarity, validity, and coherence, but also utilizes relevant modern disciplines and methodologies. *Theologia,* then, involves both intellectual formation, or *paideia,* and publicly attested knowledge, or *Wissenschaft,* though it puts the emphasis on the first. The teacher's responsibility is to facilitate students' immediate intellectual intuition of God rather than attempt to help them attain this through direct instruction about it. This process goes through four stages. First, it structures the images, beliefs, values, and rituals of faith so that some perspective can be gained on the worldview they entail, on its principal motifs and patterns, and on its relevance to present situations. Second, it inserts the concrete situation into this transcendent framework, so that both can be properly evaluated. Third, it criticizes the received tradition where the tradition results in oppression, distortion, or discrimination of particular people or groups. Fourth, it discerns and internalizes the enduring truth present in and through that tradition.

According to Farley, theological education contains five basic dimensions. The first three are the main settings in which it takes place — namely, the life-situation of the believer, leadership in the church, and theological inquiry or scholarship. All have their own integrity, and they complement one another. Farley describes the work of the church leader in terms similar to H. Richard Niebuhr's "pastoral director,"[5] though this is only one of the matrices of theological education and not the overarching goal of the enterprise. But if not a goal,

4. E. Farley, *Theologia,* p. 156.
5. H. Richard Niebuhr et al., *The Purpose of the Church and Its Ministry: Reflections on the Aims of Theological Education* (New York: Harper and Bros., 1956), p. 80.

then at least it is a horizon throughout the whole educational process. *Theologia* itself is present as a disposition in the leader: it permeates the course of studies, it orients the relevant disciplines, and it forms the criteria for developing appropriate pedagogical fields. At its center is knowledge of ecclesia and ecclesial praxis. This should be nurtured in the church as well as in the seminary.[6] The seminary then helps students to develop this disposition more rigorously and in a way that is stimulated by the academic disciplines. There are two other dimensions of theological education — namely, appraisal of the ecclesial tradition and our contemporary context. Here we move from an understanding of our world, locating what is enduring in the past experience of Christians and discerning how this experience affects our individual choices, lifestyles, and obligations, in a way that connects with our public life.

These five basic dimensions of theological education have corresponding modes of interpretation, all of which stem from the life-situation of believers in general rather than from the ministry-situation of church leaders in particular. The first three modes — interpreting the tradition, understanding its truth, and appropriate action — are introduced into life-situations by faith; these modes always coexist. The last two — interpreting faith's actual situation, and our primary vocation — are syntheses of these. All of these modes are integral to theological study and imply both a content and methodology. They should be preceded by prior foundational studies that include an analysis of the human condition, a cultural evaluation of religion and the church, and the historical investigation of Christianity. These modes of interpretation do not entail a specific curriculum, nor do they require abandoning specialized disciplines and the fourfold pattern of theological study, though we should distinguish between general pedagogical areas and more focused disciplines within the theological encyclopedia. But these modes can prevent disciplines from imposing their own autonomous boundaries and structure on theological education and could even lead to the formation of new disciplines. They would certainly

6. Further to this see Edward Farley, "Theology and Practice Outside the Clerical Paradigm," p. 38; see also *Ecclesial Man: A Social Phenomenology of Faith and Reality* (Philadelphia: Fortress, 1975); and *Ecclesial Reflection: An Anatomy of Theological Method* (Philadelphia: Fortress, 1982).

give vital theological movement and texture to all parts of the curriculum.[7]

While I have not come across a theological institution that embodies all that Farley asks for, I have worked part-time in one that contained many of these elements. This housed two separate but overlapping organizations engaged in theological education. One, the more recent, was a small but growing school of theology that trained people for pastoral ministry in the Anglican Church. The other was an Ecumenical Institute of Theology that provided graduate and adult education courses for lay people in the city. Though those training for ordination had some classes open only to them, the Institute of Theology included courses for lay people. So there was some recognition of the theological education as a wider enterprise than the training of professional church leadership. I taught one course a year as an adjunct in each of these organizations, both of which were located on the same site, sharing the same library. The main priority in the school of theology was the formation of a spiritual and theological wisdom in and through both academic study and through close daily fellowship in corporate worship and shared meals. There was a strong emphasis on understanding the wider culture, especially its indigenous Australian components, in order to properly contextualize Christian communication, church life, and so-

7. On the distinction between pedagogical fields and disciplines, see *The Fragility of Knowledge*, pp. 108-10. On pp. 174-75, Farley suggests that a new discipline centering on the hermeneutic description of situations might need to be created. This suggestion overlaps with part of Don Browning's expansion of "practical theology" in *A Fundamental Practical Theology: Descriptive and Strategic Proposals* (Minneapolis: Fortress, 1991). The possibility of creating other subspecialties is suggested by Thomas W. Ogletree, "Christian Social Ethics as a Theological Discipline," in *Shifting Boundaries,* pp. 201-39. In an unpublished paper on "Rethinking Graduate Theological Education," Farley asks whether advanced theological study excludes *paideia*. Although many would regard the specialism characteristic of such study as necessarily purging it of *paideia*, Farley argues that all three basic aspects of the latter are intrinsic to real graduate *theological* education, that is, the *paideia* of everyday truth and reality, of societal good, and of thinking. He also disagrees with those who argue that this *paideia* can be taught to those involved in graduate research. This is needed to counteract the growing complexity of advanced theological study through academic subspecializations, connections with a wider range of auxiliary disciplines, and the introduction of minority perspectives, which, whatever gains they bring, increase the risk of a more provincial or *potpourri* approach.

cial involvement. The school worked in close association with clergy in surrounding churches, a number of whom taught courses for it; pastoral formation was seen as a joint effort between local congregations and the theological college. All students had appointments in these churches, where they were encouraged under supervision to discover and express their particular gifts for ministry. In many respects, therefore, this endeavor was a contemporary reformulation of a more traditional approach to theological education, combining *paideia* and *Wissenschaft,* but with the emphasis more on the former than the latter. It is not accidental that it developed in an Anglican ethos, a tradition that alongside Catholicism and Orthodoxy remains in close touch with an earlier model of theological education. The emphasis on personal formation in this tradition also gives this school something in common with the following amplification of Farley's approach.

## B. The Significance of Personal Formation

Though owing much to Farley, others have taken his discussion a stage further. In his foreword to a symposium on the relationship between theological education and moral formation, the editor Richard Neuhaus challenges approaches to training for ministry that regard the question of moral formation as "an unwelcome intrusion." Those who advocate such training believe that:

> Theological education, like other graduate studies, is a matter of the mind. Theological education is learning and doing, and what that does or does not do for the moral character of the participants is a matter of indifference. At least it is not the proper business of the academic institution where theological education is pursued. . . . [Yet] from the New Testament era to the present, the church has always expected its leadership to be morally exemplary, or, as some ordinals put it, "to adorn the gospel with a holy life." . . . Today's disputes about the moral expectations of church leadership are not about what is *permissible* but about what is *exemplary.* . . . A persistent theme [in the following pages] is the necessarily communal nature of any useful discussion of moral formation. . . . One question addressed is whether moral formation is a necessary part of theological education. An-

24

other question involves the continuing contest over the content of moral formation.[8]

The symposium recognizes that although Farley focuses primarily on intellectual formation in his analysis of the fragmentation of theological education, to his credit he has also "set the agenda for consideration of moral formation in seminaries."[9] To understand why moral formation moved into the background, we have to go back further than the effects of the rise of the fourfold theological encyclopedia. The problem lies in the separation of disciplines that accompanied the emergence of the universities in the twelfth century.[10] To give moral formation its proper place in theological education, we also need to define *habitus* more broadly than Farley. For him, *theologia* includes reflection on virtues integral to the Christian faith as well as attention to symbols, beliefs, and practices. Such basic intellectual qualities as honesty, fairness, and respect also overlap with certain moral qualities. But these are not the only moral or spiritual qualities, and the cultivation of intellectual virtues does not necessarily result in their wider application. The virtues cultivated by *theologia* are clarity more than charity, honesty more than friendliness, devotion to a calling in general more than loyalty to specific communities of learning.[11]

While most seminary teachers recognize that moral and spiritual formation begins in the home and congregation, continues in other contexts alongside seminary, and develops afterwards in various ministry settings, there is a growing consensus that it must be an intentional part of seminary training, both inside and outside the classroom.[12] The in-

---

8. R. Neuhaus, ed., *Theological Education and Moral Formation* (Grand Rapids: Eerdmans, 1992), pp. vii, ix.

9. Merle D. Strege, "Chasing Schleiermacher's Ghost: The Reform of Theological Education in the 1980's," *Theological Education and Moral Formation,* p. 113.

10. See the comments in Richard Neuhaus, ed., *Theological Education and Moral Formation,* pp. 80-81, 91.

11. Mark R. Schwehn, *Exiles from Eden: Religion and the Academic Vocation in America* (New York: Oxford University Press, 1993), p. 18. Though he does not have Farley's view of *theologia* explicitly in view here, I think his remarks are broadly applicable to it.

12. See the lengthy report by Tilden Edwards, Jr., "Spiritual Formation in Theological Schools: Ferment and Challenge," *Theological Education* 17 (1) (1980): 1-52.

creasing presence of Catholics — and now evangelicals — in the debate has given impetus to this trend, for in such circles theological education has always had a stronger commitment to spiritual and moral formation. Among Catholics, formation takes place through the provision of programs and resources organized around clear institutional goals: among evangelicals, formation is more likely to be pursued through individual faculty contributions and extracurricular activities. Mainstream Protestants have approached this area from the side of moral rather than spiritual formation. A recent symposium on the question[13] begins with the assertion that Christian identity and commitment require moral formation as an essential ingredient. Considering the extent to which moral crisis or breakdown in ministry is currently plaguing the church, we must attend more carefully to preparing people for servant leadership in the church. As it is dominated by academic norms and values, theological education is at present ill-placed to do this, having substituted rationality for traditional notions of authority, and having created a dichotomy between theory and practice. Moral formation should be viewed as simply one dimension of spirituality, involving more than doing the right thing in specific cases. Moral formation concerns a theologically grounded obedience to Christ, and depends on participating in corporate worship, interpreting scripture, and pastoral care.

From the earliest centuries to the Reformation, the ideal of ministry focused on moral and spiritual character more than on fulfilling certain skills or functions. When Catholic seminaries developed after the Reformation, moral formation took place mainly through participating in the daily offices, through the Eucharist and retreats, and through undertaking spiritual direction, guided reading, schooling in prayer, and supervised ministry. In later Protestant schools there was mandatory chapel attendance, faculty mentoring, devotional practices, and pietistic student societies; there were also courses on the pastor's spiritual life, on duties to self and others, and on morals, manners, and health. The emphasis was primarily on personal and vocational, not social or public, formation. Much of this has evaporated, especially in Protestant circles,[14] and putting moral formation back on the agenda

---

13. On the following see the contributions and discussion in Richard Neuhaus, ed., *Theological Education and Moral Formation,* mentioned above.

14. At least until fairly recently it has been different in almost all Catholic seminaries, as John W. O'Malley points out in "Spiritual Formation for Ministry:

of theological education involves at least four steps.[15] First, the curriculum should be structured so that the moral dimension of ministry is fully addressed. Second, the norms and values inherent in this kind of instruction must be regarded as morally as well as educationally crucial. Third, alongside their teaching, the example set by faculty is fundamental. Fourth, the institutional culture of the school, and the way it is governed, should agree with the basic moral values it wishes students to develop.

At the conceptual level, recovering this dimension of theological education could benefit much from recent ethical thinking that focuses on the centrality of virtues and tradition. In view here is the work of such ethicists as Alasdair MacIntyre and Stanley Hauerwas.[16] A *paideia* thus informed would also modify the modern understanding of authority, and qualify the "expressive" and "utilitarian" individualism that is so common today, even in theological institutions. Two other writers, George Lindbeck and David Tracy, have raised concerns about the way spiritual formation is often described today in discussions about theological education. Both stress the communal character of spiritual formation over against the individualistic preoccupations of so much writing on and practice of spirituality, as well as its foundation in classical Christian traditions rather than modish sources or techniques. The first points to the danger of a false perfectionism, of a works-based rather than grace-based approach to spirituality. The second emphasizes the need to redefine spirituality in light of our increasingly pluralist and global sit-

---

Some Roman Catholic Traditions — Their Past and Present," in *Theological Education and Moral Formation*, pp. 79-111.

15. See further Dennis M. Campbell, "Theological Education and Moral Formation: What's Going on in Seminaries Today?" in *Theological Education and Moral Formation*, pp. 1-21. While definitions of morality partly reflected the cardinal Greek virtues of the dominant class of the day — prudence, justice, fortitude, and temperance — these were partly redefined through their grounding in Christ-like faith, love, and hope, the contemplation of God, and the work of the Spirit. Other virtues high on the list were chastity, honesty, and loyalty, with pride heading the list of vices to be avoided. During the last century, middle-class characteristics associated with being a gentleman also overlaid classical Christian virtues.

16. In their seminal works, A. MacIntyre, *After Virtue: A Study in Moral Theory*, 2nd ed. (Notre Dame: University of Notre Dame Press, 1984), and S. Hauerwas, *A Community of Character: Toward a Constructive Christian Social Ethic* (Notre Dame: University of Notre Dame Press, 1981), as well as in later writings.

uation.[17] This forms a good bridge to the next variant on the classical approach.

## C. The Orientation to Social Transformation

Two feminist groups of theologians, the Mud Flower Collective and the Network Center for the Study of Ministry, provide a further variation on the theme of theological education as *paideia*.[18] They are concerned more about the homogeneity, not fragmentation, of theological education — a homogeneity that stems from a failure to face up fully to the inherent pluralism of the Christian faith, and to cultural pluralism more generally. They also feel a lack of concreteness in both the process and the proposals of the theological education debate. In response to the abstract nature of the debate, members of the Collective decided to make their contribution through personal testimonies and interactions, not just the ideas and arguments. The result is a collection of stories, poetry, letters, dialogue, liturgy, conversation, and essays. In this way its members sought to model as well as explain their approach, and so to keep process and content, means and end, together.

This method of approach differs from what usually prevails. Most theological work suffers from individualism and dualism.

17. See further G. Lindbeck, "Spiritual Formation and Theological Education," *Theological Education* 24, Supplement 1 (1988): 10-32, and David Tracy, "Can Virtue Be Taught?: Education, Character and the Soul," *Theological Education* 24, Supplement 1 (1988): 33-52.

18. The Mud Flower Collective, *God's Fierce Whimsy: Christian Feminism and Theological Education* (New York: Pilgrim Press, 1985); and Lynn N. Rhodes and Nancy D. Richardson, *Mending Severed Connections: Theological Education for Communal Transformation* (San Francisco: San Francisco Network Ministries, 1991). These extend the work of the earlier symposium issued by The Cornwall Collective, *Your Daughters Shall Prophesy: Feminist Alternatives in Theological Education* (New York: Pilgrim Press, 1980). Though it predated Edward Farley's seminal contribution, this voiced some of the same concerns, such as the divorce between theory and practice, the disciplinary basis of the curriculum, claims to objectivity, and overall conformity to the academic model. Overlapping membership between the Cornwall Collective and the Network is reflected in their common search for a more holistic and inclusive approach based on collective reflection on experience, in which curriculum changes primarily flow from more basic changes in perspective.

More often than not in our educational systems, including theological seminaries, we have been taught to believe that we are very much on our own when it comes to real scholarship and academic excellence; and certainly that the intellectual enterprise is, or ought to be, separate from the world of mere experience. Here let us state emphatically our contention that the finest scholarship, the most powerful intellectual work, and the most creative thinking is done always by those whose hearts are in their work; those who acknowledge this to be the case, and gladly admit the subjective bias of their scholarship; and certainly those who understand that what they are doing has some bearing on the lives of others, for good or ill.[19]

What is true for doing theology is also true for teaching and learning theology. In accordance with the action/reflection model of liberation theology, this acts as a reminder that theory is formulated in the midst of practice. Our thinking should be embodied, experiential, and contextual, not abstract, objective, and universal. The principal characteristics of such praxis are accountability to minority groups, collaborative reflection, lives-in-relation as an epistemological starting point, cultural diversity, and shared commitment to the work of justice.

The Collective's contribution begins with an analysis of theological education's inability to embrace the meaning, value, and contribution of women or understand the pain and alienation of marginal people in general. Addressing the questions of such groups must be moved from the periphery to the center of theological reflection and education. Women are viewed as a paradigm of the power relations that inform class and racial conflicts, and as a lens through which to perceive, experience, and affirm both cultural pluralism and ordinary human experience. The Network focuses on the questions of participants who have been marginalized in the educational process. Paradoxically, the only way to overcome this marginalizing in theological education is to make it genuinely theological. *Paideia* — understood as essentially relational in character and oriented towards justice — must become central. This twofold emphasis keeps its feet firmly on the ground, addressing everyday questions relating to where people live, work, and play, not just headline issues. Theological education should be concerned with change that is both per-

19. The Mud Flower Collective, *God's Fierce Whimsy*, p. 23.

sonal and public, interpersonal and societal, in a way that acknowledges cultural diversity.

The best means of working in this direction is for people to share their stories, enabling theological reflection to focus on the God who is primarily known and experienced through relationships, to become aware of the injustice that haunts most people's lives, and to remain as concrete and accessible as possible. The chief criteria for theological discernment here are awareness, insight, critical evaluation, breadth, and respect for diversity, not the academic criteria of clarity, precision, coherence, order, and generalization. Compared with Farley, less emphasis is placed here on the role of reason; human nature is not regarded as having any universal essence. Although this kind of theology agrees with Farley that God can be known only indirectly, such knowledge occurs mainly through "overhearing" others' stories. Here there is more room for mutual learning between teachers and students, as well as between students themselves, especially where there is diversity in the group. There should be greater gender, class, and racial representation among both faculty and students. Breaking the white, male, middle-class dominance of seminaries will do more to advance theological education than the pursuit of some ideal structure or curriculum.

More than Farley, this approach places justice at the center of its understanding of God, and construes wisdom in social as well as intellectual and moral terms. Yet justice is not viewed as the external goal to which all theological education should be directed. As the foundation of human life, and as integral to the character of God, justice is an inherent dimension of *theologia* that should mark the whole process and content of theological education. Students are not just prepared for the work of justice; it should be the basis of all that is taught. This is why the first allegiance of the Collective's members is to changing structures of theological education rather than broader social structures. Theological schools must ensure that their own structures and governance operate justly and reflect diversity, and that any education or research conducted within them reflects these. Faculty should teach in a praxis-based way, and develop accountability to specific ministry contexts for classroom education. Programs should prepare people for collaborative styles of ministry, and for operating effectively in a highly pluralist culture. But emphasizing the social and political dimensions of ministry should not be at the expense of personal and corporate spiritual development. Spirituality and justice ultimately form a single reality.

30

## D. Some Critical Questions

These three variations on the proposal to retrieve aspects of the classical model pose a challenge that theological education cannot afford to ignore. Both separately and generally, however, they are open to the following criticisms.

1. It is not clear what forms the normative base of Christianity. Farley dismisses as precritical those who seek this base in "apodictically true literary texts." But the operation of critical discernment towards the biblical texts — in relation to the limits of the canon, questions of authorship, recognition of factual errors, the presence of discordant statements — did not first appear in the Enlightenment with the rise of the historical-critical method.[20] It existed in Protestant circles long before that.[21] Only if the word *critical* is equated with the inherent suspicion of the text, and only if the role of the critical element in theological reflection is overemphasized, is the association of truth with texts rendered invalid.[22] For the Collective, Christianity is so inherently pluralistic that it is not possible to identify a common set of beliefs.[23] This is highly questionable. Neither the presence of diversity nor the existence of pluralism necessitates suspension of belief in the search for truth. We can pursue truth critically within the framework of "faith seeking understanding." Doubt

20. See on this Charles M. Wood, *Vision and Discernment: An Orientation in Theological Study* (Atlanta: Scholars Press, 1985), p. 60. Wood is himself open to question on this general area. He argues that historical, philosophical, practical criticism was not born with the Enlightenment but only became more systematic, institutionalized, and professionalized at that time.

21. A good example of this comes from the inaugural presidential address at Fuller Seminary by Edward John Carnell, "The Glory of a Theological Seminary," May 17, 1955, pp. 6-7, 9. He argues that the primary role of a seminary is twofold, namely, "preserving and propagating theological distinctives inherent in the institution itself" by making a "conscientious effort to acquaint its students with all the relevant evidences — damaging as well as supporting — so that they might exercise their God-given right freely to decide for or against claims to truth." The word "freely" is the crucial term here.

22. Further on this see Richard J. Mouw, in an unpublished paper titled "Evangelical Reflections on the 'Aims and Purposes' Literature" (1992), p. 15.

23. Shortly before the debate got under way T. C. Oden, *Agenda for Theology: Recovering Christian Roots* (San Francisco: Harper & Row, 1979), challenged theologians to place classical Christian convictions in a central position in their thinking.

— "faithful" doubt as opposed to "skeptical" doubt — has a legitimate place in this.

2. In particular these approaches do not sufficiently emphasize the distinctive role of scripture in revealing and understanding God. However we define it — whether, as I would prefer, through a reformulation of the traditional approach or along postliberal lines *à la* Lindbeck — we ought to recognize the qualitative difference between scripture and later formulations of the faith. Such an acknowledgment does not rule out the creative ongoing discovery of truth, especially through the living — and especially loving — interaction of a diverse Christian community. Nor does it rule out recognition of a genuine diversity in the biblical writings themselves, and the possibility of varying, contextually shaped expressions of such diversity.

3. So far as *theologia* is concerned, Farley has not really demonstrated how it can be both a disposition and a discipline. The first has its basis in the classical conception of personhood centered on virtue that necessarily involves action, the second in the modern view of personhood centered on self-awareness that does not. Farley has not shown how these can be logically joined nor, given the contradictory philosophical frameworks of the two, is it clear that he can do so. At this point, the stronger critique of *scientia* by feminist theologians, and their preference for alternative, nonacademic criteria of what is true, is more consistent. But this raises other problems: How do we tell the difference between authentic and ideological reflection, and on what basis can the social sciences be used as reliable instruments in diagnosing injustice?[24]

4. There is also a further problem with Farley's apparently ahistorical understanding of *habitus*. Preferable here is the general approach of feminist theologians. Though they sometimes unconsciously fall into making universal judgments — particularly in relation to their commitment to radical pluralism — they do define *habitus* in a clear historical way. However, since they do not provide any transcendental criteria for distinguishing between valid and invalid contributions to this radical pluralism, they open themselves up to a form of relativism that from a Christian perspective is hard to sustain, a relativism com-

---

24. See the detailed arguments in support of this by David Kelsey, *Between Athens and Berlin: The Theological Education Debate* (Grand Rapids: Eerdmans, 1993), pp. 122-28, and, on the second problem noted below, pp. 128-34.

pounded by their failure to provide adequate ways of distinguishing experience of God from experience of others. This failure opens them up, at various points, to reductionist tendencies.

# 2. Revising Aspects of the "Vocational" Model

We turn now to the debate's second main approach to theological education. Instead of Kelsey's term to describe this approach, the "Berlin" axis, I will use the more generic term "vocational." This model stems from Schleiermacher's attempt to justify the place of theological education in the university curriculum on the analogy of training for other professions, such as law and medicine. As it happened, Schleiermacher's vision was not fully accepted; in time, other more strictly academic elements entered the picture, and a more professionalized rather than simply vocational approach became dominant. The uneasy coexistence or combination of these two elements has characterized theological education in most seminaries and divinity schools in North America and elsewhere. Recent efforts to reformulate a more genuinely vocational model have once again taken different, though related, forms.

## A. A Focus on Practical Theology

Joseph C. Hough, Jr., and John B. Cobb, Jr.,[25] agree with Farley's analysis of the fragmentation of theological education, and with his insis-

25. The first response to an early essay of Farley from this perspective came from Joseph C. Hough, Jr., "Reform in Theological Education as a Political Task," *Theological Education* 17 (2) (1981): 152-66, and later "The Education of Practical Theologians," *Theological Education* 20 (Spring 1984): 55-84. Most fully, however, see Joseph C. Hough, Jr., and John B. Cobb, Jr., *Christian Identity and*

tence that *theologia* is essential for recovering its lost unity. But they find his account of *theologia* too abstract and methodological, as well as insufficiently related to issues facing the church. They suggest that the basic problem with theological education is political rather than theological. It arises from the sociopolitical realities confronting theological schools, as they are caught in the crossfire of conflicting expectations from the secularized academy and from the professionalized church. It is by clarifying and dealing with these pressures that we will begin to overcome the fragmentation of theological education, as well as provide a clearer vocational focus and sense of boundaries for faculty caught between these conflicting expectations.

Hough and Cobb disagree with Farley's insistence that part of the problem is due to theological schools' orientation to professional church leadership. It is not this focus that is problematic, but the way such leadership is perceived. Some of the confusion and misunderstanding that surrounds the meaning of church leadership stems from inappropriate cultural expectations. Church leaders should not be viewed as pastoral managers or pastoral therapists, and the role they play should not only be the prerogative of the ordained. The chief contribution church leaders can make in the North American context today is to be "practical thinkers" and "reflective practitioners," that is, to be thinking about practice and thinking in practice.

> Some tension remains between reflective practice and practical Christian thinking. On the one hand, practical Christian thinking calls for bold vision, aggressive leadership, and strong commitment to genuine Christian practice. On the other hand, reflective practice calls for involvement of the whole community in practical thinking, and this means that leaders must be collaborative and enabling as well. Yet these tensions will finally prove to be creative. The leadership of the Practical Christian Thinker must be consonant with the church's self-understanding as a human community. The Reflective Practitioner's practice must be grounded in the identity of the church and reflection on the implementation of that identity for life in the world. Since these images are intimately con-

---

*Theological Education* (Atlanta: Scholars Press, 1985), and "Ministry to the World: A New Professional Paradigm," in Joseph C. Hough, Jr., and Barbara Wheeler, eds., *Beyond Clericalism: The Congregation as a Focus for Theological Education* (Atlanta: Scholars Press, 1988), pp. 23-29.

nected and neither is adequate without the other, we propose a characterization of the minister for today which is capable of embracing both — the minister as *Practical Theologian*. Practical theology is critical reflection on the church's practice in view of the dangerous memory of Jesus . . . [and] we can propose the image of Practical Theologian for professional church leaders without implying that practical theology should be their exclusive prerogative.[26]

Such an understanding of their ministry enables church leaders to function in a variety of ways, as problem-solvers, pioneers, and implementers as well as teachers.[27] Once this is understood, it is easier to see what kind of theological education is required. Orienting the entire theological curriculum to the vocation of the practical theologian overcomes the dichotomy between theory and practice that arose from the attempt to give theology academic respectability through introducing the theological encyclopedia. It also frees theology from being dominated by disciplines that possess atomistic, reductionistic, and mechanistic tendencies. While theology should not view itself as a discipline, this does not mean the end of disciplined thinking, specialization, or highly focused research. Even academic disciplines can find a place in the study of theology so long as they are content to play an instrumental role rather than that of an all-controlling methodology.

The task of *theologia* is to clarify vocational identity as the basis for Christian practice. To understand this identity and practice, we need to develop a theology of the nature and mission of the church in the world. This is best done by approaching the church from a world-historical perspective rather than through a study of official teachings. This highlights the unique role of the church in keeping alive the memory of Jesus, primarily through telling and enacting its basic stories in worship, but also through hearing stories from other religious perspectives. Its communal identity has several distinctive features, namely its

---

26. Hough and Cobb, *Christian Identity,* pp. 90-91.

27. Carnegie S. Calian, *Where's the Passion for Excellence in the Church?: Shaping Discipleship Through Ministry and Theological Education* (Wilton, CN: Morehouse-Barlow, 1989), pp. 7-23. Calian likewise regards the church leader as a grassroots theologian who, since the church is the primary community for international discourse, has the marketplace and world in view. More than Hough and Cobb, he stresses the complementary role of the caring, collaborative, and motivating aspects of ministry which, he feels, seminaries also have a hand in shaping.

particular institutional character, its redemptive work in the world, and its central focus on worship and holiness. Central to its identity are faith, hope, and love; and it is the unlimited love of God for humankind which models the church's approach to a just and sustainable society.[28] This prevents distortion of its identity through modern individualism and dualism. The church also needs guiding images to shape its response to pressing contemporary problems, for it is in and through its practices that it maintains its real identity. These images highlight its human, caring, evangelistic, world-affirming character — inclusive, integrating, repentant, loving, just, worshipful, and oriented to the poor.

What kind of curriculum will best serve this? (i) Biblical studies or church history should be more closely linked to the formation of vocational identity, resulting in greater gender and ethnic inclusiveness, closer attention to the wider reaches of history and other religions, and a broader focus on ministry responsibilities than just preaching. (ii) A global consciousness would be encouraged, partly through developing a multicultural student body and partly through providing appropriate immersion experiences. (iii) Theology and ethics would be less dominated by methodology, less separate from one another, and less preoccupied with systematizing, focusing instead on the church's redemptive contribution to major global issues. (iv) Neglected topics would appear in the curriculum, such as non-Western religions, the social sciences, the arts, and the mass media, as well as personal, corporate, and denominational discipleship. (v) There would be closer collaboration with local churches, with seminaries focusing on thinking about practice — through arranging complementary in-service ministry experiences (such as CPE) and exploring their own corporate practices — and congregations becoming teaching churches where, on the analogy with medical schools, internships involve thinking *in* practice.[29]

---

28. This aspect of the proposal is explored by Hough, "The Education of Practical Theologians," 59-62.

29. Stressing the role of the church in being inclusive and hospitable across normal boundaries, Calian suggests that a theological theme, such as forgiveness, might be highlighted throughout the whole theological education program. Because this must be a disposition as well as a conviction, and because it is one of the most distinctive aspects of Christianity, it would prevent us falling into a purely academic approach to what we do, and help us break out of the ideological language and orientation that so often shapes our teaching and curriculum. See *Where's the Passion for Excellence in the Church?* pp. 27-32.

Hough and Cobb's critique of the fourfold pattern and of specialized disciplines — and recommendations concerning the curriculum — are not intended to dictate any particular course of study. But a curriculum could be devised giving more appropriate expression to the indispensable connection between academic and practical work.[30] So far as teaching is concerned, faculty would instruct students in the content of significant texts. They would also engage in research, though for most this would be practical rather than scholarly in character, providing the normative basis and criteria for the work of leaders in the church — both lay and ordained, and for comprehending the social as well as private roles of church members. They would seek to cultivate a capacity for similar practical research in their students. All this needs to be done with an eye to the pluralistic world — denominationally, theologically, culturally, and religiously — in which we now live. For these writers, the challenge is to steer between the threat of "Babel" on the one hand, in which communication between different groups completely disintegrates, and "Pentecost" on the other, with its utopian promise of a single theological language (actually a misunderstanding of that event), so that we can all engage in a quest for the "common good." This creates room for rational discourse about a moral and righteous order that plays an active part in the struggle for peace and justice and in the process develops religious leadership. It is this hoped-for outcome that, they would argue, gives their approach a vocational character.[31] Hough and Cobb stress that reform in theological education along any of the above lines should be incremental. It is through the gradual accumulation of small changes that the reigning paradigm will change, not through its replacement by another model.

As I look at Fuller Seminary, I see some signs of Hough and Cobb's model already within it, and others appearing as incremental changes in its approach to theological education. Its foundation documents declare that the seminary exists "to prepare men and women for the manifold ministries of Christ and his church." These ministries include not only the usual pastoral and other church-related ministries but mission-oriented, professional, and marketplace ones as well. Another of its

30. See further John B. Cobb, Jr., "Theology Against the Disciplines," in *Shifting Boundaries,* pp. 241-58.

31. Joseph C. Hough, Jr., "Theological Education, Pluralism and the Common Good," *Theological Education* 27 (1) (1990): 8-19.

foundation documents describes what it terms "the mission beyond the mission" of the seminary. This identifies key areas of modern life, including evangelism and social action, as well as the renewal of family, church, and cultural life, that is the ultimate goal of theological education. On all course descriptions, professors have to spell out the relevance for ministry of the subject they are teaching, and they are encouraged to teach in a way that is sensitive to multicultural concerns. A growing number of faculty, especially in the applied theology areas, emphasize leadership in the church and the world as involving reflection on practice as well as practical thinking. In this way, doing practical theology becomes the primary role of Christian leaders. This affects the projects students undertake in class and at times the pedagogical character of the class as a whole. As part of this shift in understanding of theological education, more attention is given to other religious traditions and to the study of culture in both its broader and narrower senses, and at the popular and folk as well as high level. Meanwhile, especially among those teaching ethics, there is a growing fusion of ethics and theology in dealing with lifestyle, social, and environmental issues. In the ministry area, developing closer relationships with a number of designated teaching churches is closing some of the gap between the theological academy and local congregations. Some faculty would stress the inherently missiological character of the practical theological task. Although they are still too separate, and there is even some tension between the objectives and methodologies of the two, the presence of a school of world mission alongside the school of theology on campus strengthens the prospects for all training to have a missiological cast. This also creates some overlap between what happens in our institution and the character of the following variant on Hough and Cobb's model.

## B. A Preference for Contextualized Apology

Here we turn to the work of Max L. Stackhouse and his circle.[32] Unlike Farley, their basic concern is with pluralism rather than fragmen-

32. Max L. Stackhouse, "Contextualization and Theological Education," *Theological Education* 23 (1) (1986): 67-77, and especially *Apologia: Contextualization, Globalization, and Mission in Theological Education* (Grand Rapids: Eerdmans, 1988). Just as the work of the Mud Flower Collective was preceded in the

tation, though their approach is from a more global perspective. Like Hough and Cobb, they see the goal of theological education as preparing church leaders who are aware of the multiple and global contexts in which they serve. This involves religious and other types of pluralism, the pursuit of justice for marginal groups, and a quest for common truth. Developing criteria to judge the transcontextual and universal truth of Christianity helps overcome fragmentation, and a set of commonly defined beliefs would better encompass diversity.[33] Central to developing these criteria is a fresh look at what Stackhouse terms *Apologia*.

> [This] can be understood to entail several things: (1) a willingness to enter into the thought forms of those who do not always share the faith assumptions or worldviews that we hold when we enter into dialogue, (2) a willingness to attempt an account of that which we hold most dear in the face of skepticism, doubt or suspicion, (3) a willingness to hear and evaluate on their merits any alternative perspectives that are opposed to our own, and (4) a willingness to refute unsound objections to a defensible theological perspective. To be sure, all such efforts involve the presumptions that it is possible to transcend our own biases in some measure, and that we can have some prospect of knowing something reliable about God, truth, and justice in sufficient degree to recognize it in views held by others, and to preach it and teach it with humble confidence once it is discovered.[34]

*Apologia* has significant implications for the work of contextualization, globalization, and mission, for it requires translating what is perennial into a wide range of cross-cultural situations. If carried out on

---

early 1980s by that of the Cornwall Collective, one may take into account here the ground laid by the early '80s consultation recorded in A. Sapsezian, S. Amirtham, and F. Ross Kinsler, *Global Solidarity in Theological Education* (Geneva: World Council of Churches, 1981), and the later volume by S. Amirtham and S. Wesley Ariarajah, *Ministerial Formation in a Multifaith Milieu* (Geneva: WCC, 1986).

33. Implicit here is a concern with H. Richard Niebuhr's view of "radical monotheism" in *Radical Monotheism and Western Culture* (New York: Harper & Row, 1960). I leave to one side here consideration of Stackhouse's drawing on an analogy with the medieval debate between nominalists and realists, since it has the potential of confusing the real issue and is better viewed as an attempt at illustration than at categorization.

34. M. Stackhouse, *Apologia*, p. 9.

the basis of a general theory of the relationship between religion, culture, philosophy, and theology, it need not be imperialistic.

Next, Stackhouse assesses the meaning and significance of basic concepts in an *Apologia*-oriented theological education, namely, praxis (reflective action), poesis (imaginative representation), and theoria (systematic reflection). None of these can stand independently as the route to knowing and doing. He appreciates Farley's diagnosis of theological education, and for the way it makes room for poesis and praxis alongside theoria. But, Farley's model lacks an adequate understanding of how we come to know (including the role of scripture), a substantive doctrinal content (it has little place for the Creeds), a multicultural awareness (its approach is too homogeneous), and an orientation towards mission (especially to love and justice). In other words, Farley offers only a procedure for — not the substance of — theological education. Making *Apologia* central to the vocation of those in ministry can make up for these lacks. This involves both advocacy and defense. At its heart is the claim that the Christian faith is not simply an objectification of human ideas or longings, and students should have sufficient academic training to counter this Enlightenment critique of religion. This need not entail any radical restructuring of the curriculum. Moving out from Schleiermacher's modified version of the theological encyclopedia, Stackhouse proposes that biblical studies, world religions, and church history comprise "historical fields"; that systematics, ethics, and missiology be the "normative fields"; and that the various components of practical theology make up the "practical fields" on which the move from theory to application principally rests.

Since we are in the midst of challenges to Christianity as great as those during Graeco-Roman and Early Modern times, we should not underestimate the importance of this task of apologetic reconstruction. Church leaders should be able to articulate belief in God's truth and justice in a way that can be contextualized in every culture. The basic means for achieving this are word, ritual, and action. As well as communicators of a rightly based theoria, Christian leaders ought to be celebrators of an appropriate poesis, and agents of a relevant praxis. Equipping ministers to undertake this is the primary goal and unifying feature of theological education. But there must also be a concern for specific doctrines. Christianity has a conceptual core, identifiable boundaries, and criteria for judging what is true and just. Its doctrines should be accessible to human reason and experience as well as

41

to the "right-brain" dimension of life. We must pursue not only the traditional canons of clarity, precision, and coherence but more modern critical criteria. There is room here for a postcritical approach to texts, an approach that distinguishes texts of universal import, those that will make sense only in another culture, and those whose meaning is no longer relevant — even for an element of mystery.

Unlike the views so far considered, this proposal regards teachers as having an obligation to convey to students the central convictions of the Christian faith. These are: the fallen character of humanity, divine revelation in history and scripture, the Trinitarian nature of God, and Jesus' messianic character and work. Together these provide the organizing center for theological education. But teachers must be concerned about "praxiology" as well as "orthodoxy." As this relates to virtues and principles rather than specific actions, it should not be confused with "orthopraxy." At the level of practice there is room for diversity; even though "the Christian thing," as the apologist G. K. Chesterton called it, is concerned with acting rightly, it does not entail a specific set of "right actions." Through clarifying what justice involves, teachers should make it clear how theory and practice are related. Their teaching must be grounded in a spirituality that is nurtured through prayer, corporate worship, and mission, rooted in the sacraments and ministry, oriented by a world-affirming outlook, and guided by a transcultural vision centered on the love, purpose, and law of God.

Since the contribution of Stackhouse and his circle, further dialogue has taken place on the globalization of theological education. Much of this dialogue has focused on specific issues or case studies relating to the meanings of globalization and its relation to evangelism, interfaith discussion, cross-cultural dialogue, and justice, or to the implications of globalization for biblical understanding, human liberation, empowering pedagogies, institutional change, and specific curriculum areas.[35] There have also been some longer-term experiments in discovering the best ways to develop a global framework for students, ranging from short-term overseas immersion programs to longer-term

35. See the collection edited by Alice Frazer Evans, Robert A. Evans, and David A. Roozen, *The Globalization of Theological Education* (Maryknoll, N.Y.: Orbis, 1993), and the volumes given over to "Globalization: Tracing the Journey, Charting the Course," *Theological Education,* Supplement 1 (1993), and "Globalization and the Practical Theological Disciplines," *Theological Education* 20 (1) (1993).

local cross-cultural experiences with grassroots mentors or mentoring organizations.[36] Though the former add a range of interesting details and possibilities, they do not as yet amount to a systematic vision of the kind Stackhouse provides. The latter suggest valuable pedagogical possibilities, but there is some uncertainty as to whether they are fully achieving their purpose.

## C. Some Critical Questions

Alongside the difficulties with the first set of proposals seeking to reform theological education, questions have been raised about this second set as well.

1. If Farley's problem is finding a logical basis for conjoining *Wissenschaft* and *paideia,* Hough and Cobb's problem is their tendency to underemphasize the contribution *Wissenschaft* can make. Though they appreciate the results of historical-critical and social-scientific studies, they do not place much value on inducting students into the underlying methodologies. But their aim here is mostly sound, for they do not wish the scientific approach to dominate. What are we to make of another tendency in their writings, the collapsing of systematic into practical theology? Does this, as some claim, reduce the need to examine the validity claims of the Christian faith? Not necessarily, for their approach simply requires this to be undertaken in a more personally engaged rather than neutral academic way. They also rightly broaden discussion of validity to include the practical consequences of theological assertions.[37] On the other hand, there is some truth to the criticism that they do not supply in their book a good model of practical theological thinking.[38]

36. See, as an example of the second, most recently Susan B. Thistlewaite and George F. Cairns, eds., *Beyond Theological Tourism: Mentoring as a Grassroots Approach to Theological Education* (Maryknoll, N.Y.: Orbis, 1994).

37. See the exchange between Schubert M. Ogden, "Christian Theology and Theological Education," in *The Education of the Practical Theologian: Responses to Joseph Hough and John Cobb's "Christian Identity and Theological Education"* (Atlanta: Scholars Press, 1989), pp. 21-26, and Hough and Cobb, *Christian Identity,* pp. 113-20 and 121-29.

38. So Don S. Browning, "Globalization and the Task of Theological Education in North America," *Theological Education* 23, Supplement 1 (1986): 23.

2. While Hough and Cobb's focus on identity formation in church leadership is a welcome development, they define this mainly in vocational and intellectual terms. This tends to leave personal, or moral and spiritual, formation in the background.[39] Hough's discussion of the role of faith, hope, and love in forming congregational identity could help remedy this but it needs to be linked more specifically with the formation of church leaders. The stress on understanding and undertaking the church's mission in the world is also welcome. But this seems to be viewed more in terms of understanding in order to act in accordance with faith rather than faith seeking understanding. Mission is also mainly defined in terms of human development, with little reference to evangelism,[40] or the daily issues of life.[41]

3. Stackhouse's account appears confused about the relationship between theory and practice. When he is focusing on the importance of "praxiology" as well as "orthodoxy," he seems to argue that theory develops through reflection on practice; at other times he seems to fall back on the view that theory always precedes practice. Though less open to criticism in this area, Hough and Cobb's view of the relationship between these two is still implicitly one-sided. They appear to start with Christian identity and only then move to discussing the praxis it implies,[42] despite the fact that identity is partly shaped through praxis. On the other hand, they rightly avoid depending too heavily on philosophical perspectives, whether derived from Marxism or American pragmatism.

4. Stackhouse's insistence on the importance of maintaining a

39. This was pointed out by the ethicist Peter Paris, "Practical Wisdom and Theological Education," *Theological Education,* Supplement 1 (1993): 55-62, as well as by George Schner, *Education for Ministry: Reform and Renewal in Theological Education* (Kansas City: Sheed and Ward, 1993), pp. 25-29.

40. Compare Don S. Browning, "Globalization and the Task of Theological Education in North America," 43-59.

41. This is brought out by I. Carter Heyward, "Christian Feminists Speak," *Theological Education* 20 (1) (1983): 93-103, and is an issue on which feminist theological educators are generally more sensitive. Though it has also been suggested that Hough and Cobb's definition of Christian identity is too "essentialist," Cobb justifiably replies that their view involves a dynamic interaction with the Christian story. Alternatives that talk about "successive reformulations" of Christian identity risk surrendering the centrality of Christ in identity formation.

42. This is the criticism of Thomas H. Groome, "A Religious Educator's Response," in *The Education of the Practical Theologian,* pp. 77-92.

core set of Christian beliefs is regarded by some as opening up the possibility of theological absolutism. Yet Stackhouse makes room in his understanding of theoria for consideration of truth outside the Christian traditions and, within his understanding of scripture, for cultural diversity in interpretation. Nevertheless, scripture remains for him the dominant point of appeal throughout the curriculum. Its transmission and translation lie at the heart of the church's mission. He has a basic confidence in its canonical demarcation, historical trustworthiness, and general perspicacity. The emphasis here remains on its exhibiting the distinctive content of Christian revelation rather than on its being the repository of all truth.

# 3. Developing a More "Synthetic" Model

A number of approaches coming out of mainstream Protestantism seek to go beyond rather than behind the positions outlined in the first two models in the debate. Only in passing, and then polemically, does some version of a third model come into view. The goal in these approaches is to develop a higher synthesis of key elements in the first two approaches. These contributors posit a unifying goal for theological education, but avoid basing this in some ahistorical structure or essence (as Farley or Stackhouse tend to do). They endorse pluralism within Christianity and its wider culture, but seek to avoid the atomizing of theological approaches (a tendency that they discern among some members of the Collective and the Network). They work to relate theology to the whole of life, but without putting too much emphasis on the private or ecclesial sphere (as happens with some contributors to the Neuhaus symposium). They desire to maintain the strengths of both *paideia* and *Wissenschaft* but not subordinate one to the other (as Hough and Cobb are in danger of doing). The way forward, they suggest, is to provide a different conceptual framework for analyzing the issues.

## A. The Search for Visionary Discernment

Like others, Charles Wood begins by raising questions about the traditional fourfold pattern of theological studies, especially its relevance to the preparation of church leaders. In view of basic changes in theological fields and disciplines over the last two centuries, as well as definitions of the agents and work of ministry, this problem is particularly acute.[43] We can resolve this only by recasting some of the terms of the debate, especially the relationship between subjective and objective, disciplines and dimensions, theory and practice. For Wood, theology itself concerns the way that witnessing to, or passing on, the Christian tradition takes place. It is defined less by its content than by its interest in that subject matter. It is both a reflective enterprise that is functionally distinguished from, but essentially interdependent with, witness, and a critical enterprise that evaluates the validity of the content and character of that witness. It should not be confused with witness, and is not just a composite of disciplines. Whatever questions it asks of a literary, historical, or sociological kind, it also asks essentially theological questions like "Is this witness truly Christian?" (its critical mode) and "How can it become more truly Christian?" (its constructive mode).

Though this activity seems quite different from the older view of theology as a *habitus* or disposition, it can and should include this. Alongside mastery of objective content or critical methods, not just our intellects but our whole selves need to be formed and transformed by theological understanding. Theology is more than a set of objective doctrines or a professional exercise, but it is also more than a subjective disposition or attitude. Even Hough and Cobb's reformulation of the first by reference to the purposes of church leadership, or Farley's recasting of the second to include *scientia,* fails to overcome the objective/subjective polarity. The way around this apparent cul-de-sac is to view theology in its most basic sense as inquiry. Cultivating a disposition for this inquiry and the substance of that disposition, i.e., its subjective and objective dimensions, are secondary. What is meant by critical inquiry? There is no need to base this on a hermeneutics of skepticism or doubt. Critical inquiry need not be a manifestation of human pride but can be conducted in a spirit of humility and within the sphere of our obedience. There is, as he says, "a crucial distinction

43. On all that follows see Charles M. Wood, *Vision and Discernment,* part of which was previously published as "Theological Inquiry and Theological Education," *Theological Education* 21 (2) (Spring 1985): 73-93. See also his later contribution, "Theological Education and Education for Church Leadership," *Quarterly Review* 10 (2) (1990): 65-81.

. . . between questioning God's Word, and asking whether something really is God's Word."[44]

Wood then identifies three basic and two secondary dimensions of theology. The first, historical theology, encompasses biblical and historical studies, and identifies the adequate criteria for testing the faithfulness of witness to Christ and its most important examples. The second, philosophical theology, uncovers the principles by which we discern the meaning of this Christian witness and test its present truth. The third, practical theology, asks by what standards the practice of Christian witness should be evaluated, and how well these are embodied by the Christian community. Since this relates to the witness of the whole church in every area of life, it is broader than pastoral theology as traditionally defined. Though distinguishable, these three dimensions of theological inquiry are interconnected. While we may pursue an interest in only one of the three, this cannot be done without reference to at least aspects of the other two. Together they lead to two further dimensions of theological inquiry. Systematic theology is the comprehensive and constructive integration of the first three and does not just provide the theoretical groundwork for pastoral theology but includes it. Moral theology, less a distinctive inquiry than a specialized focus across all the dimensions, is distinguished from practical theology by its concern with conduct rather than witness. Since none of these dimensions depend on corresponding disciplinary arrangements, they can be pursued within each division of the fourfold structure of studies. They do not lead to new courses so much as to vital questions that should guide what goes on in all courses.

Clearly, Wood does not operate within the reigning model of theory and practice. It is not even a case of theory being developed with an eye to practice, and practice with an eye to theory. Theory and practice must be reconceptualized by setting them within a broader framework constituted by the notions of vision and discernment. Vision seeks to encompass the totality of Christian witness, discernment its particularity. Unlike theory, vision is less likely to be regarded as "irrelevant" or "absolutist" in character. Unlike practice, discernment is less likely to appear "pragmatic" and "utilitarian." Vision can incorporate the "practical" contribution provided by the social sciences, and discernment the "conceptual" clarification that comes from phi-

44. Charles Wood, *Vision and Discernment*, pp. 93-94.

48

losophy. There is a dialectical relationship between vision and discernment, with each informing and correcting the other. There can be no all-encompassing viewpoint independent of particulars, and no bare facts independent of some overarching interpretation. It is vision and discernment together that constitute theological reflection, across all its dimensions, and this means that theology is not *applied* to action but is already *part* of the action itself.

Vision and discernment have something to do with who we are as well as what we think or do. They encompass "subjective" capacities and the "objective" products of those activities. They form judgment as well as formulate judgments. The role of teachers in theological schools is to help students do both, though the first should be their principal goal. Wood thus connects the capacities required for *paideia* with those required for *Wissenschaft*. Since they are conceptual dispositions, the two have much in common. They are more character traits than just ideas or skills. This helps us understand the nature of theological education.

> Theological education is the cultivation of theological judgment. It is the acquisition of the *habitus* for those activities . . . named "vision" and "discernment": activities such as the imaginative grasp of the Christian witness in its unity, the assessment of one's own distinctive situation as a context for witness, and the testing of actual or potential efforts to convey the gospel. . . . They require intelligence, sensitivity, imagination, and a readiness to deal with the unforeseen. It is precisely this *habitus* which is the primary and indispensable qualification for church leadership. . . . But how is such judgment to be formed in the context of the present typical curriculum, and how is its formation related to the more strictly professional aspects of education for ministry? . . . This does not mean increasing the number of courses required in systematic theology, or enhancing their prestige somehow. It means, instead, understanding the entire curriculum as really and truly a theological curriculum, that is, as a body of resources ordered to the cultivation in students of an aptitude for theological inquiry. . . . The specifically professional elements of education for ministry are not simply matters of technique, to be tacked on where convenient. They are best seen as *specifications* of the broader theological inquiry.[45]

45. Charles Wood, *Vision and Discernment*, pp. 86-87.

This also prevents theological education from becoming solely spiritual formation. It involves spiritual formation, but in order to develop a mature faith this must include a critical reevaluation of belief. This can be done humbly without yielding to academic hubris, incorporating tradition, in the form of practices as well as beliefs, and interrogating function as well as content. While this is geared primarily towards professional education for ministry, it seeks to keep the non-professional ministry of lay people in view.

## B. The Quest for Concrete Divine Understanding

David Kelsey adds two basic features to Wood's general approach.[46] First, the best way to overcome residual difficulties involved in giving unity to theological education is to move away from the abstract discussion of "the Christian thing" to its concrete embodiment in congregations and seminaries. The diverse or even ambiguous expressions of the church enable us to keep both unity and pluralism in view, as well as in proper dialectical tension. Building on the contribution of James F. Hopewell,[47] Kelsey regards both congregations and seminaries as networks of complex, interconnected practices. These human, cooperative, embodied actions are historically relative, take institutional and material shape, and are inherently self-critical. Second, greater specificity can be given to the overarching goal of a theological school by defining it as

46. David Kelsey develops his own proposal in Part Two of his book *To Understand God Truly: What's Theological About a Theological School?* (Louisville: Westminster/John Knox, 1992), pp. 103-263, though see earlier "A Theological Curriculum About and Against the Church," in *Practical Theology*, ed. Don S. Browning, pp. 37-48.

47. James F. Hopewell, *Congregation: Stories and Structure* (Philadelphia: Fortress, 1987). Hopewell's program has been continued and extended by others at Emory, as documented by T. E. Frank, "Congregational and Theological Education and Research," *Theological Education* 33 (2) (1997), pp. 93-120. Kelsey is only too well aware of various objections that have been raised against Hopewell's approach, especially in the symposium edited by Joseph C. Hough, Jr., and Barbara Wheeler, *Beyond Clericalism: The Congregation as a Focus for Theological Education* (Atlanta: Scholars Press, 1988). Kelsey argues that the fear of a congregational orientation resulting in sectarian, parochial, and complacent attitudes arises from a misunderstanding of the concrete particularity and scandal of Christianity (pp. 132-35). His other arguments (*To Understand God Truly*, pp. 146-52) are given below.

seeking to understand God truly. Since understanding undergoes disciplined development, is guided by our interests, and takes place concretely through a set of practices, we can avoid the twin pitfalls of talking about some ahistorical essence or succumbing to some ideological distortion. It is because God cannot be known directly, however, that growth in true knowledge of God must take place through focusing on local churches. In this way his two proposals are vitally connected.

For Kelsey, public worship of God lies at the heart of congregational life. The redemptive mission of the church does not constitute its center but flows out of that. It is a community's self-description as belonging to Christ and its criteria for understanding this self-description, that distinguishes a church from other social and religious groups. Such a focus is saved from parochialism by orienting worship to the whole person and to the whole of life, and conducting it so that it is accessible to anyone who might be interested. Consequently, what happens in worship has a moral and political, as well as spiritual and theological, character. All this has implications for theological education. It calls for (i) a "theology of culture" which will enable it to reflect critically on the broader determinants of congregational practices and to envision more relevant ways of sharing its story; (ii) a "semiotic study" of the dominant symbols, images, and stories of the wider culture and a critique of what these reveal about its goals, values, and identity; (iii) a "social and political analysis" of the way people's identities are formed or changed and of the way power is exercised and redistributed; and (iv) historical study of congregations in relation to their own tradition and other cultures as well as social-scientific study of their practices and theological analysis of how scripture shapes their discipleship, witness, and mission.

Theological schools are constituted by a set of interrelated practices that center on teaching and learning but also include recruiting and developing, resourcing and governing, relating and worshiping. All these are directed to one end — growth in the capacity to know God more truly.

> [This] involves developing a range of capacities and abilities to apprehend God. Three points emerge: (a) Cultivating these abilities is a kind of conceptual growth that requires disciplining. (b) These abilities are guided by interests in God's peculiar ways of being present, interests in them for their own sake rather than for their

moral, therapeutic, or redemptive consequences. Above all, these interests are guided by interest in truth that requires rigorous testing as to their truthfulness. (c) Because these interests are socio-culturally situated they are diversely concrete, threatening to "fragment" understandings of God, and they are open to the suspicion of ideological bias; but because they are interests in *God* the capacities they guide also require cultivation of capacities for conversation with other concrete understandings and capacities for critique of ideological self-perceptions.[48]

This conceptual growth also involves reshaping our identities, and is judged by whether or not we act on what we learn. Central to this is the capacity to discern and respond to God's presence, and the facility to know and use scriptural narratives that illumine this. To know God truly in this way also involves its manifestation in a school's institutionalized practices. These practices are set within organizational polities revolving around different theological centers, which have a social and political impact on their wider surroundings. It is the coherence of these with the overarching goals of the school — not the type of polity or amount of social change — that is crucial. This suggests the need for ongoing institutional self-critique of all, not just educational, practices.

Though they have worship of God rather than the knowledge of God as their goal, congregations do contain educational structures, and seminaries occasionally constitute themselves as congregations.[49] The continuing relevance of a congregation's worship requires continual theological assessment, and while all its members should reflect on this, theological schools can help this take place effectively. Such reflection raises questions traditionally studied in seminaries, and invites use of the whole range of disciplines available to them. Giving focus to this reflection are three "horizons" arising out of congregations' life — the understanding of Christianity implicit or explicit in their practices (constructive theology); the fidelity of their words and actions to this (practical theology); and the criteria by which they judge these (apologetic theology). Each of these should be approached descriptively, ana-

---

48. David Kelsey, *To Understand God Truly*, p. 178.

49. Coming to similar conclusions about the extent to which the church is a seminary and the seminary is a church, is Carnegie S. Calian, *Where's the Passion for Excellence in the Church?* pp. 7-15.

lytically, and comparatively. This means that a theological school's study would be both for and against congregations, critical where they are lacking and appreciative where they are oriented to true worship. Such a focus is more basic for seminaries than wholesale curriculum reform. Much more will be achieved if each course seeks to address at least one of these "horizons," for this provides the unity that is lacking in curriculum reform, and invites a genuinely pluralist response. Other decisions about the organization and sequence of studies can be worked out by each theological school in ways that are most appropriate to its basic ethos.

Kelsey's approach seeks to gather up vital elements of both *paideia* and *Wissenschaft* in a new way. In his terms, the seminary is a kind of "crossroads hamlet" somewhere between Athens and Berlin, though facing more towards the latter. It is one with *paideia* in viewing theology as a set of capacities directed to knowing God truly, but it is one with *Wissenschaft* in endorsing the role and rigor of academic disciplines in this process. Its emphasis on developing capacities to know its subject matter rather than focusing directly on the subject matter itself allies it with Farley's approach, yet it stresses knowing God rather than developing faith and requires people to be more than participant observers in congregations. Its focus on the concrete life of congregations separates it from Hough and Cobb's model, but the two share a concern with preparing church leadership, understood not in professional terms but of the call and ministry of the whole people of God. Although the overarching goal and process of theological education relates it to the first model, and the range of areas studied and type of critical thinking employed relate it to the second, Kelsey's approach modifies both and seeks to hold them in fruitful tension. Whether it manages to do this successfully is another matter, as we shall see in a moment.

It is easier to find partial embodiments of the "classical" and "vocational" models of theological education than this more "synthetic" approach, even though in some respects it is a mutation of the first two. In my own experience of teaching in and visiting of institutions, however, I have come across occasional approaches to it in individual classes, departments, or programs. Much of my own teaching in biblical studies, theological ethics, and practical theology seeks to overcome the objective/subjective polarity through a focus on vision and discernment along the lines set out by Wood, and to move beyond seeking to transform intellect to transforming students' whole selves. In Kelsey's terms, this aims at understanding God truly and doing so by means of specific practices, not techniques, that both inform what happens in the classroom and shape what happens around it in part of the wider institutional culture. In many cases, some of the assigned work takes place as students engage in observation and experiment in their local churches. Though I teach across most of the main disciplines in the theological encyclopedia, each of my courses contains a blend of biblical studies, historical background, doctrinal/ethical reflection, and practical theology. All of these exhibit an interest in social and cultural analysis, investigation of the key images and practices of contemporary life, and commitment to personal formation and spiritual disciplines. In some respects I am both more and less traditional than either Wood or Kelsey, for I give a more normative role to the Bible and I build more practical testing out of the results of critical inquiry into the class experience itself. This makes some of what I do closer to certain aspects of the extension of Wood's and Kelsey's approach that follows.

## C. The Promise in Idea-Forming Practices

The most recent writer to attempt some kind of synthesis of earlier positions is Rebecca Chopp. While she appreciates the way Farley and Kelsey have provided a new vision of "knowledge," she is critical of the formality of their approach, arguing that what we need is practical methods for investigating concrete experiences of our struggle for transformation. The best way to do this is to focus on the actual practices of theological education, and from these construct the ideas that will both reflect and guide our actions.[50] According to Chopp, Christian feminism provides distinctive resources for this task, but only if it moves beyond its liberal egalitarian or romantic expressive forms in a more "prophetic" or "transformist" direction. Three elements of feminist theology are particularly hopeful. First, its stress on narrativity, that is, women's

50. On what follows see Rebecca Chopp, "Situating the Structure: Prophetic Feminism and Theological Education," in *Shifting Boundaries,* pp. 67-89, and "Cultivating Theological Scholarship," *Theological Education* 22 (1) (1995): 79-94 and, most fully, *Saving Work: Feminist Practices of Theological Education* (Louisville: Westminster/John Knox, 1995).

naming and taking responsibility for their own reflection, practice, and spirituality. Incorporating this in theological education requires imagination, justice, and dialogue. Second, feminist theology's redefining of ecclesia in a more inclusive, egalitarian, and life-transforming direction. The question of ordination is involved in this, not just for some women but whether it should be broadened to include all. Third, the character of feminist theology; within its broader liberationist vision of Christianity, it views itself as a practice rather than a mere set of theories. As such it is what she terms "saving work" that brings ethics and epistemology together, engages in a critique of prevailing interests and ideologies, anticipates new possibilities for the future, and contextualizes all that it discovers. Overall this offers a holistic vision of what actually takes place in theological education.

While agreeing with Farley's diagnosis, she views the dominant academic model as less the product of modern rationalism than of masculine reasoning. Therefore his suggested foundational studies should have a more pragmatic, relative, and fallible flavor. In line with this, she argues for the rhetorical rather than objective interpretation of texts, with scripture as "prototype and not archetype," and truth lying in the community's ongoing quest for understanding. The goal of *paideia* is freedom more than wisdom, and *habitus* is a concrete and historically conditioned affair. Chopp feels that even Kelsey's focus on the concrete structures of theological education is still too oriented to cognitive learning. A focus on practices broadens this, and includes intuitive, emotional, and physical dimensions of learning. It leads to a genuinely creative approach to life, a commitment to justice, and the developing of solidarity with the oppressed.

Reform in theological education will never come about by curriculum revision alone.

> If knowing God is as much a matter of right relationships as it is a mastery of correct ideas, then the present crisis of theological education cannot be fixed merely by reordering the curriculum. New relationships of imagination, of justice, of dialogue must be formed in the midst of a pluralistic world and new forms of relating, teaching and community building will have to be developed. The *how* of learning is directly related, in this notion of theological education as a process, to the *what* of learning. Indeed, the task for the subjects of theological education may be as much the doing of

new forms of relationships to God, self, others, traditions, and society as it is the articulation of right ideas.[51]

Central here is addressing important current issues in the light of past, present, and future forms of Christian praxis. This entails "doing" as well as "learning" theology, and forces us to explore the connections between theological learning and the local community. We must also give attention to symbolic patterns of religion, for only as students become poets as well as interpreters, will they be equipped to carry out their task. All this means that we will only progress in reforming theological education by undertaking a "thick description" of, and identifying "emergent possibilities" in, the present. Among others, Kelsey has welcomed Chopp's contribution as generally pointing the way forward for the debate. Especially helpful is her plea for a greater emphasis on the practices of theological education, a more holistic view of learning and knowing, and the importance to the learning community of more inclusive and participatory forms of church life.

## D. Some Critical Questions

1. Helpful though Wood's emphasis on vision and discernment is in bridging the gap that has opened up in theological education between intellectual and moral formation — which remains a problem for both the older classical and newer vocational model — it still does not go far enough. For discernment is only one aspect of moral formation, and in Wood's account the emphasis still falls on its cognitive dimension. If, as he says, a disposition for discernment is "the fruit of a certain personal and moral maturity,"[52] we need to give more attention to the stem from which this comes and to "how we may be so disposed."[53]

2. Though both Wood and Kelsey seek to synthesize the two main proposals in the debate, they have not satisfactorily explained how this can happen. Though drawing on key elements from both positions, Kelsey continues to maintain that the two models are funda-

51. Rebecca Chopp, *Saving Work*, p. 110.
52. Charles M. Wood, *Vision and Discernment*, p. 75.
53. Merle D. Strege, "Chasing Schleiermacher's Ghost," in *Theological Education and Moral Formation*, 122.

mentally incompatible. Each brings different definitions of the goal of theological study, different expectations of what is involved in teaching and learning, and different views of how teachers and students should relate. Kelsey's awareness of the problem surfaces in his carefully worded references to Wood's proposal as an "attempt" at a different model that "perhaps" amounts to a "third way," and "may" only be "something like" a higher synthesis.[54] In my judgment, like Wood's, his own approach only promises a synthesis: neither explicates how the two divergent types of thinking can be combined.[55]

3. Chopp develops a more thoroughgoing pluralist view of truth that regards personal tensions and contradictory viewpoints as constitutive for, not just instrumental in, the search for harmony. This goes beyond the Pauline conviction that "there must be factions among you" (1 Cor 11:19), according to which the expression of tension and differences is a normal part of the quest for personal consistency and theological understanding. But if, as Chopp suggests, it is less important to work through these tensions and difficulties to some resolution than to allow them to stand as continuing challenge, that is another matter. While this does not necessarily end up in complete relativism, it does leave little room for anything normative.

4. A by-product of Chopp's approach is the appearance of some vague and inadequate theological definitions. For example, she describes the church simply as the place "where the Spirit works through the lives of women and men for the realization of new life."[56] This does not sufficiently distinguish it from other groupings or activities in which believers are engaged and makes forming people for it a rather amorphous affair. Also, whatever church is, it appears to be purely instrumental to the overall good of society. It has value only as a means. In general, the lack of clear theological definition in Chopp's writings, and the blurring of important distinctions, reduces the chance of the creative and life-giving practices of theological education she favors revitalizing and transforming it in the way she desires.

54. David H. Kelsey, *Between Athens and Berlin*, pp. 215 and 200.
55. Rebecca Chopp, *Saving Work*, p. 126, also points out this inadequacy in Kelsey's proposal.
56. Rebecca Chopp, *Saving Work*, p. 52.

# 4. *Some Final Responses to the Debate*

In this concluding section on the debate I would like to offer three final responses. First, a summary of the elements on which most contributors agree, however differently they may interpret them, that represent genuine moves forward in our understanding of theological education. Second, some reservations of a more general nature, and the opening up of a new direction that could lead us beyond present impasses. Third, two reworkings of long-standing "confessional" models in light of the debate to see if they offer any helpful suggestions.

## A. Elements on Which There Is Agreement

Since up till now I have highlighted differences rather than similarities between the main proposals to the debate, let me now identify a number of matters on which there is a significant amount of agreement.

- We will only get beyond the fragmentation of theological education if the whole curriculum is oriented to some unified overarching goal.
- In moving towards that goal, all that is done at the curricular and co-curricular level must have an integral theological dimension.
- This requires students developing the capacity to do theology themselves rather than simply learning theology or how theologians go about it.

58

- Doing theology involves a combination of critical reflection on seminal texts and the exercise of other personal dispositions that are formative for thinking and acting.
- Theology is more than a set of beliefs requiring practical application, and is a holistic enterprise that integrally touches all aspects of the faith-directed life.
- The one-way relationship between theory and practice, according to which the former precedes the latter, must give way to a more complex relationship between the two.[57]
- Study should be oriented towards developing church leadership, though this should not be understood in a functional way or in terms of the clerical paradigm.[58]
- There is a public dimension to theological education, both in the intellectual criteria by which it is verified and the life-situations on which it bears.

## B. Several Significant Reservations

All of these are genuine advances in our understanding of theological education, even if there are differences in the way they are interpreted by contributors to the debate. But the inadequacies remain. Although I have already voiced criticisms about the main proposals in the debate, I would now like to spell out some reservations I have about the debate as a whole. For though it has introduced a deeper self-awareness about theological education, provided a broader analysis of key issues, and suggested a number of general reforms, it is limited by certain in-built weaknesses.

57. Though he acknowledged a place for doing as well as reflecting in theological education, H. Richard Niebuhr, *The Purpose of the Church and Its Ministry*, pp. 2-113, understood this primarily as church-related work and as providing data for learning, not as a crucial component in theory formation.

58. An exception to this latter point is the view of Dennis M. Campbell, "Theological Education and Moral Formation: What's Going on in Seminaries Today?" in *Theological Education and Moral Formation*, pp. 1-21, that *ordained* ministry is central to the enterprise of theological education. For a corrective see Donald W. Shriver, Jr., "Theological Education for the Twenty-first Century," *Crux* (1996): 18-22. In relation to the next point he argues that the focus on finding the sacred in the limits and potential of people's lives rather than primarily in the substance of daily life is an individualistic, Kantian bias that afflicts too much modern writing.

1. For all its breadth of coverage, in one sense the debate has a parochial flavor. Certainly the dominance of professional theologians has given it an advantage over most previous discussions where administrators were the main driving force. At the same time, a growing attention to the realities of seminary and congregational life, and most recently on the practices of theological education, is gradually moving it away from too abstract an approach. But there are other voices that need to be heard. Alongside women and minorities, we need to hear the voice of theological students, pastors, lay leaders, and parachurch figures. Discussions among Third World theological thinkers and practitioners should also have a greater hearing, for these have a potentially "more productive impetus toward renewal of theological education."[59] For all the recent attention to local congregations, the divorce of so many theologians from regular grassroots ministry in the church or the world results in a less concrete treatment than we really require.[60]

2. Attempts by various contributors to the debate to bring intellectual and moral formation, or theological and social transformation, into greater unity do not fully succeed. As already mentioned, Wood's helpful focus on discernment does not sufficiently close the gap. Other calls for theological education to involve seeking justice and exhibiting compassion do not explain how we can become the kinds of people who will do this. Though Hough talks about the centrality of love for local congregations, he does not discuss how it can become central in seminary life. This was implicit in the way the Mud Flower Collective approached theological reflection, but the group itself failed to become one in which love reigned. Indeed one misses in the debate as a whole a serious treatment of growth in understanding as an act of love. Chopp's insistence on the centrality for theological education of developing right relationships goes furthest towards this, but it is still the

---

59. So Robert W. Ferris, *Renewal in Theological Education: Strategies for Change* (Wheaton: Billy Graham Center, 1990), pp. 8-9. See further the survey provided and literature cited in his first two chapters, particularly the volumes edited by Bowers (1982), and Conn and Rowen (1984), on which see also note 9 in the following chapter. On my general point about parochialism, see also G. S. Wilmore, "Theological Education in a World of Religious and Other Diversities," *Theological Education* 23, Supplement (1987): 156-60.

60. Along similar lines see R. K. Martin, "Congregational Studies and Critical Pedagogy in Theological Perspective," *Theological Education* 33 (2) (1997): 137ff.

language of justice rather than sacrificial love that is being used, that language itself is too politically skewed, and little is said concretely about how this is to take place.[61] Hauerwas takes up a further issue, pointing out that you do not inculcate virtue by making it an aim in itself. "Virtues," he says, "are nurtured in activities." And he asks: "Why aren't we talking more in the language of discipleship, in the language of witness?"[62]

3. Though throughout the debate practice is given a more central place in theological education, it could be argued that it is still not central enough. Is it really possible to develop a capacity for action that is abstracted from engaging in action? It is not just that capacities can often be short-circuited (compare Paul's comments about himself in Romans 7), but that action will be devalued as a route to learning so long as it is only talked about and not engaged in. It must become part of the circle of theological reflection. This is why Kelsey's view that one need only be a "participant" not "existentially engaged" observer in the life of a congregation is inadequate. This not only models a kind of reflection that can all too easily be carried over into ministry with disastrous effects, but overlooks the fact that theological reflection has greater depth when one is actively involved. For this reason, Hough and Cobb's relegation of reflective practice to a probationary church-based year of ministry at the end of a student's course of study is also inadequate. So long as theological reflection is not an organic part of the whole curriculum, the dichotomy between theory and practice remains partially in place. It is Chopp who breaks out of this circle most fully, arguing that a focus on practice rather than ideas is the only way forward, but this is in danger of loosing practice too much from the criteria by which it may be evaluated.

4. It is questionable, as some suggest, that "perhaps the single most dramatic and important consequence of the conversation is that the 'clerical paradigm' has been thoroughly discredited."[63] For all Hough and Cobb's opening up church leadership and mission to lay

---

61. One could begin here with the section on truth as "troth" in Parker J. Palmer, *To Know as We Are Known: A Spirituality of Education* (San Francisco: Harper & Row, 1982). Note, too, the general comments on this in Mark R. Schwehn, *Exiles from Eden*, p. 50.

62. In R. Neuhaus, ed., *Theological Education and Moral Formation*, pp. 170, 192.

63. David H. Kelsey, *To Understand God Truly*, p. 162.

people and professionals, in their closing chapters they concentrate on the role of clergy.[64] Farley is better here, for his second book gives broader attention to theological education of lay people in the church and university. Apart from a passing comment by Chopp (which is placed in parentheses and followed by a question mark), these writings do not approach the more radical New Testament disavowal of clergy-lay distinctions in favor of only functional distinctions between believers' ministries in the church and world.[65] And while the growing focus on the local church in the debate has made it more concrete, it tends to marginalize those in seminaries who are training for parachurch organizations and, even more, community or justice-oriented work, or ministry in the marketplace.[66] While contributors to the debate talk about the life of church members in the world, and the wider public dimension of Christian mission, they view this primarily through the lens of the local church. This marginalizes the whole fabric of informal contacts, networks, and groups initiated and maintained by lay people outside the church. It is these that provide the basic support for the

64. In agreement with this assessment of the proposals from Farley as well as Hough and Cobb is Don S. Browning, "Globalization and the Task of Theological Education in North America," 52-53. The clerical focus also appears in Schner's work, even though he recognizes the validity of theological education for the laity.

65. Chopp's comment may be found in her section on "ekklesia" in her book, *Saving Work*, p. 50.

66. Again it is Chopp, *Saving Work*, p. 48, who makes passing reference to this. Even so, one gets the impression that people moving into some form of ministry outside the church frequently do so in response to frustration rather than as a first choice. Hough declares in one place that "Education of leaders for religious institutions is the primary justification for the existence of theological schools" ("Theological Education, Pluralism, and the Common Good," *Theological Education* 27 [1] [1990]: 18). It is not that he is wrong in saying this but that, especially in its context discussing the education of competent leadership for the major social institutions, he does not even mention anything more. For his part, Farley is behind the times, at least for many seminaries, when he says, "It is possible to envision a time when these schools will not simply be schools for clergy education" (*The Fragility of Knowledge,* p. 177). That time is already here. Indeed, in a growing number of seminaries today students on the ordained track are in the minority. This is why his additional comment that the aims of seminaries in the future "will still cluster around the education of an advanced church leadership" is unsatisfactory. Instead, seminaries must become more pluralist in the vocational directions for which they are training people.

various ministries of daily life. However much the "clerical paradigm" may or may not have been broken through in the debate, an "ecclesiastical" paradigm is still firmly in place.

5. There is a tendency in this literature to portray God as a passive agent in the whole process of theological education. Writers generally speak as if we are the active subjects in the enterprise. Surely theological understanding is ultimately about God's revelation to us, not our discovery of God; it is not so much a case of "knowing God more truly," to use Kelsey's words, as, to use Parker J. Palmer's echo of Paul's language, "to know as we are known."[67] Among these writers, only Richard Muller and Max Stackhouse include a discussion of the centrality of revelation, and they along with George Schner are the only ones who make much reference to the Spirit. Stackhouse does this mostly by means of formulating questions about how and where we can discern the presence of the Spirit today. This paucity of discussion of the Spirit is a major theological weakness in the debate. Throughout the Bible the Spirit is heavily involved in communicating with the people of God and enlightening them about God's character and work. Failure to give the Spirit a central pedagogical role in theological education demonstrates how much these writers, to some extent even those I have exempted from this criticism, still lack a fully adequate theological framework.[68]

Some of these criticisms may help to explain why the debate has not had more influence on the faculty and boards of theological institutions. Evidence shows that the main readers of material emanating from the debate have been seminary presidents and academic deans. Some seminary and university faculty have read the "aims and purposes" literature, and some administrative officers the "institutional

67. See Parker J. Palmer, *To Know as We Are Known.* Also the comment of Thomas Gillespie about the centrality of the triune God's self-revelation — attested for in scripture and confessed by the church — in the process of theological education. See "What Is 'Theological' about Theological Education," *The Princeton Seminary Bulletin* 14 (1) (1993): 55-63.

68. Richard A. Muller, *The Study of Theology: From Biblical Interpretation to Contemporary Formation* (Grand Rapids: Zondervan, 1991); Max L. Stackhouse, *Apologia;* George Schner, *Education for Ministry: Reform and Renewal in Theological Education* (Kansas City: Sheed & Ward, 1993). For an example of someone seeking to make the Spirit the epistemological starting point for theological reflection, see Helmut Thielicke, *The Evangelical Faith,* vol. 1, *Prolegomena: The Relation of Theology to Modern Thought Forms* (Grand Rapids: Eerdmans, 1974), pp. 129ff.

research" reports, but while the second of these appears to have had some influence, outside the Association of Theological Schools the first as yet seems to have had little impact on educational goals and practices. There seems less evidence of other members of seminaries, such as students and board members, being affected by the debate, and the same seems to be true for pastors and denominational leaders. Though undoubtedly there are many reasons for this state of affairs — lack of time, institutional conservatism, specialist concerns, immediate preoccupations, denominational hesitancies — part of the problem may be the abstract nature of so much of the debate, its lack of wider representation, and its focus on ideas at the expense of practices.

## C. Two Additional Rejoinders

Can any of these inadequacies be overcome by drawing on and rejuvenating two existing models of theological education — whose origins lie between the classical and modern periods — namely that found in many Catholic and evangelical schools?

1. The first seeks to rework an approach that has its roots in Aquinas. According to George Schner, Catholic forms of ministerial training have never lost the habits of theological, moral, and spiritual formation Farley and others seek, even if they do not always hold them in proper balance with other requirements. Such forms of training also tend to have a genuinely vocational rather than functional or professional understanding of ministry.[69] Schner agrees with Kelsey that Farley's model lacks a focus on the object of the habits it endorses, that is, God — God's character, work, and relation to us. It is this that ultimately orders theologia. Hough and Cobb are astray in insisting that what is determinative here is simply becoming practical theologians. And Stackhouse's emphasis on a doctrinal core stresses the intellectual rather than life-giving character of understanding God. Kelsey's proposal, however, needs more substance, and it is this that the tradi-

69. Schner, *Education for Ministry,* pp. 2-3. He argues that, mainly because of their strong insistence on vocation, Catholics have never fully succumbed to the technical definition of the professional and have always insisted on the moral and spiritual dimension (cf. also pp. 18-19). See also his article on "Formation as a Unifying Concept in Theological Education," *Theological Education* 21 (2) (1985): 94-113.

tion stemming from Aquinas, properly rejuvenated, can provide. Alongside fundamental and doctrinal theology, it opens up a genuine role for what has classically been called spiritual theology.

How would this change the character of theological study? It would emphasize more the formative work of the family, the congregation, and Christian education in nurturing it. It would also stress formation as an integral aspect of seminary life, not merely as preparation for service in the church. Indeed, spiritual formation — understood as a way of life expressing the inner life of the Trinity more than just a set of spiritual disciplines or experiences — must be viewed as a dimension of the whole curriculum and the whole institution of the seminary. This encompasses every scholarly discipline, and all our symbol-making doctrinal capacities, as well as every aspect of ministry and mission and their contextualization. According to Schner, his approach overcomes a tendency in the debate for *paideia* to be viewed too much in terms of agility in theological method and for mission to be viewed too frequently as a set of fragmented courses with a missiological dimension. Implementing it would involve, first, making liturgy, proclamation, service, teaching, and community — the basic activities of the church — the basis for reconceiving the aims of curricular change, and, secondly, faculty and students reinventing the tradition of the church and the former "parenting" rather than primarily "mentoring" the latter in it.

2. The second approach has its roots in Calvin, especially in post-Reformation perspectives.[70] Richard Muller's response to the gap between theory and practice, or seminary and church, as well as to the loss of unity and direction in theological education, is to focus on the structure of the curriculum.

Rather than rejuvenating the theological tradition stemming from Aquinas, we must develop a biblically based hermeneutics that reinvigorates the fourfold pattern of studies and orients this in a way that reflects and serves the life of the church. This need not move *sapientia* into the background, for the first formulations of the "theological encyclopedia" included a strong emphasis on it. Nor need it be a step back into a precritical approach, for the fourfold pattern has always contained a critical dimension. In contrast to Farley or Hough and Cobb, what this provides is a more objective understanding of

---

70. Muller, *The Study of Theology.*

*paideia* and more objective basis for practical theological reflection. In contrast to Kelsey or Schner it provides a more cognitive and normative scriptural basis for knowing God. Only so, says Muller, can we combine objective knowledge of God *(theoria)* and subjective union with God *(praxis),* as well as subdisciplines and competencies *(scientia),* and moral and spiritual dimensions *(habitus).* So long as the fourfold pattern of study contained broad types of interrelated and church-related fields rather than separate disciplines with their own controlling interests, it preserved this. So did use of the historical-critical method, as long as it served larger practical interpretive ends. It is the tyranny of that method and the professionalizing of ministry that fragments theological study and makes it too abstract.

Muller draws on the work of Wolfhart Pannenberg, especially his historical approach to Christianity and his adding the study of religions to the theological encyclopedia.[71] This enables him to chart a historical path through the theological encyclopedia that links its divisions and contains an overall unity.[72] The basic element and catalyst in this is a biblically impelled hermeneutics, one that recognizes the distinctive role of scripture without assuming any particular definition of biblical authority or inspiration. From this flows a hermeneutical trajectory that begins with biblical exegesis, proceeds through the study of religions, church history, and systematic theology, and concludes with the current application of scripture in apologetics/ethics and practical theology. Each specialization in the sequence should increasingly orient its subject matter to our contem-

71. Wolfhart Pannenberg, *Theology and the Philosophy of Science* (Philadelphia: Westminster, 1976).

72. At this point Muller comes close to the position advocated by Walter E. Wyman, Jr., "The Historical Consciousness and the Study of Theology," in *Shifting Boundaries,* pp. 91-117. Wyman's main arguments are that (1) historical studies should form the core of the theological curriculum, and (2) the historical consciousness ought to pervade all areas of study, not just the specifically historical areas. Where Muller differs from Wyman is in the clear, though not absolute, distinction he wishes to draw between biblical and historical studies, and in his insistence that the historically formed church witness and life form an ever present horizon throughout the whole curriculum. He argues that the plea by Gerhard Ebeling, *The Study of Theology* (Philadelphia: Fortress, 1978), for an overarching, interpretive "fundamental theology" that unites the disparate elements of the theological curriculum by requiring each to identify the truth towards which it points, offers only a direction not a solution to the problem of fragmentation.

porary situation.[73] Here, then, is an interpretive path through the fourfold pattern of study. Within this path, hermeneutics and spirituality can again become one, as can theology and ministry. So far as the problem of diversity is concerned, the challenge of contextualizing theology is not a new challenge but only more complex. As in previous times, we need to adapt new metaphors and terms from the culture in order to translate our ever relevant Christian convictions. Properly understood, contextualizing is just another exercise in putting historical method at the service of making faith understandable.[74]

How helpful are these contributions from Schner and Muller in overcoming some of the shortcomings in the debate? Their attempts to give greater substance to a focus on God by highlighting the centrality of scripture and the role of tradition, and their desire to integrate spiritual formation more closely with the curriculum and non-curricular activities, are both valuable but do not go far enough. Schner's de-

---

73. The first set of areas all have a common methodological link in historical consciousness. Biblical studies provides the foundation of the theological enterprise. Biblical theology is the link between biblical studies and the other disciplines, while church history and the history of doctrine provide the connection between the text and the present. Comparative religion and the history of religions enable us to understand the story of the cross-cultural transmission of Christianity and provide a necessary understanding of its broader context. Doctrinal theology, which draws on the full range of theological disciplines, forges a clear relationship between normative dogmas and contemporary faith-statements. Philosophical theology, lying on the boundary of the fourfold pattern and secular academic study, explicates and validates this in the light of contemporary thought. Ethics and apologetics form the place where the success or failure of our biblical, historical, and systematic theological study becomes transparent. Practical theology, with its many subdisciplines, also contains theoretical and practical elements and seeks to incorporate the social sciences within a theological framework (*The Study of Theology*, pp. 61-170).

74. One critic has accused Muller's approach of being "a textbook example . . . of 'an institutional church theology'" which is totally devoid of "any mention of the Holy Spirit" (see Ray S. Anderson, *Ministry on the Fireline: A Practical Theology for an Empowered Church* [Downers Grove, Ill.: InterVarsity, 1993], note 4). This is not quite fair, for it is less an institutional church theology than a revelation-based one that is able to criticize both church and theology, and Muller does refer to the revelatory work of the Spirit in communicating to us the mind and will of God. It is true that he does not discuss the transformative work of the Spirit in the process, structures, and outcome of theological education more generally, but this is the case with virtually all contributors to the debate.

pendence on Aquinas to legitimate modern discipline-based reflection is insufficient unless there is discussion of valuable features of post-Enlightenment thinking; Muller considers, but then dismisses, the possibility of drawing on the distinction between special and general revelation to legitimize a theological link between the two. While both effect a stronger relationship between intellectual and spiritual formation, and Schner in particular stresses the spiritual dimension of other aspects of seminary life, the personal growth that comes only from practical service of God is left out of the picture. Meanwhile their proposals are still vulnerable to the other criticisms of the debate mentioned above.

# Conclusion

Underlying a number of criticisms set out above is a final, more general, query. While in the debate the word "theological" has come in for close scrutiny, apart from Kelsey who criticizes it for its abstractness and favors the term "school," the other key term, "education," has not received the same amount of attention. Does this very term, or the more concrete word "school," assume something about training for ministry that needs to be questioned? I am aware that asking this will raise suspicions of anti-intellectualism, of which we have already had too much in the church. This is far from my intention. I ask the question in the same spirit as Farley first asked the question about use of the word "theological." He contended that the way we used that word sat uneasily with the classical meaning of *theologia*. And although he and others have used the word *paideia* to refocus our understanding of what education involves, is this sufficient? May we not still be operating within too much of a classical view of education, however christianized, when a more radically Judeo-Christian understanding of it is required?[75]

If this is the case, we need to start even further back in question-

75. In an unpublished paper by Barbara Wheeler, "Critical Junctures: Theological Education Confronts Its Future," there is a reference to some groups — especially Roman Catholics and evangelicals — challenging the adequacy of the term "theological education." Generally they prefer a term that is more indicative of formational concerns and nonseminary educational settings. My own reservations about the term go deeper and broader.

ing our assumptions about theological education. This is where we can begin to take up a possibility Kelsey mentions — what he terms the "Jerusalem" and I describe as a "missional" alternative — that is, a more integrally and distinctively Christian approach to theological education. Starting from this vantage point forces us to consider not so much the tension between "Athens" and "Berlin," or the "classical" and "vocational" models, as between "Jerusalem" and both "Berlin" and "Athens," between a "missional" and any other perspective, including the "confessional" and the "dialectical" ones. This is certainly more the issue for the majority of evangelical and Catholic schools, but it is one that mainline Protestant and university schools should also consider carefully. In the following chapter, by means of a return to the biblical documents, I want to suggest that this passing reference of Kelsey's opens up the most fruitful, as yet largely unexplored, direction for the theological education debate.

PART TWO

# BACKING INTO THE FUTURE:
# A BIBLICAL ANGLE OF VISION

When the streams of tradition have become stagnant, we must return to the fountainhead . . . to Scripture for models . . . for images that might help us reenvision the contexts and categories for theological education. The scriptures provide us with ideal constructs for cultures not our own, and it is necessary to translate these ideals carefully; nevertheless, the most significant movements for reform and revitalization in the history of the Church have always been rooted in fresh, contextual readings of Scripture.

R. H. CRAM AND S. P. SAUNDERS[1]

1. R. H. Cram and S. P. Saunders, "Feet Partly of Iron and Partly of Clay: Pedagogy and the Curriculum in Theological Education," *Theological Education* 28 (2) (1992): 43-44, 46.

# 1. The Relevance of a Biblical Starting Point

As already noted, in the debate so far there has been little reflection on what the Bible might contribute to our understanding of theological education. Given various authors' revisiting of other parts of the Christian tradition — in late Antiquity, the Middle Ages, and post-Reformation period — this omission is disappointing. If these eras have something worthwhile to teach us, why not scripture itself? For some, viewing scripture as a sub-category of historical studies rather than as a set of normative documents partly accounts for this omission. Others have a greater interest in the contemporary context than in the biblical text, or regard the scriptures of other religions as equally important. Even those who give scripture normative status in the curriculum do not suggest that it has anything specific to say about theological education. In view of the growing academic interest in formulating biblical perspectives on a variety of contemporary issues, this need not be the case. On the other hand, since biblical scholars themselves have made little contribution to the debate, they are partly responsible for this state of affairs.

At the very least the debate might have referred to the extensive OT investigation into the meaning of the word "to know." Although there is no static definition of the word *yada* in the OT, it generally refers to knowledge — of God, others, and the world — that comes through experience. It involves awareness of the specific relationship in which the knower stands with the subject or object experienced and manifests itself in action that does full justice to that comprehension. Therefore it springs from whole-hearted as well as whole-minded engagement with reality, leading to what we might call a whole-willed response to it. This stands in contrast to a detached, dispassionate, objective knowing that requires only a cognitive response. As the Wisdom literature constantly points out and the OT as a whole echoes, this distinctive kind of knowing has its genesis — and its basis — in "the fear of the Lord." Only those who acknowledge God as their Creator and Redeemer are in the right position to understand the truth and live it out in a compelling fashion. Without God as the central reference point, and apart from a living relationship with God, truth becomes distorted and behavior becomes skewed in an idolatrous and destructive direction.

This approach to knowing continues in the New Testament. It makes clear that those who do not acknowledge and express gratitude to God mistake the truth for something other than it is, and reap the harmful repercussions of this in their personal lives and relationships. True knowledge centers on a grateful and obedient response to what God has done in Jesus Christ. This involves a considered and heartfelt acceptance of the message about him, leading to a lifelong commitment to his way of life and purposes. As the letters of John clearly state, and the whole of the NT supports, this revolves around personal understanding of Christ, loving commitment to his community, and discerning obedience in the world. At the heart of this view of personal and corporate knowing — affecting mind, heart, and will — is the work of the Spirit initiating, directing, and completing our knowing. The goal is to know in as great depth and with as much intimacy, the way we ourselves are known by God, even though we will not fully realize this until we sit down with God and Christ in the new heaven and new earth that awaits us.

Implicit in all this is a Trinitarian basis for knowing, relating, and doing that requires fuller expression. It is the life of Father, Son, and Spirit in the Godhead that is both the source and exemplar of what we are talking about. Here we find not just the basis for a holistic understanding and practice of knowing, but a model of it at work. I am not thinking primarily of the inner life of the Trinity, which is difficult for us to penetrate and improper for us to intrude on. I have in mind the reflection of that inner life in the outer life of the Godhead as it faces us, relates to us, and gives itself to us. It is the "economic" as well as "immanent" Trinity that opens our eyes to the mystery of divine interaction, and we do not need to commit ourselves to a "social" instead of a more "classical" view of the Trinity to speak about this, even if the former may do so more clearly. Whatever the case, it is a biblical approach to "knowing" based on "the fear of the Lord" and the self-giving of Christ, and a theological awareness of the role of the Trinity in generating and exemplifying the fusion of truth and love, that provide the wider framework for the following investigation of ministry formation in the Bible. We shall return to this framework in the next section where, with help from a range of Christian and other thinkers, I will develop a more comprehensive theological understanding of ministry formation.

## A. On the Margins of the Debate

Biblical input into the central concerns of the debate has been minimal.[2]

1. Stackhouse's book on *Apologia* refers to two background papers drawing on scripture. The first, by W. C. Robinson, has a limited focus and examines the relationship between biblical studies and systematic theology or ethics.[3] The second, by Orlando Costas, raises the basic issue by identifying mission as the goal of the church and heart of ministry and the Spirit as the key agent in mission. But the other contributors pass it by, ignoring what should otherwise be a fruitful starting point for theological education's understanding of its task. Some argue that early Christian texts should not have a privileged position or that other ways of understanding present contexts are preferable. Others raise historical, theological, or comparative objections to the content of these texts. According to Stackhouse, Costas's paper raises fundamental questions about the relevance of a scriptural model in discerning the work of the Spirit, and whether the Spirit works the same way in different contexts, but these are virtually ignored in the remaining discussion.[4]

2. The 1984 ATS-sponsored Convocation on Theological Education did address the question of how to appropriate the biblical and historical heritage of the church regarding diversity so that this contributed to a renewal of Christian identity, but this is a secondary not primary issue.

3. There is a summary of W. C. Robinson's contribution in Max Stackhouse, *Apologia: Contextualization, Globalization, and Mission in Theological Education* (Grand Rapids: Eerdmans, 1988), pp. 51-52.

4. See further Orlando Costas, "Mission, Ministry, and Theological Educa-

2. Elsewhere in the same book Stackhouse defends the doctrine of biblical revelation as a core Christian belief. Though this implies some doctrine of inspiration, assurance of the Bible's reliability, and confidence in the church's capacity to discern its truth, it does not rule out learning about God from other texts and contexts. The authoritative role of scripture consists chiefly in its provision of a paradigmatic history and thematic framework against which other perspectives can be tested. Muller also regards scripture as the basis for historical, systematic, and practical theology, and for a coherent understanding of the practice of ministry. Because of the emergence of the critical disciplines and of our more complex cultural circumstances, it is difficult to develop interpretive links between these and the Bible. But Christian thinkers have always wrestled with this, and in some ways modern criticism helps us to understand scripture more clearly. More important than understanding relevant texts, or developing a particular doctrine of biblical authority and inspiration, is theological thinking that develops out of immersion in the totality of scripture. But despite their emphasis on the fundamental role of scripture in theological education, neither Stackhouse nor Muller suggest it might play a role in our understanding of theological education.[5]

3. Some biblical insights enter into the discussions recorded in *Theological Education and Moral Formation*. For example, biblical scholar Richard Hays expresses his discomfort at the proposal that theological education be approached through focusing on ordination. Since ordination is foreign to the New Testament we must begin elsewhere, with our more basic obedience to Christ. He also suggests that any attempt to distinguish what is essentially Christian rather than culturally ephemeral must look to the biblical writings. In the ensuing discussion, contributors sidestep these efforts to gain a hearing for scripture by referring to twentieth-century realities or to the bias of biblical scholars. Later, the ethicist Stanley Hauerwas argues that certain approaches to the role of spiritual formation in theological education lack a scriptural understanding of discipleship. These, along with other comments by Richard Hays and Geoffrey Wainwright on the ir-

---

tion in the Last Quarter of the Twentieth Century," as summarized in Max L. Stackhouse, *Apologia*, pp. 30-33.

5. Richard A. Muller, *The Study of Theology: From Biblical Interpretation to Contemporary Formulation* (Grand Rapids: Zondervan, 1991), pp. ix, 48, 97, 156, 176-77, and Max L. Stackhouse, *Apologia*, pp. 174-77.

replaceable role of scripture in helping students grow in the imitation of Christ, are not taken up in discussion.[6]

4. Two brief contributions dealing with one aspect of theological education do start from scripture. Walter Brueggemann rightly points out that education of young persons and of public advisors exhibited passion as well as knowledge, and that this prepared people to recognize idolatry and maintain the counter-cultural tone of Israel's life vis-à-vis the nations.[7] Robert Meye also helpfully sets out three canonical paradigms of spiritual formation — based on Proverbs, Jesus, and Paul — and three central marks of authentic spirituality — love, joy, and peace — derived from these.[8] Surprising in all this is that even evangelicals such as Robert Ferris, in his interesting case studies of renewal in theological education, make no mention of the role that biblical reflection might play in this.[9]

5. Cheryl Johns is an exception to this general lack of a biblical reference point. Working within a sophisticated Pentecostal framework, and operating from the sidelines more than at the center of the debate, she sets out "to reconceive theological education towards a model which attempts to incorporate a more biblical epistemological vision as a context for learning." She proposes instead "a relational model grounded in a covenantal knowledge of God," one that requires that a theological school become an ecclesial or "covenanted community of knowers."[10] In undertaking this, Johns builds on the Hebraic

6. See further Richard John Neuhaus, ed., *Theological Education and Moral Formation* (Grand Rapids: Eerdmans, 1992), pp. 141-42, 179-80, 192-94, 197-98.

7. Walter Brueggemann, "Passion and Perspective: Two Dimensions of Education in the Bible," *Theology Today* 42 (2) (1985): 173-80, and in *Theological Education* 23 (2) (1987): 89-107 (the quote coming from p. 89).

8. R. P. Meye, "Theological Education as Character Formation," *Theological Education* 24, Supplement 1 (1988): 96-126.

9. Robert Ferris, *Renewal in Theological Education: Strategies for Change* (Wheaton: Billy Graham Center, 1990).

10. See her unpublished paper "To Know God Truly: The Community of Faith Model in Theological Education," prepared for a Consultation on the Aims and Purposes of Theological Education at Fuller Theological Seminary, Pasadena. Her approach, influenced by her restorationist church tradition, the work of the Christian educationalist Lois Le Bar, *Education That Is Christian* (Old Tappan, N.J.: Revell, 1968), and the work of Thomas Groome (on which more shortly), may be described, she says, as reflecting "the Azusa Street intersection with the Jerusalem Road and the Athens Highway as well as the Berlin Turnpike"!

and early Christian understanding of knowing as experiential and relational as well as conceptual. This involves a desire to be known by God as much as to know God and others, through which the Spirit advances us to the truth that transforms us corporately as well as personally. Here scripture is not only an objective theoretical norm but an existential practical revelation requiring a response of the whole person and the whole community.

For theological education, this means viewing ordered learning and skill development within a broader vision of individual and communal formation in love. Its three basic components are (i) *enculturation* — transforming the individual by infusion of the community's culture through its practices, role models, interpersonal relationships, environment, social organization, behaviors and language, (ii) *education* — developing the individual's potential as a person, capacity for discovery, discernment, and critical inquiry, and ability to act by means of a program of learning in the context of community, and (iii) *instruction* — building the individual's competence in knowledge and skills with a view to personal and community growth. As a living system of formation, each of these processes interacts with the others and the whole, with benefit for the whole. Faculty should embody the core values of the institution, model covenant relations with students, and demonstrate the striving for truth and obedience. No subject area has priority over others on the grounds of theory before practice.[11]

Apart from Johns's thoughtful contribution, Richard Hays's complaint in one of the symposia that "the New Testament hasn't played that much of a role in our discussion, and I find that disturbing"[12] is true of the debate as a whole. By contrast, Third World theologians have continued to emphasize the importance of scripture in understanding theological education. A decade before the present North American debate there was a concern among evangelical theological educators in the Third World for "wrestling with the Text from which all texts are derived and to which they point, in order to be faithful to it in context," as well as "wrestling with the context in which the reality of the Text is at work, in order to be relevant to

11. I am drawing here also on her *Pentecostal Formation: A Pedagogy Among the Oppressed* (Sheffield, U.K.: Sheffield Academic Press, 1993).
12. In *Theological Education and Moral Formation*, p. 180.

it."[13] It is a pity that North American discussions of globalizing theological education have not listened to and interacted with these voices more fully.

## B. In Defense of a Scriptural Approach

For many, the value of revisiting scripture for the light it may throw on theological education will remain a questionable enterprise. There are several strikes against such an investigation producing anything worthwhile for our situation today:

- What could the Bible offer except scattered hints about earlier forms of ministry formation embedded in historically dubious and theologically tendentious materials? Since it does not appear to address the issue directly, its materials come from so many different periods, and so many authors have had a hand in its composition, there is little that would be of value.
- Even if something did emerge from these writings, and even if it had sufficient coherence and consonance, there is still the problem of the cultural gap between the biblical world and our own. We live in such different times — economically, socially, educationally, technically, and institutionally — that there is little in common between the two.
- The world of the church and forms of ministry are also very different. We are no longer training people for the same kind of entity or for the same kinds of roles as existed in pre-Christian or early Christian times.
- In any case, whatever we find in the Bible will mostly have to do with different methods employed in ministry formation and, hermeneutically speaking, it is inappropriate to draw on that kind of

13. S. Coe, "In Search of Renewal in Theological Education," *Theological Education* 9 (4) (1973): 237. See also, several years later, the remarks of Lesslie Newbigin, "Theological Education in World Perspective," *Ministerial Formation* 4 (1978): 3-10, reprinted in H. M. Conn and S. F. Rowen, eds., *Missions and Theological Education in World Perspective* (Farmington, Wis.: Associates of Urbanus, 1984), and the proposal by John Frame in Paul Bowers, ed., *Evangelical Theological Education Today*, 2 vols. (Nairobi: Evangel Publishing House, 1982).

information. It is the content not form of what we find in the Bible that is alone capable of interpretation for our current circumstances.

On all these counts, there seems little point to engaging in any substantial biblical investigation of ministry formation.

Let me attempt to answer these objections in turn:

1. Across the range of historical periods and diverse authors that we find in the Bible, there is enough material and sufficient consistency within it to put together at least the lineaments of a biblical approach to ministry formation. Although ministry formation is often only a secondary concern in these writings, this does not necessarily make it improper to bring it into sharper relief, as we often do in developing our theological understanding of a particular issue. In any case, at times it does come more into prominence, as with some of the major prophets' preparation of their successors, in the calling and training of the Twelve, and in the Pauline letters to Timothy and Titus. In particular, is there not something of seminal interest — irrespective of how much or how little it is capable of direct application — in the way Jesus nurtured his disciples? Should the ways we engage in ministry formation have no point of connection or lack any resonance with the way the Lord we serve undertook this task? At the very least we should suspend a decision until we see how much material there is and what it does or does not amount to.

2. Of course there are vast differences between the biblical period and our own. But this is true of a wide range of issues on which we turn to the Bible for help. Take just one example. There is little comparison between ancient and modern warfare. Both the scale and the technology are vastly incommensurate. Yet this does not — and ought not — prevent scholars examining the Bible from one end to the other to see how it handles the issue of violence. Another example is the nature of work. Between the primarily agricultural or cottage industry economy of ancient Israel or Roman Palestine it is a huge jump to the postindustrial hi-tech economy of advanced Western countries. But there is still value in examining biblical perspectives on work, images of God drawn from the workplace, and biblical figures who were based in the marketplace, in developing a response to the changing character of work and the workplace today. It is not essentially different with respect to the field of theological education.

3. Granted, there have been enormous changes in church structures and ministry between the first century and the twentieth; also in the way seminaries train people for pastoral and other work. Yet this does not prevent most contributors to the debate, beginning with Farley's original essay, harking back to past periods of Christian history from which we can relearn something vital that we have forgotten. If this is the case, cannot the biblical writings — which have a special status in our tradition — contain insights at least as valuable as those stemming from late classical (Farley), high medieval (Schner), or post-Reformation (Muller) times? Why this discrimination against the biblical writings? Surely it cannot be just because they are earlier?

4. It is true that we should always be cautious of going to the Bible for methods or structures to use now. But it is not as easy as the distinction between form and content suggests, for in some cases content partly determines form, and likewise form is simply content embodied. A distinction that may be helpful here is that between practices and methods. There are many practices in the Bible that we do not jettison simply because they are concrete ways of living out certain beliefs, realizing certain commitments, or embodying certain values. Quite apart from such practices, however, is the content of ministry formation as it comes before us in the biblical writings.

If none of these arguments persuade, let me provide one of a different kind. From one point of view, the investigation that follows is an essay in cross-cultural understanding, one that gives us an oblique vantage point from which to view and evaluate our own practice. In the light of Walter Brueggemann's recognition of the "aniconic" role of the Bible in American life, examining it afresh may help us test the integrity of our models of theological education.[14] In essence, then, to quote a precursor of the current debate, I do not view this exercise as a case of going "back to the Bible," as the saying runs, so much as going "forward with the Bible." For "as so often happens with theology, to return to primitive example is to advance."[15] Though the following in-

14. See further Walter Brueggemann, *Theological Education* 23 (2) (1987): 89-107.

15. Martin Thornton, *My God: A Reappraisal of Normal Religious Experience* (London: Hodder and Stoughton, 1974), p. 71. See also Donald E. Messer, *Calling Church and Seminary into the 21st Century* (Nashville: Abingdon, 1995), p. 75, on the critical role of biblically and theologically based metaphors in developing a more subversive approach to church and society.

vestigation derives from a technical study of the primary sources, in
the spirit of several proposals emanating from the debate I am seeking
to put biblical studies at the service of a particular interest — in this
case theological education itself. For that reason I have not gone into
detail on questions of dating and authorship, sources and historical
authenticity, sociological analysis or literary structure. Also, while I
refer to a representative number of scholarly viewpoints on key issues
raised by the text, I have not sought to document these exhaustively.
Those who wish to explore such matters more fully may do so through
comments in the notes or other works cited there.

# 2. Ministry Formation Before Christ

We cannot overlook the foundational role of parents in children's theological and practical formation. The home was the place where religious nurture, transmission of the tradition, and participation in worship — even vocational preparation — first took place (Deut 4:9; 6:7, 20-25; Exod 12:26-27; 13:7-8, 14-16; Prov 6:20-23; 13:1; 23:22-25). For this reason the wise regarded it as "as the most essential 'school' and place of education."[16] Although fathers had a special responsibility in this, it was the mother who gave children the first rudiments of an education (Prov 1:8; 6:20-23; 23:22-25; 1 Sam 1:9-11, 20-28) and sometimes played a role in adolescence (Prov 31:28-30). Instruction covered both religious matters (Exod 10:2; 12:26; 13:8; Deut 4:9; 32:7, 46) and more general education (Deut 11:18f.; Josh 4:21f.; Judg 6:13; Ps 41:2; 78:3-6; Prov 1:8ff.; 2:1; 3:1; 4:1-4; 5:1). It was essentially the passing on a whole way of life — spiritual, moral, and civil.[17] Much of this took place informally: "when you sit at home and when you walk along the way, when you lie down and when you get up" (Deut 6:9). It involved parents telling stories (Deut 5:20ff.), giving explanations (Exod 13:8; 14:6), and answering children's questions (Exod 12:26). In all this the prime teacher was God (Ps 94:10).

16. R. E. Clements, *Wisdom in Theology* (Grand Rapids: Eerdmans, 1992), p. 129.

17. See further J. Grassi, *The Teacher in the Primitive Church and the Teacher Today* (Santa Clara, Calif.: University of Santa Clara Press, 1973), p. 5.

The inter-testamentary literature also emphasized the central place of parental instruction (Ecclus 2:1; 3:1; 4:1; 30:1-13). Though the imitation of parents comes up for mention more often, this had less to do with the focus of the educational process than with the result (Ecclus 30:10). Central to this were daily family prayers, memorizing scripture, and Sabbath gatherings. While in earlier times there is no direct evidence that elementary schools existed, during this period popular education took place in the synagogue and teachers became more formally differentiated. Behind this probably lay the influence of Hellenistic models of instruction.[18]

## A. Early Jewish Roles

### 1. Community Representatives

#### i. Local Elders

Unfortunately most of what we know about the institution and practice of eldership in Jewish towns and cities is incidental (cf. Ruth 4; Job 29). It seems to have had its origin in Moses' selection of "capable men from all the people" and appointment of them as "judges for the people at all times" (Num 18:21). Each local center, however small, had its body of "elders," or lay leaders, drawn from the people to settle issues or disputes that arose. Though older men predominated in the group, it could comprise younger persons (Job 29:7) and later sometimes included women possessing a distinctive charismatic endowment or social position.

The work of elders was wide-ranging. It was a combination of what happens in a town hall meeting, school board, chamber of com-

18. See the summary of the debate on this issue in the discussion on elementary schools in Samuel Byrskog, *Jesus the Only Teacher: Didactic Authority and Transmission in Ancient Israel, Ancient Judaism, and the Matthaean Community* (Stockholm: Almqvist & Wiksell, 1994), pp. 48-52, 69-75. The early Christians continued to emphasize the role of the family. Their writings contain reports on the formative role of the family in developing their offspring's understanding of scripture (e.g., 2 Tim 3:16, which highlights the contribution of grandmother and mother) to injunctions regarding parents' responsibility (especially fathers) to "bring up their children in the instruction and training of the Lord" (Eph 6:4).

merce, and church council. Alongside their personal store of wisdom gained through life experience, there was an accumulated body of written and unwritten wisdom on which to draw (cf. the "wisdom of the wise," Isa 29:14). Some of this is recorded in the OT wisdom writings. It could be that a "school" lies behind the compilation and transmission of this material, giving opportunity to a few to gain more formal training, for which they probably paid (Prov 17:16).[19] But we have only hints of such a system, and for the most part we should reckon with nonformal, though quite substantive, mentoring processes that were "more apt to be found in the family/clan, in elder/leader training, and among the 'wise' who were experts in the wisdom tradition."[20] For example, young people could listen to the discussions of elders at the city gate, as well as to other conversations (Judg 5:10-11).[21]

## ii. National Leaders

Alongside local elders, there was training for leaders of the whole people. I take Moses and Joshua as a case study (Exod 24:13; 33:11; Num 11:28; Josh 1:1; 5:14; 24:29). What stands out is the way (i) Joshua was Moses' companion, and had been since his youth (Num 11:28). As Moses' "right hand" (Exod 24:13-14), he accompanied him where others, including the elders, did not. He was present when Moses received divine revelation for the people, and when Moses dealt with the people's response (Exod 31:17). Joshua was also the only one admitted to, and allowed to remain in, the tent set up outside the camp where God spoke directly to Moses (Exod 33:7-11). (ii) Joshua was also Moses' servant (Exod 24:13), though this did not rule out his taking the initiative at points, calling things to

19. So J. L. Crenshaw, "Education in Ancient Israel," *Journal of Biblical Literature* 104 (1985): 601-15.

20. Michael Wilkins, *Following the Master: Discipleship in the Steps of Jesus* (Grand Rapids: Zondervan, 1992), p. 65. Compare W. McKane, *Prophets and Wise Men* (Naperville, Ill.: Allenson, 1965), pp. 40-47.

21. On eldership in ancient Israel see the article on "The Elder" in V. H. Matthews and D. C. Benjamin, *The Social World of Ancient Israel* (Peabody, Mass.: Hendrickson, 1994), pp. 121-31. For the New Testament period see the wide-ranging investigation by Alistair Campbell, *The Elders: Seniority Within Earliest Christianity* (Edinburgh: T. & T. Clark, 1994).

Moses' mind (Exod 31:17), and telling him what to do (Num 11:28). This makes him more a junior assistant than a mere servant. (iii) After Moses' death, Joshua replaces him as leader and receives the promise of God's continuing presence (Josh 1:5). He has a revelation from God that is in some respects similar to the one Moses experienced on Mount Sinai (Josh 5:14). Like Moses, Joshua is described as a "servant of God" (Josh 5:14; 24:29; cf. Num 12:8). In sum, while Moses was alive Joshua was his assistant in the common task of leading the people, in the pursuit of which his formation for future leadership took place.

## 2. Specialized Callings

Other individuals or groups had a more specialized calling. Though sometimes these were full-time affairs, often they were not, or only temporarily. These callings generally revolved around a key figure for the purpose of fulfilling various clearly defined ends. The main types of callings were those of the priest, prophet, and wise (Jer 8:18).

### i. The Priests

For those moving into priestly responsibilities, it seems likely that from an early age instruction in the ways of God was part of their preparation. The ascription "father" for priests is an indication of this (Judg 17:10; 18:19). It was also one of the reasons why Samuel and Joash were entrusted to Eli and Yehoida, respectively (1 Sam 2:21, 26; 2 Kings 12:3). Though we know little about the training priests received — whether for those closely connected to a holy place or those occasionally called upon to perform priestly duties — much of it was nonformal, some more structured. Children accompanied their parents to sanctuaries (1 Sam 4:21) or to the temple in Jerusalem (Luke 2:41f.) where they would learn from the liturgy in which they participated, the sacrifices they observed, and the instruction they received. Where a young person was entrusted to a priest and moved in with him (cf. 1 Sam 2:11; 3:1), more specific training took place. Though junior figures assisted senior ones, their primary task was to "serve the Lord" under the prophet (1 Sam 1:28; 2:11; 2:18), and to follow God's personal leading (1 Sam 3:1ff.).

86

## ii. The Prophets

The prophetic writings contain occasional examples of senior and junior persons working together. Like the prophets whom they join (Amos 7:15), these associates appear to have left home and/or work (1 Sam 1:11, 22, 27-28; 1 Kings 19:19-21). There were also larger groups of prophets (Isa 8:16) numbering up to fifty persons (2 Kings 2:7), including married couples (2 Kings 4:1). Taking Elijah and Elisha as a focal example, we see that: (i) Leading prophets frequently have a younger person to follow and/or attend them (Elijah: 1 Kings 19:19-21; 1 Kings 4:38; 5:20-22, 25; cf. Jeremiah: 32:12-16; 36:4-22; 43:3-6; Ezekiel: 23:45). There is a commitment on the part of the assistant to go wherever the senior prophet goes (2 Kings 2:2, 4, 6).[22] (ii) An individual or group attached to a prophet is an "attendant" (of Elijah; 1 Kings 19:21) or "servant" (of Elisha in 2 Kings 6:1) of the prophet. Sometimes this relationship is described in familial terms (2 Kings 2:12) and the two "live" together (cf. Elisha: 2 Kings 6:1). (iii) After their death, assistants sometimes succeed the senior prophet as the primary "servant" of God in the land (cf. Elisha: 2 Kings 2:11-14), and share in the spirit of the one who has left (2 Kings 2:9).

We should think of the relationship between these people as lying somewhere between a formal "school" and an informal "fellowship." Some direct instruction took place (cf. 1 Sam 3:8; 2 Kings 4:38; 6:1).[23] There was a communal dimension to their life, but the emphasis is mainly on their working together in a common mission.[24] It was as the younger heard the words, witnessed the action, and observed the life of the older that learning occurred, as well as through the practical ex-

---

22. Sometimes a larger group has a special relationship with a leading prophet (e.g., Samuel: 1 Sam 19:20-24), and independent companies of prophets (1 Sam 10:5-10) develop a close connection with such a person (e.g., Elisha: 2 Kings 2:16: 4:1; 9:1).

23. For the debate on this, see further S. Byrskog, *Jesus the Only Teacher*, pp. 56-63. Byrskog stresses the meager amount of evidence available but comes down on the positive side.

24. As M. Wilkins, in *Following the Master*, p. 64, says of Elisha's authority over these prophets, "it is not in a school setting. The sons of the prophets were not prophets in training but were gathered around Elisha for guidance in performing their own prophetic activities." Cf. Robert R. Wilson, *Prophecy and Society in Ancient Israel* (Philadelphia: Fortress, 1980), pp. 202, 300-301; M. Hengel, *The Charismatic Leader and His Followers* (Grand Rapids: Eerdmans, 1981), pp. 17-18.

perience of working alongside them. Though this involved following and serving the lead prophet, such people were not his disciples (cf. Baruch and Jeremiah in Jer 36:26). This is primarily because it is God of whom it would be alone proper to say this.[25] On the other hand, the language of "following" is certainly present and can involve "unconditional sharing of the master's destiny, which does not stop even at deprivation and suffering . . . and is possible only on the basis of complete trust. . . ."[26]

### iii. The Wise

In the wisdom writings we find reference to a circle of advisors at the royal court (e.g., around David: 2 Sam 8:16-18; cf. 20:23-25; Solomon: 1 Kings 4:1-6; Hezekiah: 2 Kings 19:2; Josiah: 2 Kings 22:3-7). These were mostly lay people but could also include priests (1 Kings 4:5). Their varied duties included looking after the archives (Jer 36:20-21), doing the work of scribes (Jer 8:8-9), and giving political advice. They taught in the open air, at the city gates, and at the crossroads (Prov 1:20f.; 8:2f.).[27] It was partly by this means that the training of

25. The word *talmidh*, "learner," occurs only once of musicians and their apprentices (1 Chron 25:8), and *limadh*, "taught one," only once in connection with a prophet (Isa 8:16; possibly Isa 50:4). This led Karl Rengstorf to conclude that "Apart from the formal relation between teacher and pupil, the OT, unlike the classical Greek world and Hellenism, has no master-disciple relation. Whether among the prophets or the scribes we seek in vain for anything corresponding to it." Karl H. Rengstorf, "mathetes," in R. Kittel, ed., *Theological Dictionary of the New Testament*, vol. 4 (Grand Rapids: Eerdmans, 1967), p. 427.

26. M. Hengel, *The Charismatic Leader*, p. 72. So P. Hinnebusch, *Jesus: The New Elijah* (Ann Arbor, Mich.: Servant, 1978). G. Bouwman, *Folgen und Nachfolgen im Zeugnis der Bibel* (Salzburg: Otto Mueller, 1965), p. 30, suggests that a spiritual as well as actual following is intimated by the language here. However, we must be careful not to overinterpret these passages. This is easy to do in view of parallels with discipleship in the gospels (see later), and because Elisha's following Elijah has more to do with respect for, and service of, the prophet. It is interesting that the Jewish historian Josephus describes those relationships in the language of discipleship as he understood it. Where, as in the case of Elisha and Elijah, we find parallels with the gospels, e.g., receiving a call, the priority of this over family duties, following the one who has issued the invitation (1 Kings 19:19, 21 and Mark 1:19-20; 2:14), these were probably sharpened by the gospel writer himself.

27. Stuart Weeks, *Early Israelite Wisdom* (Oxford: Clarendon, 1994), ch. 3, has argued persuasively that we should not confine the wise to a group of advisors

future wise people took place. The wise also gathered students around them to whom they gave more regular training (Prov 8:32; Isa 8:16; 50:4). If the story of Daniel and his friends is any guide, this training could take place in a more intentional way by placing them in the care of an older person who taught them what they needed to know (Dan 1:3-5). In time they developed a high degree of practical "knowledge," "understanding," or "wisdom," equipping them for public "service" (Dan 1:5, 19). When they had proved themselves, they might even succeed other persons who were less gifted (Dan 2:48).

Their training embraced "academic" learning and, in some cases, "charismatic" discernment. It included the study of literature as well as the capacity to interpret visions and dreams (Dan 1:17). Only after a final oral test did they gain a position (Dan 1:19; cf. v. 14). In Israel it was probably these advisors who collected its proverbs, songs, and reflections.[28] All this has more the character of a professional "guild" inducting its younger members than of a "school" educating its students.[29]

---

at the royal court. Along with the range of locations just mentioned, note that later we read of them instructing conversationally at festive meals (Ecclus 1:16), and individually with particular persons (Ecclus 51:25).

28. Generally on this see G. von Rad, *Wisdom in the Old Testament* (London: SCM, 1972), pp. 15-23.

29. So W. McKane, *Prophets and Wise Men*, p. 22, and S. Weeks, *Early Israelite Wisdom*, ch. 8. For a cautious estimate of the presence of schools generally, see J. L. Crenshaw, *Education in Ancient Israel: Across the Deadening Silence* (New York: Doubleday, 1998), pp. 85-114. E. W. Heaton, *The School Tradition of the Old Testament* (Oxford: Clarendon, 1994), argues for a school in the more formal sense but admits that there is only indirect scriptural evidence for this, as do A. Lemaire, "The Sage in School and Temple," in J. G. Gammie and L. G. Perdue, eds., *The Sage in Israel and the Ancient Near East* (Winona Lake, Ind.: Eisenbraun, 1990), pp.165-81, and S. Byrskog, *Jesus the Only Teacher*, p. 67. An overall review of the issue comes from G. I. Danver, "Were There Schools in Ancient Israel?" in *Wisdom in Ancient Israel: Essays in Honor of J. A. Emerton* (Cambridge: Cambridge University Press, 1995), pp. 199-211. It is not until the intertestamentary literature that the word "school," *beth-midrash*, appears for the first time (Ecclus 51:23), and the role of the teacher is more formalized (Ecclus 24:30-34; 39:8; 51:23, 29). In that period — from which we have a vivid picture of the mobile and varied responsibilities of the wise — the Law increasingly became the focus of study. At this stage something more akin to a school may have developed, though probably not of a highly formalized kind.

## B. Later Jewish Groups

In later Jewish times we come across other intentional groups such as the Pharisees, Essenes, and Qumran community. Especially prominent was the role of the so-called Teacher of Righteousness in the latter. There were also the looser associations of the Sadducees and Herodians, and other occasional groups revolving around a contemporary prophet or miracle-worker. I will focus here chiefly on the Pharisees, for it is this group that appears most commonly in the gospels and it was in relation to it that Jesus mostly defined his own followers. Since, to a lesser extent, he did this through reference to the group around John the Baptist, we will look briefly at that circle as well.

### 1. The Pharisees

The Pharisees were a male lay-based movement, frequently at odds with the more socially and politically established priestly circles of Sadducees. They grouped themselves into fellowships to observe the Law diligently and to share a common meal. Respected teachers played a significant role in the movement. The Hebrew word *talmidh,* "learner," or the Greek term *mathetes,* "disciple," refers to persons committed to learning the Law through a figure (e.g., Moses: John 9:28) or movement that had significant teachers (e.g., the Pharisees: Matt 22:15-16). For them, it was essential "to get yourself a teacher" (Aboth I:6, 16) as well as a "companion" (Aboth VI:3), and some texts depict the relationship between earlier figures such as Joshua and Moses in pupil-master terms (Sifre on Num 27:18; Deut Rab 11:10). Sometimes students sought out well-known teachers (for Menahem and Hillel see Midrash Shir Hashirim Zuta) though, since it was learning the Law that was paramount (b. Ketub 96a), they were encouraged to learn from more than one teacher; schools only lasted as long as the teacher lived. In later times students were divided into two classes: those under ordinary instruction *(talmidhim),* and those who had completed their instruction but were not yet commissioned as teachers *(talmidhim chakamim).*

Teachers sat to instruct their students, with the latter at their feet. The teacher framed the questions, and there was regular repetition to drive a point home. The practice of physically "following" a teacher around demonstrated students' subservience, for they were to display the same fear and reverence to the teacher as they would to the Law he taught and embodied. Students were servants of their teacher (Aboth VI:5), fetching his sandals (T Neg 8,2), and performing other duties. They spent time in his home, accompanied him in his work, and went with him wherever he went. In this way the pupil not only listened to the teacher's words but also observed and imitated his actions. So learning was centered on a way of life rather than a set of lessons. Indeed, written texts were not at the heart of this process.[30] Though the LXX generally translates the verb "to learn" by the word *manthanein,* it was the Law to which students were discipled, not the teacher, and teachers were regarded as types of obedience rather than as individuals.[31] This accords with the fact that the student's goal was to become an independent teacher in his own right.[32]

## 2. *John's Followers*

John the Baptist also gathered around him a circle of dedicated followers (Matt 9:14; 11:2-3; 14:12; Mark 2:18; 6:29; Luke 5:33; 7:18-19; 11:1; John 1:35; 3:25; cf. Acts 18:24-25; 19:1-3). (i) As his "disciples," these followed his preaching and teaching about repentance, baptism, and obedience (cf. Luke 3:7-14 and pars.). (ii) They observed certain practices, e.g., fasting, praying, and ceremonial washing (Matt 9:14; Luke 5:33; 11:1; John 3:25), and may have imitated his ascetic

---

30. Even after A.D. 70, teaching and learning did not take place in an instructional setting divorced from concrete individual decision-making. Nevertheless, as the institution developed, it became more formal and the oral tradition became increasingly defined. For example, Gamaliel II was said to have hundreds of disciples (Sotah 49b), and the word "rabbi" only became an established title from the second century onwards. See respectively, A. F. Segal, *Rebecca's Children: Judaism and Christianity in the Roman World* (Cambridge, Mass.: Harvard University Press, 1986), pp. 52-54, and M. Hengel, *The Charismatic Leader and His Followers,* p. 44.

31. E. Schweizer, *Lordship and Discipleship* (London: SCM, 1960), p. 12. Cf. A. Schulz, *Nachfolgen und Nachahmen: Studien über das Verhältnis der neutestamentlichen Jungerschaft zur urchristlichen Urbildethik* (Munich: Kosel Verlag, 1962), p. 26.

32. See further J. Grassi, *The Teacher in the Primitive Church,* p. 9.

way of life, with its elementary diet and simple clothing (Mark 1:6). (iii) They were more than students under his instruction, or a pious community living under his rule, for they assisted him in baptizing others (John 4:1-2) and acted as his emissaries (Matt 11:2-15). Interesting in all this, especially in view of the practice in Pharisaic groups, is the lack of any reference to his expounding the Law.[33]

This group participated in a common enterprise as well as being a mobile learning center. Discipleship involved going about with John as he proclaimed, baptized, and called people to a way of life, actively assisting him and representing or defending his cause. Unlike the Pharisaic groups, teaching and learning the Law was not central to this. With its combination of radical proclamation and parabolic actions, mobile and communal lifestyle, and active service for and with their mentor, this group is reminiscent of prophetic circles in the Old Testament. Unlike these, however, John's disciples do not take his place when he dies.

## C. Some Preliminary Conclusions

There were, then, different levels and different circles within which formation for ministry took place in the biblical writings. Alongside the fundamental role played by the family and later by the school, and the largely nonformal preparation of village elders, there were the more specialized circles of priests, prophets, and the wise. For all their differences these often exhibit some common elements:

- The main purpose of associating with a key figure was to collaborate in the active service of God.
- Associates of this figure attended or accompanied him, in some cases living with or near him.
- This involved a permanent or temporary break with their normal relationships and surroundings.
- Learning occurred in diverse settings through participant observation, nonformal discussion, action-reflection, and direct instruction.

33. M. Hengel, *The Charismatic Leader and His Followers*, p. 37.

- In some cases successors emerged when the central figures passed on, whereas in others this was a by-product of the association.[34]

The Pharisees — and in differing degrees other Jewish groups in the time of Jesus — share some of these characteristics. But transmitting the tradition and developing a way of life takes preeminence over service in a common cause. The whole exercise begins to take on more of the nature of a "school," and instruction becomes more central to what takes place. The appearance of John's group signals a return to the older, specifically prophetic, approach.

34. This is generally in line with the conclusions of Michael Wilkins, *Following the Master,* p. 68.

# 3. Ministry Formation by Christ

The best point of entry for examining the way Jesus drew people into ministry is to consider his understanding of discipleship and the role of the Twelve. In approaching this I will mostly treat the gospels as a unit, and will only occasionally refer to their individual characteristics or emphases. This does not mean harmonizing them so much as looking for common elements. Throughout I will focus mostly on Jesus' attitude and practice, so far as we can recover these, and will also look at differences between Jesus' approach and that of the Jewish groups already mentioned.

## A. The Disciples of Jesus

I approach what follows by means of a set of related questions. These help relate it to some current concerns in theological education, for example:

- Who should undertake it?
- How should they be recruited?
- What are they being trained for?
- Can ministry orientations differ?

## 1. Who Were the Disciples?

The word *mathetes* (disciple) occurs often in the gospels and it is not always clear who is in view.[35] Some argue that it designates only those who accompanied Jesus throughout his public ministry.[36] The related word *akolouthein* strengthens the probability that a wider group was in view, even in Mark where this has been contested. Though, as we shall see below, this term has a range of meanings, sometimes it is virtually a synonym for *mathetes* (cf. Mark 2:14; 8:34; 10:21, 28). Jesus issues the invitation to believe and follow to the whole body of disciples, not just to his close associates. Only by interpreting that invitation as laying down the conditions for accompanying him rather than as a general call to discipleship, and by interpreting other passages to mean physically following him around (Mark 2:14), can the latter be restricted to the small group who traveled about with him. For these reasons, as is the case with the other three gospels, most scholars rightly refer *mathetes* to this wider circle.[37] On this view, the group of

35. Though the authenticity of some passages is contested, many have a strong basis in the tradition (cf. Mark 2:18, 23f.; 5:31; 6:41, 35, [37, 49]; 7:2, 5; 8:4, 6, 27; 9:18; 10:13f; 11:1; 14:12, 13, 14, 16, [27], 50?). For a detailed attempt to distinguish between references to the disciples that are redactional and passages that come from the tradition in the earliest gospel, see Ernest Best, *Disciples and Discipleship: Studies in the Gospel According to Mark* (Edinburgh: T. & T. Clark, 1986), especially the charts summarizing his discussion on pages 110-13. While not everything in the tradition necessarily goes back to Jesus, the spread and number of the passages is quite revealing. The strongest argument for the authenticity of the word is its comparative rarity outside the gospels, and it is particularly associated with the ministry of Jesus.

36. As R. P. Meye argues, in *Jesus and the Twelve: Discipleship and Revelation in Mark's Gospel* (Grand Rapids: Eerdmans, 1968), the strongest case for this can be made from Mark's gospel. Though Mark knows of wide interest among the crowd or multitude in Jesus, he never speaks of "many" disciples (unlike Luke 6:17; 19:39; John 6:60ff.), and the disciples are frequently differentiated from the "crowd" (Mark 2:18; 3:7-9; 6:33-37; 8:34). However, while it may be true that scholars have sometimes read a larger group of disciples too quickly into certain texts that do not mention the word (possibly Mark 3:33-35; 15:43), other texts containing what appear to be synonyms most naturally read as if more than the narrower group who accompanied him were involved (Mark 4:10-11, 34; 10:32). For Matthew, see P. Minear, "The Disciples and the Crowds in the Gospel of Matthew," *Anglican Theological Review* Supplement, Series 3 (March 1974): 31.

37. Luke takes this a step further by turning a specific, literal reference into a

disciples includes the Twelve, who are called out from among them and have extra demands placed on them. This interpretation is consonant with other passages where the words for disciple and follower do not appear but similar ideas are present (Mark 10:40; 15:41).[38]

The term "the Twelve" has a firm basis in the tradition (e.g., Mark 3:14, [16?]; 4:10; 9:35; 10:32; 11:11; 14:10, 17, 20, 43)[39] and — despite some suggestions to the contrary — has strong claims to stemming from Jesus himself.[40] The expression has a symbolic function connected with the restoration of Israel in the messianic community Jesus is establishing in and through his work. In this, the role of the Twelve is fundamental and unrepeatable (hence Acts 1:16, 21).[41] It is Luke's account that most

---

general, metaphorical one. Cf. E. Best, *Disciples and Discipleship,* pp. 6 and 8. Since there is no reference to crucifixion as such in the first passion prediction, talk of the "cross," as opposed to suffering or death in general may well be a post-Easter addition. See also M. Hengel, *The Charismatic Leader,* p. 59, on the stylizing of this saying by the later community.

38. This was already recognized in the classic text on the subject by A. B. Bruce, *The Training of the Twelve* (Grand Rapids: Kregel, 1971), pp. 11-12.

39. So E. Best, *Disciples and Discipleship,* p. 102; E. P. Sanders, *The Historical Figure of Jesus* (London: Penguin, 1993), pp. 169-95; and, most recently, John P. Meier, "The Circle of the Twelve: Did It Exist During Jesus' Public Ministry?" *Journal of Biblical Literature* 116 (1997): 635-72; contra R. Bultmann, *History of the Synoptic Tradition* (Oxford: Blackwell, 1963), pp. 345ff., and J. D. Crossan, *Who Killed Jesus?* (San Francisco: Harper, 1995), p. 75. Best argues that references to "the twelve" stem fully from Mark in 6:7 and 8:19, and have been added as a gloss to traditional passages in 14:10, 20, 43; 14:17 and possibly 3:14; 11:11.

40. Against G. Klein, *Die Zwölf Aposteln: Ursprung und Gehalt einer Idee* (Göttingen: Vandenhoeck & Ruprecht, 1961) and P. Vielhauer, *Gottesreich und Menschensohn in der Verkündigung Jesus* (Neukirchen: Kreis Moers, 1957), pp. 62-64, see the arguments of R. P. Meye, *Jesus and the Twelve,* pp. 192-209; E. P. Sanders, *Jesus and Judaism* (Philadelphia: Westminster, 1985), pp. 98-106. J. D. G. Dunn, in *Jesus' Call to Discipleship* (Cambridge: Cambridge University Press, 1992), pp. 95-96, points in particular to the inclusion of Judas, such details as the reference to Boanerges, and even the degree of confusion in the accounts, to support the essential historicity of a group of twelve around Jesus. See further S. Freyne, *The Twelve: Disciples and Apostles. A Study in the Theology of the First Three Gospels* (London: Sheed & Ward, 1968), pp. 33, 49.

41. For other references to this group outside the gospels see Acts 6:2; 1 Cor 15:15; Rev 21:14 (for the Twelve), and Acts 1:22; 2:14 (for the Eleven). In his classic study *The Training of the Twelve,* A. B. Bruce suggests a three-stage development from discipleship to the Twelve: (1) initially they are followers of Jesus who occasionally associate with him (John 2:1-22; 4:1-45); (2) they are called by Jesus

clearly makes the connection between the narrower and wider groups of disciples (Luke 9:13) and, though this is more precise than in Mark, it may well have some historical grounding.[42]

## 2. How Were the Disciples Recruited?

While some persons come to Jesus asking to become his disciples (Matt 8:19, 21), it is still Jesus' call which is decisive (Matt 8:22). Generally he is the one who issues the invitation. This follows a clear pattern: as he moves around he sees someone, summons them, and is followed by them.[43] Jesus addresses this call to a wide range of ordinary people as they are going about their daily lives, not while they are in the synagogue or temple. He reaches out beyond the conventional social and religious boundaries of his day, including social outcasts (e.g., lepers: Mark 14:3 et al.) and marginal groups (e.g., women: cf. Luke 8:1-3 et al.).[44] As noted above, *akolouthein*, "follow," can have either a literal or figura-

---

to became his regular companions (Matt 4:18-22; 9:9); (3) they become a select band to be trained as apostles (Matt 10:1ff. and pars.). The difficulty here is Bruce's reliance on the Johannine material, for in the synoptics it is the second of these which appears first, and what we have in John could be interpreted as John's version of that.

42. Against A. Schulz, *Nachfolgen und Nachahmen*, pp. 48-49. He rightly points out, however, that Luke blurs the lines between the two groups at points (from Markan material — Luke 5:30; 6:1; 8:9, 22; 9:14, 16, 18, 43; 18:15; 22:39; from his special material — Luke 22:39). Though in Mark's account we read in turn of the call of the first disciples (1:16-20), the selection of the Twelve from within them (3:13-19), and the separate missionary charge to them (Mark 6:7-11, earlier in Matt 10:9-14), it is hard to know how much the evangelist has imposed this structure on his gospel or how much it reflects the actual course of events. In his substantial thesis *Jesus als Lehrer*, 2nd ed. (Tübingen: Mohr-Siebeck, 1984), pp. 476-87, Rainer Riesner argues that it was after the Galilaean crisis, and denunciation of Galilaean cities (Matt 11:21-23 and par.), that Jesus, like the prophet Isaiah before him (Isa 8:16), withdrew to an inner circle of disciples. This group, he argues, may only have been created after this crisis (cf. perhaps John 6:66-70), as a collegium of twelve eschatological judges functioning as an antitype of the twelve tribes of Israel.

43. See further Michael Wilkins, *Following the Master*, p. 107; Martin Hengel, *The Charismatic Leader*, pp. 50ff.

44. This point is strongly made by J. D. G. Dunn, *Jesus' Call to Discipleship*, pp. 59-61, 89-91.

tive meaning. In other cases, it has the "sense of following him in his *wanderings* and sharing with him *his uncertain and perilous destiny.*"[45] This "calling" is not only a continuing part of Jesus' original message (Mark 2:14; 10:21, 28-32, 32; Matt 8:19-22 and pars.), but a distinctive element within it. Taking the initiative in this way was not characteristic of other contemporary Jewish figures, and highlights both Jesus' authority and his expectations concerning obedience.[46]

According to the gospels, the process involved in the call of the Twelve (Matt 10:2-4; Mark 3:16-19; Luke 6:14-16) was relatively simple.[47] Jesus spends a night in prayer alone in an isolated spot seeking discernment, takes the initiative and calls them, perhaps out of a larger assembled group. A number of these — Peter, James, John, An-

45. Martin Hengel, *The Charismatic Leader,* p. 54.

46. Jack D. Kingsbury, "On Following Jesus: The 'Eager' Scribe and the 'Reluctant' Disciple (Matt 8:18-22)," *New Testament Studies* 34 (1988): 49. Some scholars interpret "disciple" in the synoptics as more or less synonymous with "believer." So H. D. Betz, in *Nachfolge und Nachahmung* (Tübingen: Mohr/Siebeck, 1967), p. 10, argues that "following" Jesus is not the consequence of faith so much as what faith consists in or the form it takes, and F. Segovia, "Introduction: Call and Discipleship — Toward a Reexamination of the Shape and Character of Christian Existence in the New Testament," in *Discipleship in the New Testament,* ed. F. Segovia (Philadelphia: Fortress, 1985), pp. 1-23, suggests that it should be understood more broadly than the master-follower relationship of a total way of life. Against these M. Hengel, *The Charismatic Leader,* p. 88, rightly asserts that "only in the post-Easter community did 'following after' and discipleship become an expression of existence in faith, with the insistence that every believer is at the same time brought into the service of the Christ of God." S. Freyne, *The Twelve,* pp. 21-22, sees this development present in the way John's gospel uses the terms "following after" and "disciple." There discipleship is synonymous with abiding in Jesus' word (John 8:31-32), loving the brethren (13:34), and bearing fruit (15:8). Disciples are regarded as friends, not servants, to whom Jesus reveals everything (John 15:16). According to Michael Wilkins, *Following the Master,* p. 142, Matthew stresses obedience to Jesus' commandments (Matt 28:20), prayer (Matt 6:7-15; Luke 11:1-4), and life in the communal family (Matt 12:46-50), as well as certain ethical distinctives, motives, and the love and imitation of God (Matt 5–7). On the terminology of John, Matthew, and Acts see further A. Schulz, *Nachfolgen und Nachahmen,* pp. 13-155, 168-75. None of this means that G. Bouwman, in *Folgen und Nachfolgen,* p. 16, is wrong to stress the applicability of Jesus' words to the disciples to all believers (though I would not want to say this of his words to the Twelve).

47. For a detailed discussion of the similarities and differences between the gospel accounts of the call and mission of the Twelve, see S. Freyne, *The Twelve,* pp. 62-105.

drew, and Matthew (or Levi) — already had a link with Jesus (Mark 1:16-20; Matt 9:9-13; John 1:40-43). Concerning the rest, except for Nathaniel (John 1:44-50) we know less. There are other interesting connections between some of these figures, based on family (Mark 1:16, 19), business (Luke 5:10), place of residence (John 1:44), and friendship (John 1:45). In other words, Jesus does not just call isolated individuals from his disciple group but taps into existing networks of relationships. The group — which includes small businessmen (fishermen), a public official (tax collector), and a revolutionary (Simon the Zealot) — is quite diverse.

## 3. What Did Discipleship Entail?

In the synoptic gospels this call contains three basic elements (Mark 1:16-18 [20] and pars.).[48] (i) The call comes from Jesus and means becoming part of a community with Jesus. *Mathetes* normally appears in the plural and refers to a community that is described in familial terms (Mark 3:35; 10:29-30). When Jesus occasionally uses the word for disciple in the singular, he does so generically (Matt 10:24, 25, 42; Luke 6:40; 14:26, 27, 33). (ii) It is a call to engage in his mission. Jesus does not call people to be his servants but to join him in working for the kingdom. Since Jesus' initial call took place after his first public preaching (Matt 4:13, 17; Luke 4:43-44; Mark 1:14-15), it seems to involve assisting him in calling others to repent and believe in light of the coming kingdom of God. (iii) Obedience to the call entails forsaking old ties, not necessarily because Jesus demands everyone itinerate with him, but because giving primary allegiance to him has a potentially divisive effect on the families of new disciples. It is an implication of discipleship rather than mission, of the priorities of the new age rather than adopting a certain lifestyle.[49] Those who did follow Jesus

48. E. Schweizer, *Lordship and Discipleship*, p. 12. In Mark the connection between "following" and "service" appears both at the beginning of Jesus' ministry (the disciples are to become "fishers of men" [vv. 16-20]) and at its end (the women followed and "ministered" [15:41]).

49. This point is well made in the detailed and rewarding study by Stephen Barton, *Discipleship and Family Ties in Mark and Matthew* (Cambridge: Cambridge University Press, 1994). In connection with this study, on this general question of the breaking of family ties, see especially pp. 66-67, 105-7, 134-35, and 172-76.

were able to share in the insecurity and danger he experienced as he moved around and lived counter-culturally.[50] But Jesus does not require all his disciples to follow him around (cf. Mark 15:40-41; Matt 27:57; John 19:38-39), and even his closest companions sometimes move in and out of their own residences (e.g., Mark 1:29-34). Indeed, Jesus occasionally insists that a follower return home (e.g., Mark 5:18-19; cf. 10:21).

It is different with the Twelve. Jesus appoints them that they might be with him as his regular companions (Mark 3:15), traveling with him as witnesses to his ministry. Only when he sends them out to preach, heal, and exorcise (Mark 3:14; cf. Luke 6:13; Matt 10:1, 7, 8) are they not with him. Mark's use of the word *apostolos* (Mark 6:30; cf. Matt 10:2; Luke 9:10) introduces a word that was never used of the wider group of disciples, even if their commission is not dissimilar. Belonging to the Twelve not only involves severing family ties, giving up possessions, and suffering (Luke 14:26-33), but other specific, ascetic demands connected with particular mission journeys (Matt 10:9-16). These are not so much conditions of apostleship as descriptions of what it entails. The Twelve are to continue to count the cost (Mark 8:34–9:1; Matt 10:37-39; 16:24-26; Luke 9:23-27) and to grow in discipleship, as Jesus teaches (Mark 4:10-12), corrects (Matt 16:5-12), and admonishes (Matt 17:19-20) them.[51] After his death (in John even beforehand) they are active in making and baptizing new disciples (Matt 28:19-20; John 4:1; 20:21).

50. Stressing the dynamic involved in an itinerant modus operandi is D. M. Sweetland, *Our Journey with Jesus: Discipleship according to Mark* (Wilmington, Del.: Michael Glazier, 1987), p. 18. Stressing the consequences of this is Martin Hengel, *The Charismatic Leader*, p. 78. J. D. G. Dunn, *Jesus' Call to Discipleship*, p. 114, points out that the lack of guaranteed sustenance indicates "the dependence of the missionaries on the success (or failure) of their mission . . . a proof that they are sent by God will be the success of their mission and the provision of their bodily needs."

51. D. M. Sweetland, *Our Journey with Jesus,* pp. 39-41, points out that Mark depicts the call of the Twelve as including similar elements to the call of the disciples, including Jesus' taking the initiative, the centrality of service, and the forsaking of old ties. Mark uses the terms "disciples" and "Twelve" more interchangeably, though not always identically, than the other gospels.

## 4. How Were Disciples Distinguished?

There appear to have been various circles of disciples around Jesus. (i) Some disciples — such as the Gadarene demoniac and Joseph of Arimathaea — remained in their normal contexts, having only occasional contact with Jesus. (ii) Others — like the women in Galilee — accompanied him while he was in their region or for a time (cf. Mark 15:40). (iii) A number — seventy or seventy-two according to Luke (Luke 10:1-20) — undertook a task for a limited period.[52] How do followers whom Jesus did not call to accompany him permanently gain from him what they need to fulfill their discipleship? Part of the answer lies in the story of Martha and Mary (Luke 10:38-42): on the occasions when he is with them, they should give him their undivided attention. This is their way of letting go all earthly ties and duties, even the basic obligation of hospitality. Others who occasionally accompany him could, for the time in question, enter into the experience of his closest disciples. This would also be the case for those called to perform a particular task who worked with Jesus for a limited time.

The distinctiveness of the Twelve lies in their being companions of Jesus and having an apostolic role. Though some argue that the language of apostleship stems from later Pauline or Lucan influence, there are good grounds for insisting on its originating with Jesus.[53] Still, de-

52. This basic threefold categorization has more to commend it than the twofold one suggested by J. Roloff, *Die Kirche im Neuen Testament* (Gottingen: Vandenhoeck & Ruprecht, 1992), pp. 144-68. Though with respect to the Seventy, many scholars view its appearance only in Luke as suspicious. However, the fact that they never actually go to the Gentiles suggests that it is probably rash to conclude that this is merely a theological fabrication by Luke. Compare James Denney, *Jesus and the Gospel: Christianity Justified in the Mind of Christ* (London: Hodder and Stoughton, 1908), p. 220. More recent commentators supportive of this view include K. H. Rengstorf, "dodeka," *Theological Dictionary of the New Testament*, vol. 2 (Grand Rapids: Eerdmans, 1964), pp. 321-28; J. Schmid, *Matthaus und Lukas. Eine Untersuchung des Verhältnisses ihrer Evangelien* (Freiburg, 1930); and A. Schulz, *Nachfolgen und Nachahmen*, pp. 70-72.

53. Though the word has hardly any significant pre-Christian usage, there is some precedent for its use in the LXX where it means simply "to send." It is unwise with S. Freyne, *The Twelve*, pp. 54-61, to ground this partly on its links with the rabbinic notion of *shaliach*. The first official appearance of the latter does not occur till AD 140, where it referred to someone whose mission was only for a limited time and whose authority was derived from the sender rather than the message. The verb ap-

spite the gospels' distinctive application of this word to the Twelve, use of the words "disciples" and "apostles" does not always accord with the particular nuance of each term.[54] Also, since much of the work of the Twelve does not take place a long way from home but in the region of Galilee, we should not absolutize the difference between this group and those disciples who only accompanied Jesus when he was in their vicinity or did so intermittently.

## B. Jesus as Teacher

Though in the gospels Jesus is presented as the only teacher and as more than a teacher, teaching plays a significant role in his work.[55] This is evident already in the earliest gospel, despite the preponderance of narrative material over instruction.[56] In fact, proportionally Mark has the largest number of words describing Jesus as a teacher. (i) In his

---

pears already in Mark, and is therefore not dependent on Luke, who in any case uses the verbal form in Acts more broadly (e.g., Acts 13:4). On the significant similarities between ideas of apostleship in Mark, Luke, and Paul see further R. P. Meye, *Jesus and the Twelve*, pp. 183-89.

54. Matthew, for example, who does not single out the word to distinguish between the two groups, has the post-resurrection Jesus addressing the disciples rather than apostles when speaking of the universal mission (Matt 28:16). On the other hand Mark, though he uses the term "the Twelve" more often and speaks of them as "apostles," as I have mentioned, uses the terms "disciples" and "the Twelve" more interchangeably. On these differences see further S. Freyne, *The Twelve*, pp. 13, 102-5, and the summaries on pp. 148-50, 205-6, 254-55. He argues that it is Mark who most structures his gospel around "the Twelve," Matthew who most stresses their being "disciples," and Luke who majors on their being "apostles" (in Luke it is not said that they are "to be with" Jesus, presumably because they are with him already). On Mark in particular see also A. Schulz, *Nachfolgen und Nachahmen*, p. 47, esp. his excursus on pp. 49-54; D. M. Sweetland, *Our Journey with Jesus*, pp. 39-41; and, in considerable detail E. M. Best, *Disciples and Discipleship*, pp. 103, 108. According to Best: "In Mark the Twelve are normally absorbed into the disciples rather than remaining a subgroup of the disciples. . . . What is said of the Twelve, with the exception of their missionary activity, is said of the disciples." However, though the disciples "may generally represent the community as a whole there may be times when as the Twelve they represent missionaries to the world" (pp. 160, 127-28).

55. On the first point see in particular S. Byrskog, *Jesus the Only Teacher*.

56. For what follows I am drawing on R. P. Meye, *Jesus and the Twelve*, pp. 30-87.

gospel the address *didaskolos* (or its Hebrew equivalent *rabbi*) appears with the same frequency as in the other longer and more overtly didactic gospels. This appears several times more often than descriptions of Jesus as a prophet. (ii) In summary sections especially, the cognate term *didaskein* appears: this occurs several times as often as *euanggelein*, and more frequently than in Matthew and Luke despite their greater length. It is used variously in relation to a congregation in a synagogue (Mark 1:21, 22; 6:2), a crowd in the open (Mark 4:1, 2; 6:6, 34; 10:1), a group of outcasts (Mark 2:13), worshipers in the temple (Mark 11:17; 12:35; 14:49), as well as of Jesus' closest disciples (Mark 8:31; 9:31). Not only is teaching one of Jesus' customary activities (Matt 10:1), but the range of people whom Jesus teaches publicly or semi-publicly is therefore extremely broad (Mark 10:1). (iii) Mark uses the substantive term *didache,* teaching (Mark 4:2; 11:18; 12:38 et al.). Didactic motifs dominate or shape key sections in the earliest gospel, in a way that demonstrates progression. Matthew and Luke, however, do give more space to the content of Jesus' instruction, and link preaching and teaching more closely.[57]

Only the disciples have the meaning of some of Jesus' teaching explained to them, and at times only they understand what he is saying (Mark 4:11, 34; cf. 4:9, 23-24). Mark reserves a special place for Jesus' private instruction of his disciples, either when they are alone (Mark 4:11, 34) or increasingly when they are journeying together (Mark 8:27; 9:31, 34; 10:32). Even when he sets his face towards death, Jesus begins by teaching them about it (Mark 8:31; 9:31). In the other gospels we also see how Jesus, both literally and figuratively, leads his disciples into an ever deepening understanding of God's purposes in and through him and of their part in advancing these purposes.[58] Since much of this information occurs in secondary details in the texts, we can have some confidence that it reflects something of the

57. The first in particular displays a strong interest in Jesus as teacher and — even if comparatively they occur less often, in linguistic indicators of this — in the importance of understanding on the part of the disciples, and in the relationship between learning and discipleship (on which see Matt 5:1ff.; 9:10f.; 10:24-25; 17:24; 23:8; 26:17f.). See further S. Byrskog, *Jesus the Only Teacher,* pp. 200ff.

58. For this I am indebted to several conversations with — and a draft manuscript of — Professor Dieter Kemmler, of Aarau, Switzerland, who has won through to some original and profound insights into Jesus' method of training the disciples.

original state of affairs. In the beginning the disciples hear the basic message of Jesus, which introduces them to his view of the active presence of the kingdom. Next they observe, and are drawn into helping with, Jesus' healing — in the Greek "therapeutic" — ministry, through which they realize the importance of meeting people at their point of physical and emotional need. Then Jesus models for them a ministry of forgiveness, one that is not just conditional on repentance but at times a catalyst for it. Finally, they experience a developing fellowship with God and each other, through which they learn that community is integral to the process of discipleship. These four stages give us insight into the way Jesus drew people into his ministry and empowered them to work alongside him or separately on his behalf.[59]

A taste of how Jesus went about teaching and equipping his disciples, one that captures well the distinctive texture of what takes place, occurs in Mark 8–10. We do not have to take all this or regard the sequence of events as having the exactitude of a documentary report to catch something of the texture and atmosphere of Jesus' approach to learning. This section picks up and illustrates some of the points made above. Prior to the beginning of this section, the disciples have already learned various things from Jesus through hearing him teach and accompanying him in his work. The section begins with the feeding of around four thousand people in an isolated place, and here Jesus

---

59. The disciples function in other ways in the gospels. For example, apart from what they overtly learn from Jesus, and the benefits of the kingdom they experience or anticipate: (1) they act as a foil to Jesus, giving him the opportunity to teach and act; (2) they are the recipients of private instruction from Jesus; (3) they are sometimes amazed, sometimes afraid, and sometimes puzzled at what Jesus says and does; (4) they fail in action and are at points rebuked by Jesus; (5) they are mentioned or implied as present without their presence being in any way exceptional; (6) they are defended by Jesus against criticisms made of them; (7) they mediate in some way between Jesus and others, and act for or on behalf of Jesus. This is stressed particularly in some of the older, at times more homiletically oriented, treatments of the life of Christ. See, for example, James Stalker, *The Life of Jesus Christ* (Edinburgh: T. & T. Clark, 1978), p. 78, and A. M. Fairbairn, *Studies in the Life of Christ* (Edinburgh: T. & T. Clark, 1882). Matthew places the emphasis elsewhere, noting the consequent teaching and preaching of Jesus alone (Matt 11:1), and stressing the lack of readiness of the Twelve for their major mission, for which they are only equipped after Jesus has taught them more (Matt 26:1), and has also died and risen (Matt 28:16-20). See again Stephen Barton, *Discipleship and Family Ties*, pp. 172-74. He also strengthens the connection between teaching and healing, portraying the second as both the subject and visual expression of teaching.

draws them into discussion about how to respond to the need of the sizable crowd that has gathered. Highlighted at both the beginning and the end of the passage is his use of questions (8:2-5, 11-13). The centerpiece, however, is his dramatic action in breaking and distributing bread in a way that was miraculously sufficient for so large a crowd (8:6-10). The disciples' failure to bring any bread becomes the occasion for further teaching, and results in their having a substantial discussion about the meaning of what Jesus had said. This continues through a series of further questions and responses between Jesus and them (8:14-21). After walking into a nearby town, the disciples watch Jesus perform a healing (8:22-26). It is during a series of visits to surrounding villages that Jesus asks the disciples who people think he is, and what they have concluded about him. This elicits Peter's brief but accurate declaration: "You are the Christ" (8:27-30), which Jesus deflects into instruction about the Son of Man, followed by an explanation of and call to discipleship to the crowd (8:31–9:1).

Selecting three of the disciples, Jesus takes them up the mountain with him so that they can witness and learn from his transfiguration. On the way down they discuss among themselves the meaning of his projected resurrection, and this leads to a further exchange between them and Jesus (9:2-14). After a public exorcism of a possessed youngster (9:14-31), the disciples dispute secretly among themselves along the way about who is the greatest. By means of a question from Jesus and then a question from them, this leads to instruction about what greatness means, an issue involved in exorcism, and the danger of influencing others to sin (9:32-50). Again Jesus moves on, teaches another large crowd and becomes engaged in debate with some Pharisees about the legitimacy of divorce (10:1-12). An encounter with children, and with a wealthy young man, follows, both of which become rich teaching opportunities (10:16-31). Jesus then focuses on the disciples as they journey towards Jerusalem, first expanding on his prediction of his death and then discussing with them the potentially life-threatening consequences of and servant-character of discipleship (10:32-45). The section closes with a further healing (10:46-52). In all of this we see the forethought and preparation, flexibility and spontaneity, versatility and directness, instruction and participation, verbal and nonverbal character of the teaching and learning that occurred.

As this section makes clear, most of Jesus' instruction to the Twelve was occasioned by events (e.g., Mark 8:14; 10:13-16; Luke 13:1; Matt

26:50-56), disputes (Mark 10:41-45), challenges (Mark 2:18-22; 10:1-10; Matt 17:24-27), observations (Mark 4:1-40; 12:41-44), questions (Mark 9:11-12, 38-41; Luke 11:1ff.), and comments (Mark 13:1-37). Almost anything could become grist to Jesus' mill — personal or group failure, inappropriate ambition and conflict among his followers, the presence or appearance of small children, a prostitute or a sick person; everyday objects and activities in the home, fields, or countryside. In all the gospels — even those that contain long set pieces of instruction — Jesus relied mostly on dialogue, not presentation. Yet sometimes he taught in a structured way (e.g., Mark 6:8-11) and seems to have set some of his teaching in an easily memorizable form.[60] He also encouraged nonformal (Mark 9:33-37) learning, often when he was eating and drinking with his companions (Mark 14:17-21).[61] According to Martin Hengel: "With him the learned atmosphere of the school . . . is wholly lacking, with its stage-by-stage build-up of teaching, its refined memorizing technique, and the years of intensive study, aimed at the pupil himself becoming a famous teacher. . . ."[62] This is true even in the later part of his ministry; although Jesus placed more emphasis on his words than on his deeds,[63] ultimately it was his death and resurrection that were paramount. Mostly his association with, and formation of, his disciples took place "on the job" and following Jesus involved them in a kind of a mobile "seminary."[64]

60. See further G. A. Kennedy, *New Testament Criticism Through Rhetorical Criticism* (Chapel Hill: University of North Carolina Press, 1984), p. 68.

61. R. Riesner, *Jesus als Lehrer,* p. 205.

62. M. Hengel, *The Charismatic Leader,* p. 53 (cf. pp. 44-49 and 70-71.), against the approach of Stendahl and most recently Byrskog, but supported by M. Smith, "A Comparison of Early Christian and Early Rabbinic Tradition," *JBL* 82 (1963): 74.

63. B. L. Melbourne, *Slow to Understand: The Disciples in Synoptic Perspective* (Lanham, Md.: University Press of America, 1988), pp. 160-73, shows that at times "seeing precedes hearing, as at the transfiguration and before it, while on other occasions hearing precedes seeing, as at the healing of the blind man (men) and in the Olivet discourse. . . . That element which was needed the most was stressed from time to time" (pp. 164-65). He argues that the convergence of the two, without which full comprehension is impossible, comes only after the discovery of the empty tomb and the appearance of Jesus to the disciples (cf. Luke 24:31; 24:40-45). I would argue that this convergence takes place earlier, during Jesus' crucifixion.

64. E. Glenn Hinson, "The Spiritual Formation of the Minister as a Person," *Review and Expositor* 70 (1) (1973): 74.

All this raises a final question, one relevant to both the wider group of disciples and to the Twelve. To what extent does Jesus ask for imitation of what he does and says? Some scholars argue that, though terminologically different, ideas of "following" and "imitating" are closely related and virtually synonymous.[65] Others regard "discipleship" and "imitation" as distinguishable according to whether the earthly or heavenly Christ is in view, but as conceptually related around the idea of faith or conduct.[66] Yet in the gospels imitation seems to play only a small role. Jesus directs his disciples' attention more to realizing the royal will of God,[67] and imitating God's character and actions (Matt 5:43-47). Though he sets before them an example of servanthood (Mark 10:40-45), he draws attention to himself obliquely and by analogy (Matt 10:24-25 and par.). Mostly we find parallels between, rather than imitation by, the disciples or the Twelve and their master, as both pursue the work of the kingdom through preaching the same message (cf. Matt 4:17 with 10:7), exercising the same authority and compassion (Matt 9:36 with 10:5ff.), observing the same religious and social traditions (Matt 12:1-8; Mark 2:23-27), and belonging to the same family of obedience (Matt 12:46-49).[68] The

65. See first G. Bouwman, *Folgen und Nachfolgen*, p. 55; J. Grassi, *The Teacher in the Primitive Church*, p. 39; and W. S. Kurz, "Kenotic Imitation of Paul and of Christ in Philippians 2 and 3," in F. Segovia, ed., *Discipleship in the New Testament*, p. 122, fn. 2. According to Bouwman, discipleship means imitation: this is the difference between simply "following" and "becoming" a disciple. Grassi believes that the command to follow Jesus was a call to imitate him, including his voluntary poverty and typical prayer. Kurz notes that though the terms "following" and "imitation" in the New Testament are separate on the literary level, they refer to the same phenomenon, and underlying both is a common "pedagogical practice."

66. For the first, set against the background of Gnosticism, see H. D. Betz, *Nachfolge und Nachahmung*, pp. 43, 186-87; for the second, citing developments in Paul, Hebrews, and 1 Peter, see A. Schulz, *Nachfolgen und Nachahmen*, pp. 226-38, 332-35.

67. Martin Hengel, *The Charismatic Leader*, p. 53, who provided the first extensive discussion of the attitude of the historical Jesus on this issue. Though focusing on Mark's portrait of Jesus, Ernest Best, *Disciples and Discipleship*, p. 13, basically agrees with Hengel: "The example of Jesus is the pattern for the disciple and yet the disciple cannot really be like Jesus; there is a dimension in which he is unable to enter. The disciple of the rabbi in due time becomes a rabbi; the apprentice philosopher becomes a philosopher; but the disciple of Christ never becomes a Christ."

68. Michael Wilkins, *Following the Master*, p. 132.

imitation of Christ is only a secondary motif in the gospels, and it is not accidental that the call to the Twelve omits any reference to it.

## C. Some General Comments

1. Though reflecting some of the characteristics of the priest, prophet, or wise man, Jesus is clearly more than these. In some respects he seems to act as a first-century "rabbi." But unlike these figures he had no fixed location or salary (Luke 8:3), and did not regularly cite the authority or seek the fellowship of other learned teachers (Aboth I:4b; II:4b; III:2b; III:6 and IV:4). Nor does he encourage his disciples to seek other teachers so that they may receive the fullest education. He does not present himself as an interpreter of the Law so much as the one by whom the Law is interpreted and to whom it points.[69] Interestingly, the gospels do not portray the disciples primarily as his "students." The word *manthanein* occurs only once undisputedly in the gospels in close connection with teaching, and even there in relation to the parables (in Mark 13:28/Matt 24:32).[70] While, like the rabbis' students, his disciples occasionally do make arrangements for him (Mark 6:35-44; Mark 11:1-7; 14:12-16; Luke 9:52), Jesus' basic insistence is on their serving others, not himself (Luke 22:26f.). The only comment suggesting otherwise is an extended simile, not a direct description (Matt 10:24; cf. John 15:20). In fact Jesus himself is among them "as one who serves" (Luke 22:27), providing food for them at times (Mark 6:30-43; 8:1-13; John 21:4-14) and (according to John) once washing their feet. All this suggests that Jesus was a teacher in a different sense to his contemporaries. Whether the terminology of "friendship" rather than servanthood goes back to Jesus or not, it rightly conveys the spirit of his association with his followers (John 15:12-15). Though we should not understand this in contemporary egalitarian terms, John indicates that it involved mutuality and love. The Jewish scholar C. G. Montefiore rightly observes that accompanying Jesus

---

69. On this see Martin Hengel, *The Charismatic Leader*, p. 55 (contra A. Schulz, *Nachfolgen und Nachahmen*, pp. 33-45 et al.), and for the second Robert Banks, *Jesus and the Law in the Synoptic Tradition* (Cambridge: Cambridge University Press, 1975).

70. A. Schulz, *Nachfolgen und Nachahmen*, p. 56. Elsewhere redactional activity is clearly evident.

was oriented to *service* more than just study. As such it was a *"new thing,"* which did *"not fit in"* with the usual rabbinic approach.[71]

2. With respect to those whom Jesus gathers about him, we appear to have the following circles:

  (i)  the twelve apostles, within which there is an inner group of three;
 (ii)  a wider body of people, including, among others, Mary, Martha, Lazarus;
(iii)  the broader group of followers who live in various places, plus, on a one-off basis, the Seventy.

On occasions, we find a subgroup within one of these circles, such as the inner core within the Twelve (Mark 5:37; 9:2; 13:3; 14:33) with the "beloved disciple" at its center (John 13:23; 19:26; 20:2).[72] The main difference between the first group and the rest is that they accompany Jesus on special occasions (Mark 5:37ff.), receive privileged insights into his status (Mark 9:2ff.), are the only audience for some of his teaching (Mark 13:3ff.), and are present during his darkest hour (Matt 26:7ff.). Yet Jesus does not make any qualitative distinction between these groups. The wider group of disciples has a familial relationship with Jesus, even though they do not go about with him (Mark 3:35). They cast out demons (Mark 9:14-29) and share the

71. C. G. Montefiore, *Rabbinic Literature and Gospel Teachings* (New York: KTAV, 1939), 218. Cf. G. Bornkamm, *Jesus of Nazareth* (London: Hodder & Stoughton, 1960), p. 145. Throughout his study A. Schulz, *Nachfolgen und Nachahmen,* consistently overdraws the parallels between the historical Jesus and the other first-century teachers (e.g., pp. 56-62). In his discussion of the portrait in Matthew's gospel, J. Roloff, *Die Kirche im Neuen Testament,* pp. 154-57, describes the disciples as, *inter alia,* students, but places them within the broader context of their having a personal relationship with Jesus, participating in a distinctive communal lifestyle, and serving the kingdom of God. Meanwhile, W. T. Shiner, *Follow Me! Disciples in Markan Rhetoric* (Atlanta: Scholars Press, 1995), distinguishes Mark's depiction from that of followers in several non-Jewish authors.

72. Others who could be added include those who do not know Jesus but who are not against him (Mark 9:38-40), and those who in principle are childlike, the poor and the sinners, but these seem to be categories of a more generic kind. We note also that some disciples seem to have brought along people with them (Mark 1:36), that some people are around Jesus even though not disciples (Mark 4:10), and, perhaps on the analogy of the Twelve, some of his followers seem to have generated their own disciples (Mark 9:38-40).

news about what Jesus has done for them (Mark 1:45; 5:20). This means that:

> There is a functional distinction between Jesus and his followers, but very little of functional specialization between these followers. Among the Twelve there is some rudimentary role specialization. . . . Generally speaking, however, "the Twelve" and/or "the disciples" act together as a homogeneous unit, all of them able to perform the same functions. . . . This means that members of the laity are no longer relegated to the position of second-rate Christians. The Twelve are nowhere shown within the Gospels as functioning within the wider group of Jesus' disciples in any kind of hierarchical rule. They are closer to him and act as assistants and missionaries but have no intermediary function. . . . There is no suggestion of the Twelve functioning as "priests" to others' "laity." . . . The pattern for relationships within the community of Jesus' disciples is . . . a quite different model.[73]

Also, we do not find here any qualitative distinction between service performed towards other followers and towards those in the world. Peter, for example, is to help look after the flock but is also among those who are to make disciples. Peter even returns for a time to his work of fishing as a means of support.

3. For Jesus, instructing his disciples in a way that was spiritually and morally formative was not everything. Failing to see this is the mistake of William J. Lunny's otherwise perceptive account of Jesus' attitude to his followers.[74] He brings out vividly the holistic and communal training the disciples received as they accompanied Jesus. This took place partly through verbal instruction such as in the Sermon on the Mount and the parables (which he regards as primarily addressed to the disciples), partly through such actions as healing miracles and exorcisms, exercising forgiveness, as well as undergoing persecution, and partly through their eating, drinking, and praying together. However, he insists that the purpose of *all* this was to prepare and train the Twelve. In other words, Jesus set up a series of "training sessions" and

73. D. M. Sweetland, *Our Journey with Jesus,* pp. 97, 64; J. D. G. Dunn, *Jesus' Call to Discipleship,* pp. 106-7; and O. Dibelius, *Paul* (Philadelphia: Westminster, 1953).

74. William J. Lunny, *The Sociology of the Resurrection* (London: SCM, 1989), pp. 41-103.

"immersion experiences" for them. On the contrary, it was not *preparation* of the Twelve *for* mission that was uppermost in his mind, but *engagement* of the Twelve *in* mission.

4. Nevertheless, we should not think of the lifestyle of Jesus and the disciples as always marked by activity and business in the work of the kingdom. Much of it took place at a different pace to the work of ministry today, even when crowds were present or needs were great. One only has to note the rare references to any activity in the evenings. And while healings sometimes took place on the Sabbath, there is no hint that Jesus viewed this generally as a working day. As well, there was a regular pattern of activity and withdrawal, of public ministry by, and private fellowship between, its members. Often they were on their own, in isolated or less populated places. As noted, it was often as they were walking from one place to another that teaching took place, in a conversational way. We should not necessarily interpret this as a leisurely rather than organized way of teaching, for some of it probably had at least an orderly character. Nor should we necessarily think of this as informal as opposed to instruction, for much of it was more likely nonformal in kind, and at times may have included a formal component. Overall we should remember that there is an eschatological atmosphere about their time together — not incompatible with engaged learning but different from the pressured learning that marks so much modern seminary life.

# 4. Ministry Formation After Christ

One of the difficulties in exploring the ongoing relevance of Jesus' relationship with his disciples is his unique status. Because of his distinctive character and work, we have to be careful about the wider conclusions we draw for theological education. For example: (i) His call to discipleship involves a kind and degree of personal attachment that would be inappropriate elsewhere. (ii) The number of the core group has symbolic significance for Israel, and its make-up reflects the role of males in first-century Jewish society. (iii) His messianic role differentiates him from others engaged in the service of the kingdom. (iv) The probable three-year duration of Jesus' link with these groups was partly a function of his early death. None of this means that his example is irrelevant to the debate over theological education. But before we pursue this further, we need to look at the way early Christian leaders, especially Paul about whom we know most, engaged in ministry formation.

First-century Greek philosophical groups — Stoic, Epicurean, neo-Platonic — provide the background here. Mostly these stemmed from a revered teacher or exemplar. Alongside these groups were a number of imported mystery cults from the East. These drew initiates into a close relationship with and imitation of a spiritual guide.[75] According to Betz, it was in the classical Greek mysteries, such as the cult of Dionysius, that the idea of imitation came into prominence, first in

75. H. D. Betz, *Nachfolge und Nachahmung*, pp. 60ff.

connection with the ritual, then broadened to cover the whole of life. It was from there that it began to influence pre-Socratic philosophy, Plato, and the post-Platonics. In such circles there seems to have been a shift from learning a particular tradition or learning from a particular figure (one did not need to be a disciple in the personal sense but could follow a revered teacher from the past) to imitation of that figure, though some form of instruction and learning continued to be central.[76] For Paul, it is the language of collegiality, of partnership not discipleship, that provides the best point of entry for investigating his link with those around him. Though Luke continues to use the term *mathetes* (e.g., Acts 4:32; 6:2; 9:26; and 11:26), in the Pauline writings it drops out of sight altogether and other expressions come to the fore. It is probably Jesus' removal from the scene that explains this change in vocabulary. The presence of the Spirit, not just the memory of Jesus (Acts 1:1ff.), forms another bridge between the group around Jesus and the group around Paul. The Twelve, whose number was restored after Judas' defection (Acts 1:12-26), form a more explicit connection. Although initially attention focuses on Peter and James, it is not long before it shifts primarily to Paul (Acts 9:1ff.; 12:1ff.; and Gal 1:18–2:10).[77]

Careful investigation of Acts and Paul's writings[78] shows that the apostle almost always had others with him on his missionary travels. On the rare occasions when he was alone, it is never long before he moves on to find one of his companions (2 Cor 2:12-13). This collegial approach to his work — in which Paul was certainly the major figure — has its basis in: (i) the pattern set during his earlier days at Antioch, when he was drawn in by Barnabas as a junior partner in ministry (Acts 11:25-26); (ii) his desire to embody the corporate implications of

76. M. Wilkins, *Following the Master*, pp. 77-78. In classical and Hellenistic Greek, imitation ranged from physically mimicking another person to following and emulating them. The idea of imitation affects even the Greek translation of the Old Testament, which places a greater stress than the Hebrew version on the imitation of both exemplary human figures and God.

77. Outside Acts, another of the core group, John, appears as a source for some of the gospel, letters, and revelation attached to his name.

78. Though I think that the Pastorals come through Luke rather than directly from Paul's hand, and accept that the account of Paul and his journey in Acts reflects some of Luke's interests, these writings can still help us reconstruct Paul's approach.

the gospel of Jesus as well as preaching the gospel (1 Thess 1:4-7; cf. Gal 3:1); (iii) the need to provide resources for churches that he could not visit by reason of imprisonment or other responsibilities. Paul the apostle, then, "was essentially a teamworker. His roving little community of apostles was at once a training school, a miniature Church, and a mutual source of support in a very difficult vocation."[79] All told, at some time or other, upwards of forty people linked up with Paul in this way, including Jews (e.g., Acts 4:36; 15:22; 18:8), Gentiles (Acts 16:10; 19:29; 20:4), and people of mixed parentage (Acts 16:1). Though men predominated, the group included women (Rom 16:7, 12; Phil 2:2-4), singles, widows, and marrieds (Acts 18:1-3). There were younger people in the group (1 Tim 4:11; 2 Tim 2:22) along with those who had more experience, and there were slaves as well as masters (Col 4:9; Philem 1:8-21). The composition of this group crossed the religious, ethnic, gender, and status lines in a way that was unparalleled at that time.[80]

## A. The Colleagues of Paul

### 1. Who Were Paul's Colleagues?

I will follow here the same pattern of concerns as in the previous investigation of Jesus and the disciples.

This circle around Paul waxed and waned according to circumstances. Building on, but also revising, W. H. Ollrog's detailed investigation we can discern three main groups of coworkers.

1. The smallest circle comprised those who worked with him for a substantial period of time (e.g., Barnabas and Silas) or permanently (Timothy). This group was either regularly traveling with Paul or traveling on his behalf (2 Cor 8:16-17). Within it Timothy was the one who worked most closely with the apostle (Phil 2:20; 1 Tim 1:2; 2 Tim 1:2).

2. The larger group included representatives (cf. Epaphroditus)

---

79. Joseph Grassi, *A World to Win: The Missionary Methods of St. Paul the Apostle* (Maryknoll, N.Y.: Orbis, 1965), p. 81.

80. Robert Banks, *Paul's Idea of Community: The Earliest House Churches in Their Social and Historical Setting* (Peabody, Mass.: Hendrickson, 1994), ch. 15.

from various congregations founded by Paul (cf. 1 Cor 16:15-18; Phil 2:19f.; Col 1:7f.; 4:12f.; Philem 13).

3. There were also key figures in local churches founded by Paul, indeed sometimes whole churches, with whom he spent time on his journeys (e.g., Acts 20:17ff.).

An additional one-off group contained representatives from the churches who joined with Paul and Titus to carry out a particular task, namely the collection for the saints in Jerusalem (1 Cor 16:1-4; 2 Cor 8:1-7, 22-24).[81]

## 2. On What Basis Were They Recruited?

Interestingly, none of these people were involved in what we term today "full-time" ministry, not even the first group. We know that Paul himself regularly worked with his hands, and we have no reason to believe that his colleagues acted otherwise. The second group came and went from their usual churches and occupations. The third group occasionally received financial support from fellow-believers, but served the church mainly from the base of their ongoing secular work.

How did these people connect up with Paul, and what role did they play in his work? With respect to the inner core around him, it was Paul who chose them (cf. Acts 16:40), though he sometimes took advice from a church beforehand (Acts 16:1-3). It was the local communities who selected these leaders and encouraged them to accompany him for a time before returning.[82] In many respects they acted as his surrogates (Titus 1:5ff.; 1 Cor 4:13). As the prevalence of compounds formed from the prefix *sun-* indicates, especially the term *sunergoi,* "workers," Paul viewed these people as partners or colleagues, not as servants or even apprentices, even though they might from time to time have made arrangements for him or undertaken

81. Somewhat to one side were those, like Apollos, involved in independent missionary work with whom Paul occasionally collaborated. On all this, see generally W.-H. Ollrog, *Paulus und seine Mitarbeiter: Untersuchungen zur Theorie und Praxis der paulinischen Mission* (Neukirchen-Vluyn: Neukirchener, 1979), p. 108.

82. The second of these meanings affects even the Greek translation of the Old Testament, which places a greater stress than the Hebrew version on the imitation of both exemplary human figures and God.

things on his behalf. Others accompanying him assisted him in practical ways, e.g., Mark, who may have been a scribe (2 Tim 4:11), and Luke, who may have acted as his physician (Col 4:13). Increasingly he handed over major responsibilities to some close companions, while others who came and went continued in work similar to his own.

### 3. How Did He Relate to His Colleagues?

The relationship between Paul and his coworkers was analogous to the diverse relationships with churches he visited. He worked with independent apostles like Apollos in the same mutual way he related to churches he had not founded (1 Cor 3:5-9; cf. Rom 1:11-14). With colleagues converted through him and selected by him, Paul did not place himself "over" but "alongside" them, as partners rather than disciples, as he did with churches he founded (2 Cor 1:24). Though they undertook responsibilities on his behalf, he looked for their agreement with what he asked them to do. Though he was the dominant person in the group, the pivotal figure was Christ (1 Cor 3:5-15) or the Spirit (Acts 14:6-7), and it was the whole group or relevant members who made the basic decisions about its activities (cf. Acts 16:6-10; 2 Cor 8:16-17).

### 4. What Was the Purpose of the Group?

The purpose of the group was evangelism, church planting, congregational nurture, and networking (2 Tim 4:1-5). This was what we would describe as a parachurch enterprise, working alongside and for local churches. Sometimes members operated together as a larger team, sometimes in a smaller group, and sometimes separately from the apostle but on his behalf. Some have described these associates as "apprentices" who were being prepared for further ministry through present practical learning. This is not quite accurate. While they may have been younger and less experienced in ministry, they were still his colleagues rather than apprentices. They represented him fully when he could not visit a particular church, and they shared in writing the letters he sent to various congregations (1 Cor 1:1; 2 Cor 1:1; Phil 1:1; Col 1:1; 1 Thess 1:1; 2 Thess 1:1; Philem 1). In all these ways — working with Paul in preaching, pastoring, teaching, as well as connecting and interpreting churches to one another — they had a part in instructing Paul's converts.

## B. Paul as Teacher

Paul presents himself explicitly as a "teacher." His regular practice was to teach people "publicly and from house to house" (Acts 20:21), and he refers more than once to the importance of his hearers "living according to the teaching" they have received (e.g., 2 Thess 3:6). So highly does he rate teaching that he places it alongside prophecy as one of the two basic gifts of the Spirit (1 Cor 14:6; cf. 12:28). Elsewhere, he describes himself by means of other terms and images that include reference to teaching, such as father (1 Cor 4:15; cf. 1 Thess 2:11) and nurse (1 Thess 2:7-8). He also speaks constantly in his letters about the importance of his hearers or readers "knowing" and "learning," or of their "receiving" instruction or tradition at his hands (1 Thess 2:13; 1 Cor 15:3). As the content of certain letters indicates, especially Romans and Ephesians, Paul sometimes engaged in more systematic instruction. His most common way of teaching probably comes before us in Acts 20:7-12, where it says that Paul "dialogued with" (not preached to) the church at Troas (until midnight), and later "conversed" with them over a meal. This suggests that his favored way of proceeding was an opening presentation leading into questions and answers about concrete situations, followed by more general discussion about all manner of things.

Many scholars have called attention to the educational dimension of Paul's work. According to E. Glenn Hinson, "Timothy had been schooled on the job with the Apostle Paul." For Joseph Grassi, "Paul's traveling school provided a very valuable training opportunity for others who would carry on the same kind of work."[83] Though we lack detail on what went on at this level, Paul's writings contain sufficient clues for us to piece together a general picture of what happened. This suggests that the language of "school" is not altogether apt. While there is overlap with what took place in circles of philosophical

83. E. Glenn Hinson, "The Spiritual Formation of the Minister as a Person," p. 75; Joseph Grassi, *The Teacher in the Primitive Church*, pp. 76-77.

instruction at the time,[84] especially in seeking the truth in order to live
well, Paul's group was primarily a community action in which learning
and maturing also took place. This is why the term "students" is not
the most accurate term for Paul's companions. As already mentioned,
and as Romans (and Ephesians) suggests, this does not mean that systematic instruction was absent from Paul's teaching; certainly both
formal and nonformal instruction took place as he and his group prepared for and evaluated their common work, as well as occasionally
with a wider group of key figures (cf. Acts 15).[85]

A concrete example of how Paul went about teaching and equipping those who accompanied him comes before us in his letter to the
Philippians. This is certainly from the hand of Paul and gives us some insight into his association with his long-term assistant Timothy, a representative from a local church called Epaphroditus, who worked with
him for a season, and key members of the church in Philippi itself, with
whom he had a special relationship. We are informed at the outset that
Paul and Timothy jointly composed the letter (1:1). Not only does this
tell us something about the shared nature of the apostolic work they
were doing, but suggests that they must have had considerable discussion about its contents. In the opening section of the letter, Paul refers to
his arrest and imprisonment for the gospel, and explains that this did not
discourage leading local believers or his assistants but spurred them instead to step into his place and courageously and fearlessly speak the
Word (1:14). Here we have further reference to the work of mission as a
shared responsibility, not dependent on the work of the pivotal figure.

84. In "Paulus und die Weisheit," *New Testament Studies* 12 (1965-6): 231-
44, Conzelmann argues that the presence of reinterpreted wisdom materials in
Paul's writings indicates the existence of an actual Pauline school in Ephesus from
which qualified helpers went out in an organized way to other centers. However,
his exegesis of certain passages is unpersuasive (e.g., Rom 1:18ff.; 10:6ff.; 1 Cor
1:18ff.; 2:6ff.; 10:1ff.; 11:2ff.; 13; 2 Cor 3:7ff.), and he overlooks the missiological
or pastoral rather than educational context of Paul's dealing with a range of issues.

85. In his study of Paul's coworkers, W.-H. Ollrog, *Paulus und seine Mitarbeiter*, pp. 118f., overreacts when he says that hardly anything is going on educationally. He can only do this by ruling out wholesale any use of Acts. While Paul's
energy is primarily directed to the churches in which he ministers, not the coworkers with whom he ministers, he allows that there must have been a pedagogical
side to Paul's missionary endeavors. Perhaps, reflecting his German background,
Ollrog is too dominated by the "formal schooling" model of education to appreciate the variety of ways in which this would have occurred.

Yet his link with a colleague like Timothy is extremely close. It is a special relationship, more akin to the affectionate bond that can exist between a father and his adult son than between a superior and a subordinate. Despite the difference in age and maturity, and despite Paul's remaining the central figure in their common work, however, the emphasis is on the way Timothy has served "with" him, not as a servant "of" him, in the work of mission. Timothy has "proven" himself through this service, graduated we might say with distinction (2:22-23).

Paul's relationship with Epaphroditus, the church's representative, is also a close one, and is described in brotherly terms (2:25). Epaphroditus was so committed to the work of mission alongside Paul that he risked his life and almost died in its service (1:27-29). A little later there is a reference to Paul being a general "example" and "pattern" to those around him (3:17). This leads into a reference to the way in which other local church leaders, including two prominent women who had since fallen out, worked side by side with him in the cause of the gospel (4:2). He does not command them to overcome what separates them, but issues a plea for their reconciliation. Though in other letters he refers to the teaching he left them with — and no doubt that was as true for the church in Philippi — he does not do so here but only refers to their association in accomplishing a common task (4:3). It is only their working together in mission, not their studying under him, that he calls to mind. Indeed, he says of this church that it took up "partnership in the gospel from the first day until now" (1:5), and has "always obeyed" the implications of the salvation they have received (2:12). His desire is not primarily that its knowledge will grow — though that in itself involves heart and will as well as mind — but that its "love may abound more and more in knowledge and depth of insight" and that they may be "filled with the fruit of righteousness that comes through Jesus Christ" (1:9-10). In this letter we have an open window into the priority of mission, the character of the relationships, and the supportive role of knowledge in Paul's connection with the inner, intermediate, and outer circle of coworkers.

Scholars have rightly discussed the imitation-of-Paul motif in connection with his general teaching directed to his churches rather than that specifically directed to his coworkers.[86] There is no doubt

86. The main contributions are reviewed in Elizabeth A. Castelli, *Imitating Paul: A Discourse of Power* (Louisville: Westminster/John Knox, 1991), pp. 21-

that basic for Paul is the imitation of God (1 Cor 4:16; 11:1; Eph 5:1; Phil 3:17; 1 Thess 1:6; 2:14; 2 Thess 3:7, 9) as reflected in Christ (Eph 4:32; 5:2). Imitation of Christ does not consist in any literal following of Jesus' example but has to do with Christ's attitude and approach being reproduced in the lives of all God's people (e.g., Rom 14:1; 2 Cor 8:8-9; Phil 2:5; 1 Cor 11:1; 1 Thess 1:6). Christ is basically a model for the Christian life in general, not for the ministry of any particular group. When Paul asks others to imitate him, it is because he in turn imitates Christ (1 Cor 11:1; cf. 1 Cor 4:16-17; Phil 3:17-21; 1 Thess 1:6). Although he can recommend some of his specific activities for people's imitation (2 Thess 3:7, 9), Christ's example is probably never far away (cf. Acts 20:33-35). Basic to the whole process is following and handing on the teaching about Christ (1 Thess 3:6-9),[87] at the heart of which is the redemptive power of the cross and resurrection (2 Cor 4:16-17).[88]

---

33. As already noted, for some scholars his idea of imitation, though terminologically different from talk about discipleship in the gospels, conceptually overlaps with that. Against W. Michaelis, *TDNT*, vol. 4, pp. 659-74, who argues that the imitation of Christ was not a central feature of the Pauline writings. A. Schulz, *Nachfolgen und Nachahmen*, finds the imitation of both Christ (pp. 270-89) and of the apostle (pp. 308-14) to be a Pauline theme, though only at a modest level. See also H. D. Betz, *Nachfolge und Nachahmung*, and the unpublished dissertations of D. M. Williams, "The Imitation of Christ in Paul with Special Reference to Paul as Teacher" (Ph.D. diss., Columbia University, 1967), and B. Fiore, "The Function of Personal Example in the Socratic and Pastoral Epistles" (Ph.D. diss., Yale University, 1982). On the "imitatio" motif as a fundamental perspective in Paul see also R. A. Wild, " 'Be Imitators of God': Discipleship in the Letter to the Ephesians," in F. Segovia, ed., *Discipleship in the New Testament*, and G. Bouwman, *Folgen und Nachfolgen*, pp. 66ff., 73ff. Bouwman suggests that all Paul's ethics can be derived from this.

87. As Joseph Grassi remarks, in *The Teacher in the Primitive Church*, p. 63: ". . . since his own life is the direct link with Christ, he can present himself as a concrete example of Christian tradition that is to be handed on to others."

88. In keeping with the concrete nature of Paul's approach, it is only in churches he has founded that we find him speaking this way: elsewhere he talks more generally of doing something in conformity with Christ. His letter to the Philippians is a case study in his approach to the question of imitation. To them he says: "Practice what you have learned and received; what you have heard me say and seen me do" (Phil 4:9). The letter brings out forcefully the radical grounding of imitation in the servant-oriented coming, life, and especially death of Jesus. Although the incarnation of Jesus is mentioned here it is not the central focus. Paul takes this as the example all believers should follow.

Paul presents himself as a model to believers generally — including his associates — in the following ways: how he and Apollos operate (1 Cor 4:6), his celibate state (1 Cor 7:6-7), his practice of glossolalia (1 Cor 14:6, 19), working with his own hands (1 Thess 2:9; 4:11-12), encouraging others (1 Thess 2:11; 4:18; 5:11), self-effacement on behalf of the weak (1 Cor 10:31–11:1), offering forgiveness (2 Cor 2:10), approach to Jewish food regulations (Gal 4:12), striving for as yet unattained perfection (Phil 3:12-14), bearing the marks of Christ's suffering (Gal 6:17).[89] Interesting here is the focus on concrete stances or actions, not on lists of virtues or vices as was conventionally the case. In the Pastoral Letters, because they are are addressed to two of his close associates, there is a more specific stress on Paul as a model for their imitation. Highlighted here are his hardships and suffering (2 Tim 1:8-9; 2:3), his teaching, faith, and love (2 Tim 1:13; 2:2), his way of life, purpose, patience, and endurance (2 Tim 3:10). But even here Timothy is also presented as exemplifying these characteristics "with" Paul (cf. 2 Tim 1:8; 2:3) and "with" the help of the Spirit (2 Tim 1:14), not through slavish copying of the apostle.[90] It is not on the basis of some incarnational model of ministry but a servant-like model of the Christian life, that imitation of Paul should occur. It is primarily God or Christ who his colleagues are to imitate, not Paul himself. While it is proper for believers to imitate him, they should also imitate others like Apollos (1 Cor 4:6), as well as his coworkers (e.g., Phil 2:29). So, in the main, we should regard imitation of Paul as more a general theme in Paul's teaching about the Christian life and only a secondary feature in his teaching about the conduct of ministry.[91]

89. See also the use of the expression "ways" for Paul's way of life (1 Cor 4:17; 7:17; 11:16; 14:33, 36) and many other precepts (1 Cor 1:10, 31; 3:21; 4:1, 5, 16; 5:9, 12-13; 6:18, 20; 7; 8:9; 10:10, 12).

90. See further B. Fiore, "The Function of Personal Example," pp. 332-35. He explores the differences in emphasis between the approach to imitation in these and the undisputed letters of Paul on pages 417-19.

91. Nor is the incarnation ever presented as a model for ministry in the Gospel of John. I owe this point to Marianne Meye Thompson, who has written extensively on the Johannine literature. She points out that an emphasis on the incarnation and ministry, particularly where the latter is regarded as a function of only some believers and not the whole people of God, all too easily leads to the opposite of what is at its heart, that is, to a sense of superiority rather than humility. Viewing the *imitatio* motif as secondary in Paul partly overcomes the objection to *imitatio* language maintained by Elizabeth Castelli (Elizabeth A. Castelli, *Imitating*

## C. Some Common Features

What are we to conclude from this examination of the biblical writings? For all the differences in ministry formation before, by, and after Christ, there are some clear lines of continuity:

1. There were different levels of association with the key figure. First, around that person there was a relatively mobile core group made up of a limited number of people. Second, an intermediate group containing people who came and went for various periods of time. Third, a broader group who had only occasional contact with such a person. On occasions there was also a one-off group with a specific commission to fulfill, generally made up of people from the first two of these groups. There are no status distinctions between these groups, and functional ones are more a matter of degree than kind, and are determined more by the place where ministry takes place. The composition of these groups is exceedingly diverse and increasingly inclusive. They encompass people from all walks of life, people who differ strongly from one another in personality, occupation, and politics. Over the course of time women begin to feature more strongly, and ethnically they become more representative. Overall there is a growing orientation to the global scene, as that was defined at the time.

2. Those who join such groups require a significant degree of commitment. A direct call or recruitment, followed by testing, is most

---

*Paul,* esp. pp. 21-22, 35-38, 49-50, 57-58). She argues that in relation to the dynamic between Paul and others involved in imitation, scholars have tended to spiritualize the idea or regard it as unproblematic. In doing so, they have masked the one-sided flow of power it depicts, and so opened it up to ideological manipulation. Those who imitate Paul or Christ are either bound to an authoritative textual tradition, or to a simple obedience to Paul which keeps them in a dependent position. Although she does not claim that Paul necessarily intended his words to be understood this way, Castelli fails to see the way Paul puts the *imitatio* motif in its place, and so prevents its operating in a hierarchical or oppressive way. Paul uses the language of collegiality rather than imitation for those working and learning with him, and where he uses the language of imitation, underlying it is the image of the cross which overturns all human notions of hierarchy and power. In any case, Castelli's understanding of personhood is affected too much by contemporary ideological concerns, namely a focus on equality rather than on unity (or community), and a tendency to equate imitation with sameness (or identity). A discerning response to Castelli and treatment of the *imitatio* motif have now been provided by Andrew D. Clarke, " 'Be Imitators of Me' ": Paul's Model of Leadership," *Tyndale Bulletin* 49 (2) (1998): 329-30.

common for the inner group. For the intermediate group it arose from someone's offer to join, a person brought by them, or the arrival of representatives from a church. For the broader audience it entailed only a willingness to embrace the key figure's message and way of life and to give him priority when he was in the vicinity. The initial encounters with people in each of these groups frequently arise in the most everyday settings. The core group did have to break some family ties, but seem to have maintained occasional links with their place of origin. For the intermediate group the opposite is the case, since they only leave their regular surroundings for a shorter time. In the broadest group, unless accepting the gospel itself necessarily led to it, they did not have to forsake existing family ties.

3. For the core group, associating with the key figure includes living, learning, eating, and praying with him, that is, sharing in his total life. Except when sent away on a mission without him, members experience this on a daily basis. The intermediate group is able to take up the opportunity to live and work with the key person from time to time. The broader group must make the most of that person's intermittent visits or larger gatherings, and give their undivided attention to these when these occur. Unexpected circumstances, even persecution, might limit the amount of time in the group. During moments of special challenge or opportunity, there is an urgency and intensity to their common work. When a longer association is possible, associates have greater opportunity to undertake tasks on their own.

4. The purpose of these groups was not increase in knowledge of their basic traditions, progress in moral or spiritual formation, or the development of skills associated with ministry or leadership. It was active service or mission in furthering the kingdom, as initially defined by a key figure and progressively clarified by the whole group. Within that framework, however, spiritual growth and practical development, as well as substantial learning, also took place. Such learning was often in-service and nonformal in character; at other times it was more extensive and systematic. Instruction touched on matters of conduct, belief, rituals, and mission. Companions of key figures learned about key scriptural teachings, significant historical traditions, and major theological and ethical convictions. They also received direction and resources to undertake God's work. The point of departure for such instruction was often the life-situations of individual members, the group as a whole, or the context in which they were operating. As a re-

sult, it took varying forms, including presentation, dialogue, questions, and private conversation.

5. The associates' spiritual and character formation had already previously begun in their homes and local communities, but was enhanced through engaging in service alongside a key figure. To the extent that they are with the central figure, it takes place as they prepare for, participate in, and evaluate their common tasks and as they observe and learn from the way that person operates. For the core group there tended to be specific instruction in — and modeling of — service to God and others, as well as in overcoming challenges and disappointments encountered in the work. By these means associates learned how to obey and relate to God, to deal with tendencies towards pride, ambition, and failure, to operate as a community under God, and to serve others in word and deed. Within this there is only a secondary place for imitation of the key figure, understood more as developing the same orientation to God and others, not specific copying of their ways. For the disciples, this meant less following a tradition *about* Jesus than living a tradition *in* Jesus, central to which — particularly after the resurrection — is the role of the Spirit, who brings this about in ever new and diverse ways.

# Conclusion

Standing back from all this we can agree that the key figures we have considered were "not geared to mass production. It needed intimate participation and sharing both in a lifestyle and in a common action. This takes a great deal of time as well as intense exposure" and "is only possible in a group that comes in close contact with one another and their teacher."[92] This applies in the fullest sense to the inner core of associates around a Samuel, Jesus, or Paul, but in some measure to those in the intermediate and outer circles as well. It is important to note that the orientation of this formation was not just or even primarily to the church. Much of what took place was in the world at large, in a wide range of settings, even including the workplace.

At this point we need to remind ourselves of what we have discovered about the basic similarities between people in these different circles. All receive a challenge to undertake the same type of service, and this means they need to learn some of the same basic things. We do not find status divisions between them. Distinctions are basically numerical — for example, "the Twelve" as opposed to "a number of the disciples" or "the whole group of disciples" — or geographical — the Twelve as "apostles" are more "sent" ones than "stay-put" ones, with the intermediate group partly sedentary and partly mobile. While we do read about people being commissioned for various responsibilities, either by the key figure or by core groups in churches, this is a

92. Joseph Grassi, *The Teacher in the Primitive Church*, p. 107.

functional affair, and does not imply the presence of a religious hierarchy such as ordination later introduced.

All of this has implications for the way we envision and undertake theological education:

- It ought to comprehend the broader people of God not just as an elite cadre, though special attention should be paid to a core group and, to a lesser extent, to an intermediate group.
- It should orient itself primarily around "in-service" ministry activities, within which intellectual, spiritual, and practical concerns form a seamless whole.
- At its center should be a living and working partnership with an experienced person who, for different periods of time, offers his or her whole self to those in such a group.
- The break with home, occupation, and often family, involved in attending a seminary, or the residential requirements in extension centers, mirrors something of what we find in the biblical narratives. So does the general development of residential campuses, extension centers, and continuing education or distance-learning programs.
- The growing desire to have a stronger interconnection between the seminary and the church, and between study and practice, is well based.
- In a limited way echoes of Paul's collegial approach appear in the one-on-one or small-group academic mentoring of advanced students, who are regarded as junior members of the community of scholars.

There are, then, real continuities and overlaps between our present practice in theological education and these biblical antecedents. But there are also some significant differences. How much these antecedents should inform or change our present practices requires exploration of our changed cultural and ecclesiastical circumstances. We also need to look at the contribution of several contemporary thinkers who are moving in directions that have something in common with these biblical approaches. This will form the centerpiece of the next chapter.

# PART THREE

# DEVELOPING A MISSIONAL MODEL: FROM THE MARGINS TO THE CENTER

For historical reasons Christian theological education in North America is inescapably committed to two contrasting and finally irreconcilable types or models of what education at its best ought to be. They are normative models, models of "excellent" education. . . . Although persuasive theological arguments can be given for adopting each of these types, neither of them can be said to be somehow theologically mandated by the very nature of Christianity. Indeed, Tertullian's ancient question, "What has Jerusalem to do with Athens?" might suggest that, with its roots in "Jerusalem," Christianity in fact mandates a third type of excellent schooling altogether, one hitherto ignored by major Christian communities.

DAVID KELSEY[1]

1. David H. Kelsey, *Between Athens and Berlin: The Theological Education Debate* (Grand Rapids: Eerdmans, 1993), p. 5.

# 1. Beyond Mission-Oriented and Missiological Education

## A. Developing a New Trajectory in Theological Education

In my view, the quotation from Kelsey is the most significant and overlooked statement in the whole debate on theological education. Is there not a more distinctively Christian approach than the proposals we have been considering? Having raised the possibility, Kelsey does not pursue it, focusing instead on what "is the case *de facto*" in North America today rather than "whatever the theologically normative case might be." This is a pity, because it is precisely the focus on developing a *theological* understanding of theological education that distinguishes the present debate. While we must do our thinking concretely — in conversation with our existing patterns of theological education — and while we ought preserve valuable elements in our current model, we should not limit ourselves to these.[2] Nor, unlike Kelsey and others, should we resign ourselves to living with two logically contradictory models without trying to incorporate vital aspects of both into a more consistent one. If, as Kelsey says, there is an approach that is "theologically mandated by the very nature of Christianity," we are under a

---

2. So far as I know, the only other person to highlight the importance of this statement by Kelsey is Norman J. Kansfield, "Beyond Athens and Berlin," *Perspectives* (October, 1994): 10-12, who does so, however, because of the need to have a more global conversation about the issues, not so much on basic theological grounds.

theological imperative to explore it. In the previous chapter I have sought to lay the basis for doing just that.[3]

What follows falls into four main sections:

i. I begin developing a missional model by examining those who talk about mission as a dimension of theological education, those reflecting on the future shape of missiological education, and the praxis-oriented approach to education by key people working in the Third World. Because of the increasing number of Christian professionals undertaking some theological education — as noted earlier, in my previous seminary we had a full-scale school of psychology — I also wish to say something about recent trends in thinking about the education of those involved in the professions.

ii. I then return to some of the key issues in the current debate — for instance, fragmentation and unity, pluralism and uniformity — to see how they appear from a missional perspective and whether this resolves them more satisfactorily than other approaches. I also revisit the hermeneutical issue and extend what was said in the previous section.

iii. Next, I identify contributions to, or alongside, the current debate from a range of other fields — especially education and philosophy — that consciously or unconsciously point towards such a model. I try to preserve key elements in the other proposals, while overcoming their shortcomings and offering more than they can provide. It is not hard to revise and incorporate these elements within the approach I am proposing.

iv. Finally, I explore how all this affects what lies at the heart of theological education, that is, the nature and practice of teaching and learning. I attempt to do this as practically as possible.

---

3. Kelsey's lack of interest in exploring this actually perpetuates the systematic ignoring of it by major Christian communities, on which he himself comments. The only other contributor to the debate who hints at the model I will develop, in a way that predates Kelsey's typology but in relation to a classical approach, is Douglas John Hall, "Theological Education as Character Formation," *Theological Education* 24, Supplement 1 (1988): 53-79, and especially pp. 57 and 75.

## B. Some Mission-Oriented, Missiological, and Mission-Friendly Approaches

### 1. Echoes of a Mission Orientation

Before developing the model more fully, it is worth looking at other discussions of theological education using the language of mission. Such language is not absent from the models I have already examined, for example, the Network's and Mudflower Collective's insistence on social transformation and, as mentioned, Hough and Cobb's emphasis on the worldly dimension of ministry. But in each of these the reference to mission functions primarily as the horizon or goal of theological education rather than as an actual practice within it. Other contributors to the debate, however, begin to move beyond the language of goal or horizon.

#### i. Theological Education as a Dimension of Mission

Orlando Costas begins with Kähler's well-known dictum that mission is "the mother of theology." Mission generates communities of faith and obedience that are ceaselessly searching for understanding, and influences the flow of understanding that shapes and renews the future of the church. Mission also stimulates theological education, as through the church institutions are created by the Spirit "to teach the basic elements of the faith, to reflect on it critically and systematically, and to equip leaders for ministry."[4] Theological education is a dimension of mission and has a vital missiological content; it is an aspect of the teaching ministry of the church involving specialized testimony to the kingdom. It fulfills this educational service of the faith by (i) forming character, abilities, and thought, (ii) informing mind, praxis, and contemplation, and (iii) transforming values, people, and communi-

---

4. O. Costas, "Theological Education and Mission," in C. Rene Padilla, ed., *New Alternatives in Theological Education* (Oxford: Regnum, 1986), pp. 5-6. See further David Bosch, *Transforming Mission* (Maryknoll, N.Y.: Orbis, 1991), p. 16. Costas, quoting the work in Spanish of Aaron Sapsezian, Gerson Veiga, and Daniel Schipani, claims that this linkage of theological education and mission is strongly represented in Latin American approaches to the philosophy of education. From one denominational angle see now the volume edited by Nancy R. Heisey and Daniel S. Schipani, *Theological Education on Five Continents: Anabaptist Perspectives* (Elkhart, Ind.: Institute of Mennonite Studies, 1997).

ties. Its model is: "what Jesus did with his disciples: inviting them to follow him, helping them to listen and to understand his Word, training them to be obedient, and gifting them with the transforming power of his Spirit."[5] Theological education has three main goals, namely, preparing lay leaders to help in the educational ministry of the church; preparing ministers of the "Word and sacraments" to equip the whole people of God, develop leaders for mission, and help the church articulate its faith; and producing teachers of ministers and "doctors" of the faith. Only by maintaining its close links with mission will it remain relevant to changing circumstances, and hold true to the missionary impulse that gave rise to the church and theology.

Costas rightly places mission at the center of God's purposes and recognizes that it is a responsibility of all the people of God. He understands that theological education is a significant expression of mission, identifies Jesus' relationship with his disciples as the basic model it should follow, recognizes the missiological background to the major divisions of the curriculum, and affirms the informational, formational, and transformational character of all aspects of ministry training. He is one of the few to highlight the basic role of the Spirit in theological education. Yet for him the teacher's primary task is to *form* people *for* the service of the kingdom via a *problem-oriented* approach, not *engage* people *in* it through *actual ministry*. The key missiological contribution of theological institutions is *formal teaching*, rather than *in-service instruction*. For him, theological education certainly involves (i) *cultivating* love of God and neighbor, (ii) *training* to articulate the faith accurately and relevantly, and (iii) *developing* discernment of the times for faithful obedience to the kingdom. But he sees these primarily as *preparation for* future ministry rather than reflective *experience of* ministry. His approach is missiological rather than missional. So while Costas' contribution takes us part of the way, it does not go the full distance.

### ii. A Ministry-Centered Approach to Theological Education

A more radical approach to mission appears on the edge of other contributions to the debate. This goes beyond the Network's main empha-

5. O. Costas, "Theological Education and Mission," p. 9.

sis on contextually based teaching and learning, in which practitioners and people help shape students' curriculum and learning.[6] Such "immersion education" is valuable, but it mainly concerns *interpreting* the ministry context with a view to *confronting* it later rather than now. It also goes beyond Hough and Cobb's recommendation that theological education culminate in church-based internships. This already happens in a number of places but should be at the *center,* not the *end* of, ministry training, and involves modeling of ministry by faculty, not just by others.[7] Both of these approaches contain helpful elements but do not go anywhere near far enough.

Glenda Hope argues that the best form of ministry studies centers on the practice of ministry rather than on learning in the classroom. This could take the form of students doing ministry in a parish or agency for twenty hours a week while taking several classes a semester across the whole curriculum. Ministry and classes then interact with one another, with some courses being taught by practitioners, and each student working on site with a field-faculty person. This revisioning and restructuring of theological education leads to (i) faculty and students cooperating in and outside the academy, (ii) abandoning tenure in favor of alternating periods of time in the seminary and in a parish or agency, (iii) reappraising the goals, recipients, sources, processes, and materials of theological scholarship, (iv) seminaries divesting themselves of their property, (v) replacing comfortable intellectual and therapeutic approaches to learning by the uncertainties of public communal discipleship.

## 2. Insights from the Discussion of Missiological Education

### i. Recent Thinking on Missiological Education

As one author has acknowledged, the burst in recent thinking about missiological education has not come from the old academic centers

6. See Lynn N. Rhodes and Nancy D. Richardson, *Mending Severed Connections: Theological Education for Communal Transformation* (San Francisco: San Francisco Network Ministries, 1991), pp. 51-53, 56-58.

7. Joseph C. Hough, Jr., and John B. Cobb, Jr., *Christian Identity and Theological Education* (Atlanta: Scholars Press, 1985), pp. 121-23. This applies to field education generally, on which see Donald F. Deisswenger, "Field Education and the Theological Education Debates," *Theological Education* 33 (1) (1996): 49-58.

but from schools and institutes, networks and movements that have been peripheral, dissident, and innovative.[8] In some of this thinking there is a move to recapture more of a biblical worldview in understanding and undertaking mission, though at the level of theological education this mostly highlights the significance of biblical studies in the curriculum rather than leading to a new look at training for mission as a whole. In some quarters there is also a greater stress on missiological education for the lay person as well as professional missionaries.[9] The best way of implementing this is off-campus, through new syndicated courses and theological education by extension. These allow lay people to learn in the settings where they live and work, and avoid the danger of clericalizing or professionalizing them.

This involves recognizing various types of vocational outcomes, ranging from informal lay mission and unpaid para-professional mission work by those who have had less or more nonformal missiological education, through bi-vocational short- or long-term missionaries who often have a mixture of formal and nonformal theological education, to mission team leaders or administrators and international mission communicators or statesmen who have formal theological qualifications.[10] Or, thinking more of the church, we could enumerate lay leaders of small groups and congregations who require informal and nonformal modes of learning, evangelists and leaders of larger congregations who require in addition some formal education, and leaders of associations of churches and parachurch ministries who require primarily nonformal and formal theological

8. See G. H. Anderson, "The State of Missiological Research," in J. D. Woodberry, C. Van Engen, E. J. Elliston, eds., *Missiological Education for the 21st Century: The Book, the Circle, and the Sandals* (Maryknoll, N.Y.: Orbis, 1996), p. 25.

9. So Paul G. Hiebert, "Missiological Education for a Global Era," in *Missiological Education for the 21st Century,* pp. 37-41, and L. Grant McClung Jr., "Pentecostal/Charismatic Perspectives on Missiological Education," p. 61. For an earlier discussion of some of the same issues, mostly preceding the current debate, see Harvie M. Conn and Samuel F. Rowen, eds., *Missions and Theological Education in World Perspectives* (Farmington, Mich.: Associates of Urbanus, 1984), especially the preface by David Bosch, and articles by Lesslie Newbigin, Chung-Choon Kim, and Irene W. Foulkes.

10. Cf. Edgar J. Elliston, "Moving Forward from Where We Are in Missiological Education," in *Missiological Education for the 21st Century,* pp. 238-40.

education.[11] For some missiologists, more institutional approaches to theological education must reelevate service to a status alongside reflection. Service should not only take place through weekend assignments divorced from reflection, and reflection should involve more than just preparation for ministry practice.[12]

## ii. An Apprenticeship Model of Theological Education

Missiologist Charles Van Engen takes a step further. In view of the dramatic changes taking place in the world today, formation for ministry must also undergo a radical shift. This requires us to go back to the earliest model of ministry formation. Down through the centuries, we have seen in turn models based on (i) apprenticeship (found in the Bible), (ii) monasticism (from the fourth century onwards), and (iii) the university (during the early modern period). It was the last of these that for the first time emphasized *knowing,* at the expense of *doing* and *being.* Denominational and interdenominational seminary education draws something from each of these models — encouraging relationships between faculty and students but primarily in the classroom, cultivating worship and seeking communion. But mostly this is co-curricular, and the major emphasis is on knowledge-based and classroom-dependent instruction. The professional school model now dominates, and this continues to ignore the *being* of the student, to exalt professionalism over calling and vocation, and to broaden the gap between the formally trained person and the amateur in the pew.

According to Van Engen, seminaries should recapture the priorities maintained during the last 150 years by Bible institutes and Bible colleges, for these continue to emphasize spiritual formation and skills development. What is primarily lacking in seminaries is "in-ministry formation." The Theological Education by Extension (TEE) movement in the Third World rediscovered this as it searched for a way to keep *being, knowing,* and *doing* together. Such a model focuses primarily on devel-

11. As in Mark Young, "Planning Theological Education in Mission Settings," in D. Elmer and L. McKinney, eds., *With an Eye on the Future: Development and Mission in the 21st Century* (Monrovia, Calif.: Marc, 1996), p. 78. See also Darrell L. Guder, ed., *Missional Church: A Vision for the Sending of the Church in North America* (Grand Rapids: Eerdmans, 1998), pp. 216-17.

12. Note especially here Ted W. Ward, "Evaluating Metaphors of Education," in *Missiological Education for the 21st Century,* pp. 45, 50-51.

oping real leaders rather than with issues of ordination. It encourages congregations to help those developing leadership among them to pursue further training, it holds fast to the importance of "the priesthood of all believers," and it regards formation as a process more than a program. In other words, theological education can only enhance ministry in progress, not prepare people for ministry. Central to this is pairing more and less experienced people, whether lay or ordained, in a mentoring or apprentice-style relationship. Within this whole process, student excellence is redefined in terms of maturity, wisdom, and influence. It is congregational and denominational groups that should evaluate people's capacity for ministry, not seminaries.[13]

This approach is more holistic than any of the others articulated in the debate and comes very close to what I am advocating. Particularly noteworthy is its stress on the "person to person" characteristic. There are three differences, though at times these are more a matter of degree than of kind. First, the approach focuses on the role of "the church in the world" and does not bring into view that of "the Christian in the marketplace." In other words, it speaks more about what congregational organizations and projects can achieve than about the contribution of individual Christians or interdenominational groups in the workplace, community, or wider culture. In this respect it remains too ecclesiastical in orientation. Second, although in places it hints at a wider process of formation for all the people of God that takes place in service outside as well as inside the church, at other times it separates professors from practitioners, who alone provide modeling and mentoring. The more these two groups of "teachers" overlap, without necessarily fusing them, the closer this approach is to a missional model. Third, its stress on apprenticing is a welcome move in the direction of learning-through-doing alongside other forms of learning, and is certainly an element in a missional model; but there, as in the biblical materials, the primary emphasis is coworking or partnering.[14]

13. Charles Van Engen, *Shifting Paradigms in Ministry Formation* (Glendora, Calif., 1994). A shortened version of this appeared in *Perspectives* 9 (8) (1994): 15-17.

14. An ecclesiastical, indeed quite clerical, orientation is also the chief weakness of the approach by the M. J. Murdock Charitable Trust in its *Review of Graduate Theological Education in the Northwest.* See "A 21st Century Seminary Faculty Model," *Faculty Dialogue* 23 (1995): 9-22. Its emphasis on spiritual formation, its insistence on classes becoming long-term learning cohorts or communities, and the

## 3. The Relevance of Praxis-Based and Professional-Training Approaches

### i. A Praxis-Oriented Approach to Theological Education

Drawing on the work of Paolo Freire and Ivan Illich, Terry Harter develops a critique of and alternative to Western theological education.[15] He argues for a curriculum based on action-reflection even in the classical disciplines, and through field education and internships that directly confront the major fault lines of oppression and injustice in our society. Such an education should help students develop a critical awareness of everyday realities, devise ministry projects that now as well as in the future help them transform society, and provide learning resources and personal empowering for all kinds of ministry. Since speech based in and interpretive of reality is itself action, the classroom can become the crucible for an individual and communal praxis that helps create a more just and whole society. But for this to happen properly, all levels of theological education must become globally networked, open to pedagogical experiment, and more inclusive of minorities. The difficulty here is that though Harter's approach strengthens the connection between theological education and ministry or life situations, it still tends to think too much in terms of reflection *on* rather than reflection *in* ministry and life.

A more radical approach, one that stands closer to Freire's original vision, exists among those involved in what J. Luis Segundo calls "second level" rather than "first level" liberation theology. The latter is more the product of the study, classroom, and library; while its content may differ from that of the West, its academic context, materials, and form do not. "Second level" liberation theology takes place primarily in the basic Christian communities and their surrounding urban

---

central role given to lay or ordained mentoring are admirable. On the revelance of the apprenticeship model, see also the comments by S. Escobar, "The Training of Missiologists for a Latin American Context," and, in part, J. Dudley Woodberry, "Till the Final Book Is Opened in the Final Circle," in *Missiological Education for the 21st Century*, pp. 104 and 276 respectively. Van Engen himself has an interesting discussion in this same book on the relationship between the integrative and conceptual dimensions of missiological education.

15. Terry Harter, "A Critique of North American Theological Education from the Perspectives of Ivan Illich and Paolo Freire" (unpublished Ph.D. dissertation, Boston University, 1980).

settings. Its context is the people, church, and barrio, and the resulting theology takes a variety of forms in accord with the purposes and au- diences in view. It trains people in their present occupational and con- gregational contexts instead of a residential setting that often distances students from both, equipping them to reflect theologically and practi- cally on the everyday issues they and their people confront.[16] If any- thing, it sometimes focuses too much on the world and not enough on the church, with issues of justice rather than redemption, and on the usefulness of Marxist categories. In its general dynamics, however, this is close to the kind of model I am proposing.

During the eighties, I flew up to Australia's most northern and tropical city, Darwin, to teach a two-week intensive at Nungalinya College, the theological training center for Aborigines from all over the country. Most of these were tribal Aborigines from the North or Center, though some came from large urban cities in the South. Classes comprised small groups of around a dozen students, men and women, of varying ages. Some were elders in their tribes, others well-regarded younger believers. Most of the time these students were away from the campus, going about their ordinary ministry and reflecting alongside and through this with the assistance of distance-education resources and qualified local tutors. Interspersed through the three-year learning program was time on campus. This involved study oriented to prac- tice, and both personal and communal formation. Although all ele- ments of the traditional theological encyclopedia were present, this framework did not determine the structure of the curriculum. There was a strong emphasis on the importance of praxis in the framing and teaching of courses, as well as on conversation as a key medium for learning. Along with their theological courses they undertook other courses on community development and related subjects. One of the courses I taught was titled *Paul: The Walkabout Apostle*. This focused not on the role of walking in Paul's apostolic activity, but on walking as his central metaphor for the Christian life. All this connected with

16. See further J. Luis Segundo, "Two Theologies of Liberation," in A. Hennelly, ed., *Liberation Theology: A Documentary History* (Maryknoll, N.Y.: Orbis, 1990). This has more to offer, I think, than basing theological education around counterparts of the ashram in India. See further K. Klaudt, "The Ashram as a Model for Theological Education," *Theological Education* 34 (1) (1997): 25- 40. For all the strengths this contains, it is more consonant with a version of Farley's paradigm than one revolving around mission.

the central Aboriginal tradition of the annual "walkabout," when the whole tribe set off for several months to follow the food chain and visit sacred sites, along the way inducting younger members of the tribe into the basic stories governing the community's life. The course encouraged students to engage in walking as a context for discussing, learning, and implementing what was coming out of the study of Paul. Some class members told me afterwards that it resulted in their reclaiming the importance of walking as a learning and nurturing activity for their children, and as a way of training younger associates in ministry into the nature of the work itself. An evangelical, inner-city, Western variation of this theme will be discussed later in the book.[17]

## *ii. The New Look at the Training of Professionals*

Relevant here is the work of Donald A. Schon on how professionals think in the course of their everyday work. In his study of the way architects, psychotherapists, engineers, town planners, and managers operate on the job, he describes this process as "reflection-in-action," an approach that differs from both the "theory-to-practice" or "action-reflection" schemes. Schon finds three levels of connection between thinking and doing; when these take place, he says, a person becomes "a researcher in the practice context."

> He is not dependent on the categories of established theory or technique, but constructs a new theory of the unique case. His inquiry is not limited to deliberation about means . . . but defines [means and ends] interactively as he frames a problematic situation. He does not separate thinking from doing.[18]

Inherent in the way professionals work, then, is not just problem-solving, but problem-setting, an activity that clearly has a theoretical component; not just finding answers, but formulating hypotheses.

17. Eldin Villafañe, "Seminary-Based Theological Education," in Rodney L. Petersen, ed., *Christianity and Civil Society: Theological Education for Public Life* (Maryknoll, N.Y.: Orbis/Cambridge, Mass.: Boston Theological Institute, 1995), pp. 121-33.
18. Donald A. Schon, *The Reflective Practitioner: How Professionals Think in Action* (New York: Basic, 1983), p. 68. The whole section on "the structure of reflection-in-action" (pp. 128-67) is worth reading, as also his discussion of "the patterns and limits of reflection-in-action" (pp. 267-83).

However, Schon argues that alongside reflection-in-action there is a place for ancillary outside-the-context learning that enhances the practitioner's capacity to think-in-doing.

In his recent book on the crisis in the professions in America today, William Sullivan takes up Schon's insights and draws out their educational consequences. What is required, he says, is

- rehabilitating nonformal modes of rationality that create room for the practical and moral standpoint of the subjects and objects of knowledge;
- identifying the social factors that inhibit the potential such practical rationality has for transforming professional life;
- developing more effective ways of spreading and communicating this knowledge within and through educational institutions.

This reorientation, however, requires that faculty and practitioners develop mutual trust. It also requires that they reshape professional disciplines away from rigid bodies of established knowledge into supple interactive networks of investigators. This involves restructuring the structure of disciplines and the system of rewards.[19]

Issues this raises for seminaries include (i) empirical assessing of the practical value of theoretically oriented classes; (ii) evaluating the whole curriculum in light of desired competencies and values; (iii) investigating how well the life experiences of students and practitioners are drawn into the educational process; (iv) discerning how well learning contributes to personal formation, values, and lifestyle; (v) questioning whether those entering pastoral ministry see the need of networking with other professionals to further the common good; (vi) examining faculty reward systems to see how far they encourage collaborative projects and creative pedagogical approaches; (vii) identifying other institutional factors that could block innovative developments.[20]

19. William L. Sullivan, *Work and Integrity: The Crisis and Promise of Professionalism in America* (San Francisco: Harper, 1995), p. 188.
20. On this see Elizabeth A. Dreyer, "Excellence in the Professions: What Theological Schools Can Learn from Law, Business, and Medical Schools," *Theological Education* 33 (1996): 1-21. Dreyer gives special emphasis to the need for trainers of "religious leaders" in both the church and the community.

Reorienting training for ministers in this direction would not only assist those who are heading into professional work in the narrower sense, e.g., counselors, therapists, psychologists in the marketplace, but all those whose sphere of work involves community building, empowering others, Christian education, and spiritual guidance in the congregation. Support for this general approach is now coming from educational studies into the enhanced learning that takes place when community service and classroom instruction are properly integrated instead of being kept separate or related to one another only obliquely.[21]

21. See "Integrating Community Service and Classroom Instruction Enhances Learning: Results from an Experiment," *Educational Evaluation and Policy Analysis* 15 (1993): 410-19.

# 2. Recasting Major Issues in the Debate

## A. Distinctive Characteristics of the Missional Model

Before revisiting some key issues in the current debate on theological education, it may be helpful to summarize and clarify some of the differences between what I will call a "missional" model and other approaches to theological education. By mission I mean not just "mission-oriented," but an education undertaken with a view to what God is doing in the world, considered from a global perspective. This is the way Hough and Cobb, or Stackhouse and his circle, talk. I also mean something more than what "missiological" education generally covers; I'm thinking rather of reflection, training, and formation for work on the mission field, whether the latter takes place overseas or locally. This is the language of schools of mission and many Bible colleges. While "missiological" or, for that matter, "mission-oriented" theological education may contain elements of what I am proposing, these tend to be secondary to what mainly happens. By "missional," I mean theological education that is wholly or partly field based, and that involves some measure of doing what is being studied. This may take the form of action-reflection or reflection-action, distinctions that in any case are useful only up to a point, since effective action involves some element of or relationship with reflection, and effective reflection involves some element of or relationship with action. We could also talk here about theological education involving more than participant observation, as Hough and Cobb or Kelsey define it: a missional approach also requires observant participation, which is not the same thing.

It may be helpful here to set the three main models discussed in the first chapter side by side, along with the neo-traditional approach of people like Schner and Muller.

- The "classical" model, as outlined by Farley, the Collectives, and the Neuhaus symposium, places the main emphasis on theological *formation,* on acquiring a *disposition* to think theologically about the whole of life that also shapes a person's moral and spiritual character, and provides direction in the conduct of ministry. On this view theological education is primarily though not exclusively concerned with the *process* — intellectual and moral — of Christian *faith* and therefore places greatest emphasis on acquiring cognitive *wisdom.*
- The "vocational" model advocated by Hough and Cobb, and with an apologetic emphasis by Stackhouse and his circle, places the main emphasis on theological *interpretation,* on developing a *skill* in relating Christian tradition to contemporary issues that also influences personal identity and values and shapes the definition and practice of ministry. On this view theological education is primarily though not exclusively concerned with the *goal* — reflective and practical — of the Christian *story* and therefore focuses mainly on acquiring cognitive *discernment.*
- The "dialectical" model developed by Wood, Kelsey, and Chopp draws on the first and last of these approaches, allowing them to work alongside one another as they contribute to an overarching *vision* or *practice* that focuses on God but also affects personal, vocational, and societal life. On this view theological education is primarily though not exclusively concerned with the *ethos* — mindful or behavioral — of the Christian *"thing"* and focuses on acquiring cognitive, but more-than-cognitive, *insight.*
- The "confessional" model reworked by Schner and Muller places the main emphasis on theological *information,* on gaining an *understanding* that gives systematic shape to Christian beliefs and provides direction for personal growth and for the practice of ministry. On this view theological education is primarily though not exclusively concerned with the *content* — doctrinal and ethical — of Christian *revelation* and therefore focuses mainly on acquiring cognitive *knowledge.*

143

In contrast to these, though it also overlaps in particular ways with each of them, the "missional" model of theological education places the main emphasis on theological *mission,* on hands-on *partnership* in ministry based on interpreting the tradition and reflecting on practice with a strong spiritual and communal dimension. On this view theological education is primarily though not exclusively concerned with actual *service* — informed and transforming — of the *kingdom* and therefore primarily focuses on acquiring cognitive, spiritual-moral, and practical *obedience.*

## B. Revisiting Central Themes in the Debate

We can gain a clearer perspective on a "missional" approach by focusing on two major issues in the present discussions, that is, unity versus fragmentation and pluralism versus uniformity.

### 1. Unity and Fragmentation

We need to go behind attempts to locate the fragmentation of theological education in the rise of modern critical methodologies, post-Reformation theological encyclopedias, or medieval university structures, to the earlier separation of learning from active service of God and neighbor. This had already begun in the first Christian "schools" in Alexandria.[22] These were probably a continuation of the school for catechumens attached to the main church there, and flourished from the late second to early fifth century. These do not seem to have possessed buildings; teaching took place in homes. Financial support probably came from teachers' outside work, the church, and some honoraria from students. Teaching did not follow set hours, and discussion sometimes went on all day or into the night. Students were of both sexes and included

22. See further the dissertation by Vasil T. Istavridis, *Theological Education in the Alexandrian School* (Boston: Boston University School of Theology, 1951). See also the work by Clement of Alexandria, *Christ the Educator,* vol. 23 of *The Fathers of the Church,* trans. Simon P. Wood (Washington: Catholic University Press of America, 1954), and on the implications for present Christian higher education Keith R. Anderson, "Clement of Alexandria: Patron Saint of Higher Education?" *Faculty Dialogue* 20 (1993-94): 59-72.

students of philosophy (not all of whom were Christian) preparing to become teachers themselves or embarking on pastoral ministry.

The first level of teaching, *paedagogia,* focused on personal readiness for learning through cleansing of soul and mind from passions. Then came *didaskalia,* which moved from philosophy and science through ethics to theology, the latter including Bible and tradition. These schools arose to serve the church and worked in close connection with it. Throughout there was a serious attempt to connect the teacher's instruction and the student's experience. Because of the presence of Jews or heretics, instruction had a practical, apologetic dimension. But the earlier Christian focus on learning through mission began to move into the background in favor of group spiritual and intellectual formation. Integrating theory and practice, and correlating objective and subjective, is still in evidence here but only with the goal of helping individual students develop a mature relationship with God. Clement's approach certainly gave room for life experience and issues to arise, created opportunities to reflect on these, enabled them to do in community, and encouraged their dialogue to be as much with God as with each other. But for all its intellectual breadth and pedagogical depth, we still see here the beginning of a separation of theological education from direct corporate life and witness in the world.

From a biblical perspective, the unity of theological education does not lie primarily in spiritual formation. Those, like Farley, who follow the "classical" model rightly view this unity as integral to theological education. But they interpret this mainly with a view to the forming of a disposition to act rather than action itself. Outside the official debate others, like the late Henri Nouwen, have called for theological education to move away from a more secular preoccupation with professional training to focus primarily, though not exclusively, on a spiritual formation that brings students into increasing conformity with Christ. This results in a close relationship with God, each other, and fellow human beings, and it requires theological reflection on the painful and joyful realities of daily life. But here, too, the emphasis is not on reflection in the midst of personal and vocational struggles so much as on reflection largely alongside them.[23]

23. See further Mary Kate Morse, "Henri J. Nouwen: A Pastoral Voice for the Re-Formation of Theological Education," *Faculty Dialogue* 23 (1995): 33-40, and Nouwen's comments in *The Living Reminder: Service and Prayer in Memory*

Those, like Hough and Cobb, who advocate a "vocational" model, rightly put ministry in the center, but emphasize intellectual preparation for ministry rather than reflective practice in it. This wrongly locates the unity of theological education in its goal rather than its actual dynamics. Truest vision and discernment come to us as we engage in the work of ministry itself and reflect on it, as the example of the apostle Paul and many others so vibrantly demonstrates. And while knowing God truly is the foundation for both of these and for the work of service itself, it is only in and through the serving itself that full knowing of God takes place. The biblical approach to knowing, which includes obedience as well as understanding, confirms this.

One way of articulating a more satisfactory approach to solving the problem of fragmentation in theological education is to insist that it is not *theologia* or *apologia* that gives coherence to the enterprise but *missiologia*. As the missiologist Samuel Rowen argues, this applies not only to missionary work in the traditional sense, or just to pastoral, educational, and diaconal work in the church, but to the work of teaching and spiritual formation. Scholarship can also find its place here, if viewed as pushing back the boundaries of understanding and reclaiming territory for Christ otherwise lost to the cultured despisers of religion.[24] However, as in Rowen's case, there is still a danger of regarding *missiologia* as only an academic discipline and not as an active discipling of others, of converting cultural structures into Christ. Once this life-engaging mission is removed from the center of theological education, parts of the latter begin to whirl off and develop a life of their own. This fragmentation is compounded by the theory-practice split that became more pronounced in the medieval university, by the curriculum subdivision that gained strength from the introduction of the theological encyclopedia, and by the overspecialized disciplines that resulted from the rise of critical methodology.

- It is not *paideia* revolving around *theologia* that can overcome this. To the extent that this provides a unifying center for these

---

of Jesus Christ (New York: Doubleday, 1977), p. 73; *The Way of the Heart: Desert Spirituality and Contemporary Ministry* (New York: HarperCollins, 1981), p. 47; *In the Name of Jesus: Reflections on Christian Leadership* (New York: Crossroad, 1989), pp. 68-69.

24. Samuel F. Rowen, "Missiology and the Coherence of Theological Education," in *With an Eye on the Future*, p. 96.

dichotomies, divisions, and disciplines, it results in a partial privatizing of faith, and — in Farley's version at least, with its narrower intellectual definition of *habitus* — opens up a gap between theory and practice within persons themselves.

- Nor can *scientia* revolving around practical theology do what is required. So far as it provides a unifying center, especially when people culminate their studies in reflective or apologetic praxis, its predominantly intellectual focus and classroom setting separates the formation of vocational identity from the exercise of public ministry.

- When vision and discernment, or truly knowing God, move into the heart of the process, this provides even greater unity for the fragmented enterprise of theological education, broadening *habitus* to include imagination and practical reason. It places God, not just faith seeking practical understanding or understanding seeking faithful relevance, at the center; and it goes part of the way to overcoming the dichotomies between objective and subjective and between theory and practice. But it does not supply the existential and integrated orientation that focused action, in real space and time, offers teaching and learning. Nor does it provide the decisive and public assessment of whether effective teaching and learning have taken place.

Turning from the student's to the faculty's role, in all three approaches teachers are also mostly separate from the sphere of public ministry. Instead of being theologically formative practitioners they are at best exemplary models of theological formation or professional exponents of practical theology. Their students are not coworkers in ministry whose learning is further stimulated through active service, but at best good novices gaining untested tools for future service. In such a setting, problems of relating the subjective and objective aspects of learning are bound to arise.

## 2. Pluralism and Contextualization

A more holistic approach to theological education opens up a fresh approach to the issues raised by pluralism and contextualization. Challenges along these lines were not alien to the people of God in biblical

147

times. (i) In the Old Testament, faith in God was expressed in a variety of overlapping ways — priestly, prophetic, sapiential — which on occasions were in tension with one another. In the New Testament there were distinctions and sometimes divisions between Jewish, Hellenistic-Jewish, and Gentile Christian believers, as well as between churches founded by different apostles. (ii) Israel's life involved a constant struggle with other faiths inside and outside its borders, especially during the conquest and the exile. The early Christians contended with followers of other religions within their homeland, and encountered the full variety of these as they spread into the wider Mediterranean world.

Where theological education revolves around doing as well as teaching, issues of pluralism and contextualization become more acute but can be resolved more satisfactorily. With respect to pluralism, the Mud Flower Collective moved in this direction by bringing together a diverse racial group around a particular task, namely writing a book on theological education. While discussion within the group failed to achieve agreement or harmony among its members, it did manage to pull itself together sufficiently to complete this objective. What it could not do by focusing on its *internal* tensions, it could do by focusing on an *external* challenge. So long as the group concentrated on its own formation, or with ways of potentially transforming society, it reached an impasse, but by focusing on this common objective it managed in part to get beyond this.[25]

With respect to contextualization, we turn to Stackhouse's placing this at the center of the debate and highlighting *religious* pluralism as the basic issue. Unlike other contributions, his volume unabashedly regards this as an exercise in *apologia,* not just *dialogia.* There is room for dialogue, but only as the process, not as the essence of the matter. Dialogue can assist in discovery of truth but should not do so at the expense of fundamental Christian convictions. It makes room for a wide range of diversity, but is not an end in itself. While the Collective helpfully highlights the gender, ethnic, and class dimensions of pluralism, it runs the risk of relativizing a Christian understanding of these.

---

25. In other respects the Collective was pluralist in only a limited sense. It was made up only of women, from a similar class background, who shared considerable theological agreement. It was not as diverse a group as we find, for example, in Paul's circle of associates.

Still, what both *apologia* and *dialogia* have in common is a tendency to deal with the issue of religious pluralism and contextualization at one remove, that is, only through practical reflection *on* them rather than through reflective practice *of* them. This is not to deny the importance of such reflection. But if such practical reflection were occurring in tandem with actively confronting these concerns where they appear most sharply, it would win through to a more concrete, versatile, and creative way of dealing with them. Also, there is a tendency in these writings to approach contextualization more abstractly than do missiologists.

To some extent Kelsey's proposal, centered as it is on the actual life of the congregation, provides a concrete reference point. Such a focus is adequate for some purposes, but its influence is limited to those who are already meeting as or with the church. A more effective strategy calls for a team of people that reflects the pluralistic nature of those they are seeking to serve in the world. Paul's diverse band of co-workers is an excellent model. Those who call for more representative faculties and student bodies in theological institutions also provide a more concrete reference point. This enables more sensitive multicultural or cross-cultural *learning* to take place. Better still are smaller groups in such institutions *working* together in a multicultural or cross-cultural way. As they do this, deeper learning also takes place within the team itself, even though this is not the main point of the exercise, and it models the inclusiveness of the gospel to those outside and inside the institution.

## C. A Further Look at the Hermeneutical Issue

By this time, several objections to a more holistic missional model may come to mind. I have delayed raising these until the general contours of the model were apparent. Now it is time to deal with them.

### 1. Is the Missional Model Anachronistic?

Despite my earlier remarks about the legitimacy of drawing on biblical writings in thinking about the future of theological education, some might still feel that this fails to come to terms with current realities.

Have not historical developments over the last two millennia rendered this naive or passé? Does it not result in a betrayal of the basic intellectual calling of seminaries? It should at least be clear by now that I am not interested in simply preserving or restoring biblical approaches to theological education. We cannot resurrect the approach of the biblical prophetic bands, disciple groups, or apostolic teams. Like everyone else in the debate, I hope to discover the most effective contemporary approach to theological education. But for me this will only come about if it resonates in certain fundamental ways with these earlier approaches. As mentioned earlier, each of the proposals before us have their roots in the past — the "classical" in late antiquity, the "confessional" in the late medieval or post-Reformation period, the "vocational" in the flowering of modernity — and therefore are all in certain respects anachronistic. This means that, in one sense, the debate is about exactly what from the past has the most to offer us. While my proposal goes back further in time than these, it does not do anything essentially different, and by no means excludes integrating vital elements from other periods. Also, quite apart from the biblical materials themselves, it is possible to locate and draw on later traditions that in some way mediate the approach contained within them. In other words, there are other traditions in the history of the church than those discussed by Farley and company, on the one hand, or by Schner and Muller on the other.

Still, are there particular changes in our ecclesiastical and cultural circumstances that would make resort to certain biblical emphases in theological education questionable? First, since biblical times, churches and other Christian organizations have undergone significant institutional development and diversification; and the formation of the ministry has taken on comparable complexities. People often mention here the need for newer managerial and counseling skills. Second, in modern societies, education has become part of life in a way that has no historical parallel. Whatever the effectiveness of our educational institutions and systems, those called to ministry in the church must now have as comprehensive an understanding of theology as many members of their congregations have of their own occupational fields. Over the last 150 years, a majority of churches concluded that founding seminaries was the most effective way of doing this. But the need for more substantial theological education than in earlier times does not require wholesale abandonment of a more holistic model, only its formulation in a way that does full justice to our present situation. Nothing in my proposal seeks to diminish the importance of high-level theological reflection, involving all the prevailing critical approaches and social scientific resources. It is only a question of where, when, and how best to incorporate these.

## 2. Is the Model Vulnerable to a False Distinction?

In the last two decades the traditional distinction between Jewish and Greek ways of thinking has been under serious challenge. Scholars have challenged such influential works as Adolf Harnack's multivolume *History of Dogma,* with its critique of the "hellenization" of Christianity, and Thorlief Boman's widely read *Hebrew Thought Compared with Greek.*[26] Some might assert that the proposal I am developing entails a basic distinction between biblical and Hellenistic approaches to knowing, learning, and teaching, and overlooks the positive influence of the Greek tradition on Christian theology and instruction. But as scholars have argued, we should not draw too sharp a separation between Hebraic and Hellenistic thinking, partly because of the pervasive presence of the Greek language and of Hellenism generally in early Christian times. The early church fathers often made fruitful, and not uncritical, use of some of the categories and components of Greek philosophy.

In response, I would point out that the biblical writings themselves make room for the mind alongside the will, but also contain the basis for a doctrine of what later came to be called general revelation. I shall say more about this later in another connection. Here I wish to focus on the encouragement this gives us to draw on a range of fields and disciplines in theological education over and above what we can learn from the practice of ministry or through scripture, spiritual disciplines, and community. A holistic approach to theological education

26. Adolf Harnack, *History of Dogma,* 7 vols. (New York: Dover, 1961); Thorlief Boman, *Hebrew Thought Compared with Greek* (London: SCM, 1960). For a critique of some of this way of thinking, see James Barr, *The Semantics of Biblical Language* (Oxford: Oxford University Press, 1961), and, with some differences and in a more limited way, David Hill, *Greek Words and Hebrew Meanings: Studies in the Semantics of Soteriological Terms* (Cambridge: Cambridge University Press, 1967).

therefore lives up to its name in this connection as well. As Paul says: "all things are yours" (1 Cor 3:21), and "whatever is true" (Phil 4:8), no matter from where it comes or how it is arrived at. This should always have scripture as its reference point and norm, and should benefit from spiritually discerning its value in practice. This is why I prefer the term "general revelation" or the general work of the Spirit through our world and life, to the description "natural theology," for the latter suggests too large a place for human reasoning and its products.

## 3. Is a More Academic Model Required Today?

Some would argue that in today's more specialized world there has been a legitimate breakup of what was once an organic whole. So the holistic way that mission, instruction, and formation took place in biblical times now spreads over a range of institutions. This is a natural outcome of the broader "division of labor" characteristic of modern societies. We can still gain an experience of the whole through participating serially or simultaneously in a number of institutions. For example, a student may develop some spiritual maturity through small groups and retreats before linking up with a theological institution, may be engaged in urban mission through a parachurch organization alongside this, and after leaving, may discover ways of relating theological knowledge to the everyday life of the people of God. Why not allow seminaries and other theological institutions or programs to concentrate on helping them to deepen their theological knowledge and encourage them to make the most of these other opportunities for gaining a rounded training for ministry? A growing number of students coming into theological institutions are second or third career people with more life experience than earlier generations of seminarians. Some are working pastors and members of church staffs who need to gain theological credentials: in some cases these possess greater practical theological wisdom than junior faculty persons. So, in our more institutionally diverse and specialized society, should not seminaries focus on what other Christian organizations provide least, and simply major as they mostly do on teaching the Bible, church history, systematics, and pastoral theology?

There is something to be said for this. The mandate given to us by God to disciple all nations and to exercise trusteeship over creation gives us the freedom to create a whole range of institutions. Our only obligation is to ensure that these do full justice to their own spheres of responsibility, and that they do not detract from others with adjoining or overlapping concerns. We should also develop ways in which institutions with such concerns can cooperate rather than compete and so enhance their individual effectiveness. What does this mean for our current institutions of theological education? Once again it is helpful to look back at the early church to see whether there are any parallels to our present situation. We find reference, for example, to Timothy joining Paul's apostolic team after he had already gained a basic understanding of scripture (2 Tim 3:14-17), and had proven himself in ministry to his local church (Acts 16:2). Even so, in and through his being a partner in Paul's work he experienced ongoing learning (1 Tim 6:20-21; 2 Tim 1:13-14; 2:2, 7) and formation (1 Tim 4:7-12; 2 Tim 2:22; 3:10-13).[27] Paul himself, through his Pharisaic background, had experience of an approach to learning that, while formational, contained more of a "schooling" element.

## 4. Is Biblical Illiteracy a Determining Factor?

Others might argue that the paucity of biblical and theological understanding among students today reinforces the need to concentrate on instruction in basic theological traditions. It is not only congregations that are to blame for this state of affairs but also Christian parents. In any case, these days a growing number of students come into seminary as relatively new converts with little knowledge of the Christian tradition. We do need places where this initial or remedial education can take place — places that encourage people to read through the whole Bible, gain a little understanding of their church traditions, discuss a few basic theological books, and work through some elementary ministry issues. But is this what seminaries are for? Are they there to provide people with the knowledge that families and congregations should really be transmitting? If this is not enough, cannot other institutions take up the slack by providing preliminary theological studies? Or through encouraging such people to

---

27. Even when separated from him, Paul expected Timothy to continue in this fashion (2 Tim 3:14).

enroll first in a Bible institute, a Christian college, or a discipleship program course?

Here are two well-proven examples of what can be done in this remedial area, either through the seminary appointing people to look after this aspect of their program or through cooperating with some other institution. A nine-month biblical overview course, developed in Canberra, Australia, and already mandatory for incoming students in one seminary, gives people a basic knowledge of scripture in a way that connects with their personal questions and ministry responsibilities. Six to eight people contract to read through five or six chapters of the Bible a day, five days a week, over a nine-month period. They meet once a week, beginning with a meal or refreshments, where they build community and begin to talk about their work and lives. This is followed by a two-hour discussion on what they are reading, similar in style to the conversations people have about books they have read or films they have seen, treating the Bible primarily as a story, indeed as "the greatest story ever told." Members of the group talk about what excited, puzzled, or disturbed them in the section they have read, who they did or did not identify with, why people said or did what is written of them, and how the story challenged or encouraged them. Each person follows through a theme of their own choosing, related to some issue with which they are grappling, and regularly reports to the whole group on what they are discovering. Various scholarly aids, e.g., a dictionary, commentary, history, or atlas, are available to be utilized at any point, and at least one person each week reads a scholarly treatment of what they will be discussing. The pedagogical approach, communal ethos, and practical orientation of this method of studying the Bible recreates some of the family or ecclesial ethos most conducive to learning, yet also treats persons as responsible adult learners. Exactly the same approach can and has been used with the study of church history and systematic theology, and would work equally well with a course on apologetics, ethics, or practical theology.[28]

A broader example of what is possible is the Aston Training Scheme in England, which is a two-year, part-time foundation program for students who have potential for further ministry but are not yet ready or able to enter seminary. In the midst of their ongoing lives

28. On this see further R. Banks and J. Banks, *Conversational Bible Study* (Sydney: Albatross, 1997), pp. 81-171.

a demanding program of study, experience, and reflection takes place through a mixture of intensive residential events, private study, and regular personal interaction with a pastoral tutor. This contains both rigorous self-assessment and external assessment. Learning is built on the wealth of skills, experiences, and abilities that students already have, and there is a preference for self-directed, participatory, and experiential approaches. Families are expected to participate fully. The scheme embodies the conviction that "a high level of self-awareness, group and personal skills informed by habits of spiritual discipline and theological exploration, are prerequisites in ministerial formation." The benefits of the scheme vary according to the individual, and include (i) developing personal life, working through disabling experiences, gaining self-confidence and greater personal integration; (ii) testing the strength of vocation and its effect on families, as well as broadening spiritual discipline; (iii) gaining a deeper understanding of the nature of society and its systemic ills as the context for ministry; (iv) acquiring study skills and academic self-confidence. Central to the whole endeavor is the integration of all aspects of students' lives, including a proper balance of family, work, leisure, and study.

A related issue is the narrow range of ministry experience some students bring with them into their formal theological education. This is partly a function of the specialized character of ministry inside or outside the church today. It is also partly a consequence of set or trendy forms of church life or Christian work that restrict the available possibilities for ministry. As already mentioned, there is also the question of relatively new converts, at times even serious seekers, applying to seminaries to learn more about the Christian faith. This situation could further justify developing a model of theological education that places a high priority on active mission. The difficulty is that people who have little or inadequate ministry exposure should really gain more experience in this area before coming into seminaries, Bible colleges, or lay theological institutions. The focus there should be on more advanced ministry experience. It is churches and parachurch organizations, or intentional Christian approaches to ministry in the workplace and wider community, that can best supply what others require. While it is not the seminaries' responsibility to provide or arrange a basic ministry experience, through their faculty and students they could help congregations, Christian organizations, and marketplace believers develop a framework for understanding and undertaking such ministry.

The issues raised by these objections should remind us that, whatever seminaries contribute to their members' theological education, it is only part of what should be a lifelong process. As R. Paul Stevens says: a theological institution "can only engage a part of that purpose, a truth usually not appreciated by incoming students."[29] This has at least four consequences. It should

- help us appreciate the limits of what we can achieve, and inject a degree of realism and humility into our efforts;
- incline us to discover what background students have in these areas so we can best help them to take the next step;
- encourage us to collaborate more with other agencies, particularly with families, congregations, and parachurch organizations, to complement and enhance each other's efforts;
- direct us to finding ways of strengthening what goes on through these other channels, or assisting new or existing institutions to remedy what is lacking.

All this calls for closer links between theological institutions and other structured forms of Christian life.[30] The more students are based in their own localities, congregations, or occupations during any formal theological education they undertake — the more their attachment is like those in the second or third concentric circle around a prophet, Jesus, or Paul — the more important this becomes. In such instances other Christian institutions continue to play a greater part in all levels of what they do.

29. R. Paul Stevens, "Marketing the Faith — A Reflection on the Importing and Exporting of Theological Education," *Crux* 28 (2) (1992): 9.

30. Compare here the comments of Merle D. Strege, "Chasing Schleiermacher's Ghost," in Richard John Neuhaus, ed., *Theological Education and Moral Formation* (Grand Rapids: Eerdmans, 1992), p. 131.

# 3. The Nature of Learning
## in a Missional Model

It is important now to clarify two basic elements in a missional model of theological education: that between action and reflection and between theory and practice. I will do this in conversation with some thinkers on the edges of the debate or those who are dealing with parallel issues in their own areas of concern. Before embarking on this, however, it is helpful to have a reminder of the breadth of learning this model envisages, and how it relates to the field of Christian education. First, this approach has a view of learning that revolves around active involvement in ministry through both practical reflection and reflective practice. While it also stresses the importance of learning the tradition — biblical, historical, theological — this should take place in a formational and life-oriented way. Indeed, such learning should have reference to all the basic dimensions of a person's life — family and friendships, work and neighborhood, church and Christian organizations, voluntary and civic involvement — and at crucial points it should be guided by specific people who have a special understanding and calling to such work. Clearly this approach involves more than the usual foci of theological education — evangelism and discipleship, preaching and leading corporate worship, pastoral work and counseling, social action and mission — and encompasses the ministry of all the people of God, not just a select few.

Second, this means that theological education is not a higher stage of Christian education, but a dimension of everyone's Christian education, depending on their stage in life and calling. This is obscured by the widespread ambivalence about serious learning, the undue professionalizing of both theology and education, and the prevailing homiletic paradigm of how faith occurs and matures.[31] The presence of continuing education programs in seminaries already suggests that theological education and Christian education are not as separate as is generally thought, as does the introduction of home-grown theological studies in some large congregations. Those engaged in formal theological education tend to regard these as second-class citizens.[32] A better way of viewing the connection between the two is to regard an initial theological education — what is now called general Christian education — as something that helps ordinary believers assess the meaning of mature discipleship, apply this to their witness in the world, and review it as they continue to learn. Further — what we call formal — theological education builds on this by helping believers pursue this process in a more integrated, discerning, and sophisticated way. The first encourages Christians to *live out* their faith authentically in the world, the second to *model it* more to others there.

In recognizing theological education as simply a more intensive form of Christian education, Wood is not untypical of most contributors to the debate, and I can perhaps use him as a base here from which to go further. Underlying his differentiating the two is a distinction between the implicit ministry of most Christians — a ministry that takes place largely through everyday activities, and more explicit forms involving ordained and lay church leaders.[33] It is better to talk merely of differing types of ministry; otherwise value and status judgments about their relative importance tend to intrude. Speaking this way finds support from the wide range of everyday symbols, images, metaphors, and analogies in the Bible that describe various aspects of God's work. This divine work, as Wood acknowledges, is the model for all ministry.[34] In line with some others, Wood also suggests that to

31. On these see Edward Farley, "Can Church Education Be Theological Education?" *Theology Today* 42 (2) (1985): 158-71.

32. For a new way of envisaging and implementing lay theology and theological education see my book *Redeeming the Routines: Bringing Theology to Life* (Wheaton, Ill.: Victor, 1993).

33. On this and what follows see C. Wood, "Theological Education and Education for Church Leadership," *Quarterly Review* 10 (2) (1990): 65-81.

34. Robert Banks, *God the Worker: Journeys into the Mind, Heart and Imagination of God* (Valley Forge, Penn.: Judson, 1994).

fulfill its proper role, theological education should not focus *directly* on forming us spiritually, mediating the Christian tradition, equipping with leadership skills, or practicing Christian witness. It should concentrate instead on developing habits of critical self-reflection on spiritual formation, faith, leadership quality, and practice that *indirectly* will influence these important areas of life and ministry. Otherwise we lose the unique contribution of theological education. While I am in agreement that we must not lose sight of the distinctively theological nature of theological education, this again opens up an inadmissible gap between action and reflection. Only by overcoming this can we *do* as well as *learn* theology, indeed *do* we actually *learn* theology in the fullest sense.

## A. A More Immediate Connection Between Action and Reflection

A missional model places greater emphasis on action than the other models we have been considering, even those using the language of praxis. It is now time to clarify the relationship between action and reflection. Since the debate has not produced a significant discussion on this matter, we need to look elsewhere for assistance.

A good place to begin is with those working in the field of Christian education for whom this is an issue, especially where they view Christian and theological education as being on a continuum, rather than separate endeavors. A key person here is Thomas Groome.[35] For him, the primary locus for theological education is not academia, or even the church, but human history. This praxis of God, as he calls it, is the primary text for Christian or theological education. To understand what God is doing we must bring the scriptures into dialogue with our situation, for they already reflect elements of divine truth that are present in it. We can do this in five stages: (i) encourage people to express or name their present praxis; (ii) engage in critical reflection on this; (iii) bring the results into contact with the Christian story and vision; (iv) al-

---

35. T. Groome, "Theology on our Feet: A Revisionist Pedagogy for Healing the Gap between Academia and Ecclesia," in Lewis S. Mudge and James N. Poling, eds., *Formation and Reflection: The Promise of Practical Theology* (Philadelphia: Fortress, 1987), pp. 55-78.

low a genuine conversation to take place between the two; (v) follow this through to a new or renewed praxis. We need to be clear that, according to its original Marxian usage, praxis refers here not just to actions but to the reflection that lies behind and within them. Too often the word is simply a synonym for action rather than for reflection on life oriented towards and involved in action. This distinguishes it both from abstract reflection on, or a pragmatic response to, concrete situations.

This action-reflection model of learning provides a helpful starting point, but in several respects it needs strengthening. For instance, we require more objective criteria in discussing reflection on action. Helpful here is Don Browning's more detailed explanation of practical theological thinking. He regards this as relevant to teaching the whole theological encyclopedia, not just ministry-oriented subjects.[36] Alongside Groome's stress on action criteria in reflecting on our actual situation, we can ask five basic questions: (i) What kind of world do we live in? (ii) What should we do? (iii) What are the basic needs, tendencies, and values we should satisfy? (iv) What constraints does our present cultural, sociological, or ecological context place on our actions? (v) What are the concrete rules and roles we should follow? After we have asked these questions and begun to build a solid descriptive theological understanding of the situation, we can explore what the Bible and the Christian tradition have to offer. Then we can engage in more systematic theological reflection on it. With the help of other disciplines and accumulated experience, further strategic practical theological thinking will lead to specific principles and guidelines for action. If this process sounds too one-sidedly cognitive, we should remember that each of the ethically oriented questions mentioned above has its counterpart at the level of personal formation. Our task as teachers is to train students across the whole curriculum to help ordinary people ask and answer these questions. It is important that they "act out," not just "learn from," the educational process.[37]

While these suggestions fill out the meaning of action-oriented thinking, they do not go far enough. The role of scripture is still too

36. On what follows see Don Browning, "Practical Theology and Religious Education," in *Formation and Reflection*, pp. 79-102.

37. He develops this approach further in Don Browning, ed., *Practical Theology: The Emerging Field in Theology, Church and World* (San Francisco: Harper & Row, 1983), but most extensively in *A Fundamental Practical Theology: Descriptive and Strategic Proposals* (Minneapolis: Fortress, 1992).

marginal: it appears to have only a central illuminative status. Both writers view the Bible as a revelatory book that helps us discern more clearly what is going on in the world and what to do about it. Groome in particular emphasizes its narrative and visionary character in a way that brings out more vividly the Bible's link with action, but it does not play a normative role. There is another side to this. Drawing on the Bible's own evaluation of the power of words, on our own experience of this taking place, and on contemporary philosophical discussions about "speech-acts," we should recognize that *speaking* is one of the key expressions of God's past and present *acting*. Meditating on the Bible, and bringing it into conversation with life, is not always the second but is sometimes the first step in the process of learning and doing. Apart from anything else, it can raise questions that help us identify areas of life excluded from our concern, or discern the problematic nature of certain situations for the first time.

It is not only the role of scripture that requires more emphasis, but the context of ongoing mission in the world. There are two ways in which this can happen. First, we should understand the process and setting of theological education itself as more than the place where active reflection on life takes place. It is also the place where this can be put into practice. There are two ways in which a seminary, Bible college, or lay center might encourage this to happen. One is to view it as a *working model* of the world in the sphere of education.[38] Here the seminary becomes an analogue or laboratory of the everyday world, in which we can learn to reflect on and respond to its demands and challenges. Out of this we develop the character necessary to equip others for mission, and the ability both to reflect on action and to act on reflection vis-à-vis everyday life. The sequence of courses would facilitate learning how to learn, learning how to use learning for others, and practicing the learning this involves, all of which could still culminate in a year of apprenticeship in ministry. In this way we are not only *preparing* people for ministry but *inserting* them into it, if only in situations in theological institutions analogous to those they will meet outside. As teachers, we should also model how to address real-life issues

38. Some of what follows was stimulated by an unpublished paper by Tim Dakin, "Faith Seeking Understanding for Faith" (1991), that was written for the Church Army to help it reform its approach to training people for urban evangelism.

in our institutions and the kind of relationships we want those learning with us to have among themselves and others.

This view of theological institutions as working models of outside structures casts spiritual formation in theological education in a somewhat different light. Instead of it being viewed mainly as building inner resources and character for future ministry, it becomes an essential component in carrying out present ministry in the place where one is learning. According to Douglas John Hall, we would strengthen this aspect of theological education further if we substituted for the language of spiritual formation, relying as heavily as it does on the idea and practice of spiritual *disciplines,* the language of *discipleship* itself.[39] This would require us to focus less on how to integrate spiritual formation into theological education, and more on how theological education — at both the initial and more developed level — can illuminate and facilitate a contemporary form of discipleship. Rather than concentrating on the inner life of the believer, this orients it to, and contextualizes it in, the here and now of daily life in the service of the kingdom. As students do this by adopting a language that links their common life with the life of the church, they engage in a form of discipleship appropriate to their setting. This will lead them beyond adding a set of spiritual practices to deepening their covenantal commitment to God, and help them develop a discerning discipline of interpreting the Word of God, a discipline that involves prayer as well as study.[40]

39. See further Douglas John Hall, "Theological Education as Character Formation," pp. 53-79. In affirming the renewed emphasis in theological education on spiritual formation, he is nevertheless worried that too direct a focus on the spiritual disciplines overlooks the grounding of spiritual formation in divine grace rather than human works. There is also a danger of forgetting that spiritual maturity is attained through losing ourselves in the service of others rather than finding ourselves through contemplation of God.

40. Cf. also the approach of Richard Mouw, "Spiritual Identity and Churchly Praxis," *Theological Education* 23, Supplement (1987): 88-112, who in this connection discusses the indivisible relationship between *orthodoxy* and *orthopraxy,* though he prefers to talk the language of *orthopathy.* The heart-felt, heart-torn essence of what it means to the divinely appointed "go-between" between God and the people. Yet Mouw's approach, like Hough and Cobb's on which it is partly dependent, leaves unclear how this divine pathos is to become deeply implanted in those undergoing theological education, especially when the process of teaching is generally separated from the conduct of ministry. It is not clear how the dynamic connection he desires between reflection and action can be fully experienced in a theological institution, for vitality in prayer is also partly dependent on

According to these views, theological institutions are more than a setting in which rehearsals for ministry take place — the equivalent of a firing range in which military exercises are conducted. The reason for this is that "real life" happens inside as well as outside such institutions. This is why viewing these institutions as an analogue to what happens in the so-called "real world" is an advance on seeing theological training as only a preparation for ministry. But the experience of real life in these settings is limited in scope and in some measure sheltered from the full force of life experiences. Accordingly, we do not find here as broad a range of encounters, opportunities, and challenges that a missional approach offers.[41] Only up to a point can teachers model what being practical theologians — and reflective practitioners model what doing ministry — involves, and only to a degree can students serve the wider world other than through learning about it. It also means that the spirituality exemplified by teachers, and that developed by learners, cannot compare with that nurtured in a range of situations by involvement in joint mission.

## B. A More Complex Relationship Between Theory and Practice

We can pursue the link between action and reflection further by focusing more specifically on the relationship between theory and practice. As with the word *praxis* above, we need first to clarify the meaning of these terms. Sometimes people talk as if the classical disciplines provide the theory for the practical areas, or for specific ministry practices. But it is often difficult to show persuasively how the first two relate in that way, and specific ministry areas frequently operate with their own implicit or explicit theories drawn from psychology or edu-

---

the everyday opportunities and challenges of ministry. While ministry to others can and does take place within theological institutions, divine pathos is intimately connected to the world at large. Perhaps this in part explains the frequently observed phenomenon of a loss of enthusiasm for relating to God among so many seminary students.

41. The language used by people who adopt these approaches betrays this. For example, Dakin calls for "faith seeking understanding for faith" rather than also obedience, while Hall talks about the "metaphor" rather than the "reality" of discipleship.

cation. Sometimes the words refer to criteria for particular activities, and may be used in a normative or explanatory way. Rather than placing the two terms in separate categories, we should recognize that theory is embedded in practice, and practice embodies theory. Since theory has to do with the standards and goals of practices — and practices are internal to the life of a person, organization, or church — theory does not exist "outside" but "inside" what empirically takes place. And in the same way that facts cannot be "value neutral," practices cannot be independent of theory.[42]

Such an approach to the relationship between theory and practice takes us beyond what usually short-circuits a full-ranging discussion. It means that we can do more than compare and contrast curriculum areas, focus on non-theological materials by which ministry or other religious practices are evaluated, and assess materials theologically just from the point of view of right understanding. At this point it is helpful to look at Matthew Lamb's fivefold typology of the relationship between theory and practice.[43] He outlines the following possibilities:

- the simple application of theory to practice,
- the movement from practice to the formulation of theory,
- theory and practice in a constant state of tension,
- fusing the two from the side of practice,
- combining theory and practice from the side of theory.

Ben Ollenburger's understanding of practice moves us immediately beyond the first of these positions. As noted earlier, all sides to the debate acknowledge that the relationship between theory and practice is more complex than any simple application of theory to practice.[44] Mul-

42. On this see further Charles Taylor, "Social Theory as a Practice," *Philosophy and the Human Sciences*, Philosophical Papers, vol. 2 (Cambridge: Cambridge University Press, 1985), pp. 91-115.

43. Matthew L. Lamb, *Solidarity with Victims: Toward a Theology of Social Transformation* (New York: Crossroad, 1982), pp. 66-86.

44. Ben Ollenburger, "Theory and Practice in Theological Education," a paper read before the Lilly Project on "The Aims and Purposes of Evangelical Higher Theological Education," to be published in a forthcoming volume. See further on this David Kelsey and Barbara Wheeler, "Mind Reading: Notes on the Basic Issues Program," *Theological Education* 20 (2) (1984): 11-12, a comment made early in the debate that still holds true.

ler and Stackhouse sometimes sound as if they are advocating the first position, but in varying degrees move more in the direction of the fifth. Chopp, the Collective, and some in the Network hold to a version of the second that I have already queried. What are we to make of the last three possibilities?

The fourth position, Lamb's own preference, has received some support from Browning among others. One of these, James Fowler, now proposes a more "dialectical" approach closer to the third option. He argues, rightly in my judgment, that those who advocate fusing theory and practice from the side of practice fall short of giving the moments of emergent truth that arise from moving between theory and practice the status of revelation. At the root of this, he suggests, is a tendency to substitute for practice the *idea* of practice, and so to sublate praxis into theory.[45] This preference for metatheoretical method over reflecting on concrete situations relies on critical reason to overcome its own limits instead of recognizing the priority and objectivity of divine initiative. He would prefer to see an approach that gives more credit to, and recognizes a more complex connection between, both poles of the equation. Actual practice rather than just the idea of practice should receive attention, but so should the revelatory, not just illuminating, nature of theory. This is true, but still leaves revelation too much on one side of the line. Also, how theologically adequate — from a biblically informed perspective — is a purely dialectical as opposed to a genuinely dynamic view of the relationship between theory and practice?

We can overcome these two problems and move to a less abstract and more theological account of the fifth position in the typology by drawing on a helpful distinction in systematic theology. Doing this can also help overcome the danger involved in a too-abstract theory-based approach to integrating theory and practice. What would help in this whole discussion is a better appreciation of God's broader communication through the creation and culture, yet one that is not fused or identified with God's clearer communication through scripture. The form this takes in classical Protestantism is preferable to that in classical Catholi-

---

45. Like Groome he uses the word *praxis* over against *theory*, and I have sought to clarify this by substituting the word *practice* in the text. See James Fowler, "Practical Theology and Theological Education: Some Models and Questions," *Theological Education* 42 (1) (1985): 54-55. He goes on to suggest that drawing on H. R. Niebuhr could help here, since he was unafraid to talk about revelation occurring at such moments.

cism: it is better to think in terms of general revelation rather than natural theology. In other words, alongside some of the building blocks for theory given us in scripture are those provided through our personal and collective human experience, in which the providence and Spirit of God are active. While this is not generally self-interpreting, by the same token we can sometimes understand scripture itself only through what we learn in the created and human order.[46]

So we have two divinely related and practically inseparable conduits of revelation, one in the biblical tradition and one, however partial, in creation and culture. We can fill out this suggestion further. Turning first to general revelation, we should view this as encompassing the genuinely illuminating insights that come from activities as diverse as personal observation and reflection on various constancies in the human and natural order, accumulated experience and wisdom crystallized in enduring proverbs and stories, and technical investigation and research in different areas of knowledge based on scholarly disciplines. Since these all come to us influenced by flawed human, unconscious cultural or shared ideological considerations, we cannot accept them uncritically. Since their results sometimes stand in tension with one another, they do not always provide a complete picture, and say little about the wider framework for understanding them. They remain incomplete. Turning to special revelation, we can call back into view Wood's emphasis on the role of vision and discernment in understanding and interpreting the biblical story. Stressing the role of imagination helps us break out of a reliance on critical reason even in developing such a scriptural perspective. We could extend this in a more intentionally doxological direction, in relation to understanding and responding to what we learn of God from scripture and Christian traditions. This creates room for directly addressing God, not only in moments of personal or corporate worship, or even in the classroom when overcome by some insight into God but, as with Anselm in the *Proslogium,* as a way of engaging in theology or theological education.[47]

46. This subject has been opened up again in a stimulating way — though one hindered by the language of natural theology rather than general revelation — by James Barr, *Biblical Faith and Natural Theology* (Oxford: Clarendon, 1993).

47. The best discussion of this may be found in D. W. Hardy and D. T. Ford, *Praising and Knowing God* (Philadelphia: Westminster, 1985). See now also C. M. Lacugna, *God for Us: The Trinity and Christian Life* (San Francisco: Harper, 1991), pp. 356-67.

Some philosophical studies provide further insight into an approach to theory and practice that stresses their dynamic interconnection. In his seminal work on the role of action in personal life, John MacMurray underscores the presence of rationality *in* action, not just as its precursor or aftermath. At its best, action is embodied rationality. Sometimes it is the form rationality chiefly takes.[48] This should not be strange to anyone who has a dynamically sacramental view of baptism, where it is the tangible way believers demonstrate their new-found faith in Jesus Christ. Inherent in this is the core of a new outlook on life, a new worldview, a new understanding of reality. Mostly what we *do* is in some sense dependent on what we *know*. There is a knowledge base for actions directed towards some target. Sometimes, as has been persuasively argued, this knowledge is tacit. We know more than we can say.[49] Since such knowledge contains certain assumptions about reality, about the sort of knowledge available to us, about human nature and social interaction, and about what constitutes acceptable forms of explanation and inquiry, there are implicit or explicit theoretical, indeed theological, insights underlying our actions, including ontological and epistemological ones.[50] Theory, then, is at least embryonically present on the practice side of the equation.

The dynamics of everyday thinking supports and extends this.[51]

48. John MacMurray, *The Self as Agent* (London: Faber & Faber, 1957). Related to this is the work of Parker J. Palmer on the cognitive dimensions of "love," or "love" as a form of knowing. See again *To Know As We Are Known: A Spirituality of Education* (San Francisco: Harper & Row, 1982).

49. Michael Polanyi, *The Tacit Dimension* (London: Routledge and Kegan Paul, 1967), J. V. Apczynski, *Doers of the Word: Toward a Foundational Theology Based on the Thought of Michael Polanyi* (Missoula, Mont.: Scholars Press, 1977), and R. K. Martin, "Theological Education in Epistemological Perspective: The Significance of Michael Polanyi's 'Personal Knowledge' for a Theological Orientation of Theological Education," *Teaching Theology and Religion* 1 (3) (1998): 139-53.

50. See further B. Mazibuko, *Education in Mission/Mission in Education: A Critical Comparative Study of Selected Approaches* (Frankfurt: Peter Lang, 1987). For an approach to some of these issues from an anthropological and cultural studies perspective, with implications for theology, see also Kathryn Tanner, *Theories of Culture: A New Agenda for Theology* (Minneapolis: Fortress, 1997), pp. 69-72.

51. On what follows see Agnes Heller, *Everyday Life* (London: Routledge and Kegan Paul, 1984), esp. pp. 211-15. Interesting also in this connection is the discovery in some areas of life that immediate, perception-based, precognitive responses to challenges, for example hitting a target at a great distance, turn out to be far more accurate than carefully considered ones. They possess an inbuilt, only

Though daily life is essentially pragmatic and oriented to action, various types of theorizing occur in people's ordinary thinking processes. There is "anticipatory thinking," which takes place when we cogitate in preparation for a specific activity. It is present in so-called "daydreaming," which is not only the basis of art but often pregnant with theoretical possibilities. It is there in "postmortem reviews" of an already completed action. Though such reflection is separate in time and space from the action, it is an inseparable part of it. The role of contemplation alongside action, and the description of qualities of events or objects beyond what is necessary for action, point to the presence of theoretical elements in everyday life even when more formal theorizing is absent. This is why an implicit worldview to give direction to our actions — one that answers our personal and collective need to know why we are here, what we should do, and how we should react — exists in the popular myths and folk wisdom of all races.

There are two other general philosophical approaches that are relevant here. Some have suggested that the influential American movement known as pragmatism could further clarify the complex relationship between theory and practice. Others prefer to take advantage of the broader cultural shift that is taking place from modernity to postmodernity. Philosophically, one way of handling this transition is to develop an understanding of theology, and by extension, of theological education, that views the process of theological thinking and learning more in terms of a research project than theory construction. It is not only experts and those working with them who can develop and test this process, but the experience gained by ordinary people as they grow in communal wisdom. This general approach has much to commend it and is worth exploring further.[52] While philosophical pragmatism and less relativist forms of postmodernist philosophy can provide some support for what I am proposing, they only take us so far. Both of these still tend to stop short of a stronger orientation to praxis and practice as partial embodiments of theory and as resources for building theory.

---

later demonstrable, rationality. See further E. S. Tauber and M. R. Green, *Prelogical Experience* (New York: Basic Books, 1959), p. 71.

52. On the implications for theology, see especially the stimulating discussion by Nancey Murphy, *Theology in an Age of Scientific Reasoning* (Ithaca, N.Y.: Cornell University Press, 1990).

# 4. Reconceiving Teaching as a Missional Practice

What consequences does a missional approach to theological education have for the role of the teacher and for the practice of teaching? Teaching lies at the heart of current approaches to theological education, and remains central to all proposals to reform it.

In the initial survey of current proposals to the theological education debate, I took careful note of their various implications for teaching. Though discussed less, these have implications for teachers themselves as well as for their role and task. Since teachers and teaching are central to theological education, we have to give special attention to what a missional model means for these. There is another reason for giving them special consideration here. Because of their very centrality, recasting these is the most likely way to initiate substantive change in the way seminaries function. One person who understands this is Cornel West, who argues that if change is to take place: "the best place to start is with the most delicate and difficult: *the self-images and self-identities of seminary professors.*"[53] We can broaden this to include those teaching in other kinds of theological institutions. It is a delicate and difficult area, for we have such a large personal investment in our professorial images and identity. Sometimes these are simply a function of what we do, so that our vocational understanding determines our self-understanding. Criticism of the one is regarded as criticism of the other. Calls for change in one are interpreted as calls for change in

53. C. West, *Prophetic Fragments* (Grand Rapids: Eerdmans, 1988), p. 276.

169

the other. This is often too threatening. It is because of the general tendency today to find not just our professional but our personal identity and meaning in our work that calls for change frequently meet with so much resistance.

Yet our basic identity and meaning lie in our relationship with God and others, not in our work. Otherwise we are personally diminished when we come up for retirement, are incapacitated in some way, or become aware that as teachers we are only in the second rank. In any case, our effectiveness as teachers flows ultimately from who we are and how we relate as much as what we do.[54] Unless animated by, and visibly expressing, the faith, love, and hope that make our efforts effective, we do not achieve much in the classroom that endures. There may be much sound and fury of ideas there, and when students go out into churches or other places of ministry they may do so full of strong views and great plans, but this too will not amount to much. But alongside our being fully committed and increasingly matured persons, we also need an accurate understanding of our role and task. For Cornel West, the key element here is the fullest reveling in the life of the mind and putting this at the disposal of the people of God. For him, the chief obstacles to this are the self-seeking careerism and self-excusing cynicism that are so endemic to the academy, or the myopic preoccupation with numbers and influence that is so widespread in the church. If, as teachers, we are to fully serve the concerns of the kingdom of God, then we must be prepared to live on the margins of both these institutions. Great teachers, he says, have always operated this way, and this is why they continue to exert influence today. If a larger number of present-day faculty would follow in their footsteps we would begin to see "full-scale reform" in theological education.

Although more is required to move theological education in the right direction, West has put his finger on a crucial aspect of the role and task of the teacher. We need more vital Christian thinking, espe-

54. Even if it is expressed somewhat differently, the seminary faculty model for the twenty-first century suggested by the "M. J. Murdoch Charitable Trust," *Faculty Dialogue* 23 (1995): 17-21, rightly puts personal integrity and character at the head of their list of key characteristics. It follows this with reference to understanding traditional Christianity and contemporary realities, with academic excellence and skill in application, and with shared seminary and church appointments. Though the report suffers from being oriented only to the training of pastors and to the work of the church, in general it is pointing in the right direction.

cially in a period when professors have difficulty finding time to read, reflect, and research, and when so much of their writing and teaching is technical and dispassionate. He rightly insists on teachers subordinating their work to the concerns of the kingdom rather than to academic or ecclesiastical goals. Quite rightly he focuses our attention on our responsibility to the people of God rather than on purely clerical or professional forms of ministry. But while theological institutions should accord a central place to the life of the mind, especially where this takes place in a creative and prophetic way, this is only part of our educational task. As Howard Gardner and others have argued, there are other forms of intelligence that require nurturing. Alongside our linguistic and logical abilities, there capacities arising from our feeling and intuition, as well as others of a physical, spatial, or musical kind.[55] I have already referred to the existence of emotional and intuitive rationality at the everyday level, and the first is presently receiving increasing attention alongside the cognitive.[56] It is precisely because some faculty suffer from a lower emotional and relational intelligence, a less intuitive and practical wisdom, that they are less effective as teachers. But all this is only another way of talking about the formational and practical dimensions of theological education discussed earlier.

## A. Teaching as Sharing Life as Well as Knowledge

In order to gain a clear understanding of what teaching comprehends, recourse to some further theological reflection, informed again by the biblical witness, is helpful. We have already seen that teaching was significant for all the biblical figures we examined in the last section. In differing ways and degrees they were also working models of what they taught. The prophets, Jesus, and Paul not only shared the truth with others, but also their lives — with, at times even for, them. Why? Because this was the central truth they were conveying, and teaching it involved living and sometimes dying

55. Howard Gardner, *Frames of Mind: The Theory of Multiple Intelligences* (New York: Basic, 1985). He also discusses educating the intelligences (pp. 331-66).

56. At a popular level see Daniel Goleman, *Emotional Intelligence: Why It Matters More Than IQ* (New York: Bantam, 1995).

the truth as well as declaring it.[57] We can take Paul as an example. As he says to the Thessalonians: "Our gospel came to you not simply with words, but also with power, with the Holy Spirit and with deep conviction. You know how we *lived* among you for your sake. You became imitators of *us* and the *Lord*" (1 Thess 1:5-6). It is through the sharing of a person's life as well as their beliefs that life-giving change comes to others. Truth must be embodied as well as articulated, incarnated as well as revealed. Doing this sometimes drains the life out of the one who is sharing with others, but it is precisely this that brings the greatest life to them. It is, as Paul says, a case of "death in me, but life in you" (2 Cor 4:12). This is the ultimate *wisdom* of God. The *theologia* of which Farley and others speak comes to most profound and powerful expression in suffering. Luther, for one, fully understood this, when he insisted that the chief qualification for a theologian was suffering.[58]

We see the underlying reason for this more clearly if we step back and consider how each member of the Trinity functions.

1. The culmination of Jesus' teaching in and through the cross reminds us that transformation of others ultimately comes primarily through self-sacrifice on their behalf. Ideas, no matter how profound or persuasive, are not enough: it is only in lives that embody and on occasions risk all for the truth that this happens. Yet, it is precisely here that divine wisdom is most fully revealed (1 Cor 1:21-25). For those who hold a classical view of the atonement, there is something contradictory about believing in the power of teaching alone to transform their students. There is a disjunction here between their doctrine and their pedagogy. Jesus did not have an impact on others' lives simply because he was a great teacher, but only as he poured out his life for them.

57. On Jesus as teacher see Marcus Borg, *Jesus: A New Vision: Spirit, Culture and the Life of Discipleship* (San Francisco: Harper & Row, 1987), though one does not have to buy his whole understanding of the work and person of Jesus to appreciate much of what he says. This accords well with the earlier approach of T. W. Manson, *The Teaching of Jesus* (Cambridge: Cambridge University Press, 1935), and, with a different set of interests in mind, the view of J. D. G. Dunn, *Jesus and the Spirit: A Study of the Religious and Charismatic Experience of Jesus and the First Christians as Reflected in the New Testament* (Philadelphia: Westminster, 1975), that Jesus is presented in the gospels as a model for Christian living or spirituality.

58. See further H. G. Haile, *Luther: An Experiment in Biography* (Princeton: Princeton University Press, 1980), pp. 304ff.

2. For all the Father's instructing of the people and the inscribing of that teaching in the Bible, Christianity is not primarily — unlike Islam — a "religion of the book." Without the Father's authoring of the book we would not know what was primary, and that is why both its contents and teaching of them is crucial. But what most reveals to us the heart of God is our experience of God's grace, redemption, and transformation, all of which are dependent on God's unfathomable and inexhaustible self-giving and love. If we are to instruct others in a way that is consistent with God's education of us, our own "courses" must take a similar self-giving "course" as we find in our divine mentor.

3. The Spirit is not just an advocate or guide, not just one who trades in enlightening and inspiring words. Words are certainly central, as is clear from the Spirit's role in proclaiming Christ (John 16:14) and inspiring scripture (2 Tim 3:16). But the Spirit is also a reconciler and healer, who not only gives us direct instruction in the scriptures, but who also reveals to us the mind, heart, and will of God by fashioning people into role models and examples and by building communities that express the divine life. One could do no better than explore the breadth of the word "edification" to see the diverse and interconnected ways in which the Spirit brings people to knowing God fully "with all our heart, mind, soul, and strength" (Matt 12:33). It is this rather than "education," a word it only uses of the Law (Gal 3:24), that should primarily guide our thinking and practice of ministry formation.

There is another side to this perspective on the work of teaching. What we do not only has God's self-giving as its ultimate role model but also as its power. It rests on divine grace rather than on our human efforts. As Craig Dykstra reminds us: "We are not responsible for making people whole or training them for ministry. Our approach should be a grace-based not work-based one. This is the very opposite to the view that if anything is going to happen we must make it happen."[59] In a paradoxical way, then, teaching involves giving more of ourselves than is customarily understood, yet at the same time involves relying on ourselves less than is often the case. This is where a belief in the sovereignty of God, the presence of Christ, and the power of the Spirit comes profoundly into its own. Strangely enough, sometimes

59. Craig Dykstra, *Growing in the Life of Faith* (Louisville: Presbyterian Church, 1989), note 24.

one or more of these is absent even in contexts where these beliefs are a central part of an institution's theological tradition.

Parker J. Palmer brings this out in an arresting way. Our deeply rooted Western tendency, he says, is to externalize truth in order to communicate it to others. Yet truth is not essentially a purely objective phenomenon that we can analyze, describe, or point others towards. While it does have a real existence outside ourselves, it is more like a subject to whom we are pledged and with whom we are in relationship. The word "truth" comes from the word "troth," and embracing it is sometimes a very personal — even private — affair. Indeed the metaphor "affair" is not at all out of place. It conveys something of the intimate relationship we should have with truth. If it is to become fully part of us, we must not only learn it but become "betrothed" to it. As we share it with others — which we do best through "courting" them so that they can experience as well as hear it — we seek to "betroth" them to it as well. All this is in accord with the biblical understanding of knowledge, which involves both assent and action, understanding and obedience, communication and commitment.[60] We do not just *present* truth, we must *represent* it to others. We do not just relate the truth in the hope that others might comprehend it, we relate to them in a way that helps them begin to be apprehended by it. In biblical terms — and this forms the title of Palmer's book — the goal both for ourselves and for others is "to know as we are known" (1 Cor 13:12). In the spirit of this metaphor, we could say that in offering a "course" on a subject we are inviting students to have "intercourse" with it.[61]

## B. Teaching as Active as Well as Reflective Practice

How can those involved in teaching put into practice this biblically informed theological definition of their role?

---

60. See generally Keith R. Anderson, "The Ancient Hebrew Faith as a Model for Teaching," *Faculty Dialogue* 12 (1989): 69-78.

61. Parker J. Palmer, *To Know As We are Known,* pp. 31-32, 42-46. Note also Stephen Webb, "The Voice of Theology: Rethinking the Personal and the Objective in Christian Pedagogy," *Journal of the American Academy of Religion* 65 (4) (1997): 763-81.

## 1. Some Basic Considerations

1. Alongside technical knowledge of their subject area, teachers require an intimate acquaintance of the One who is present in it and animates it. Our language is interesting here: we talk about "subjects" but often communicate them as objects. Only if teachers are in vital touch with the presence of God in their area of expertise, whatever that happens to be, will they be able to communicate this in a life-giving, life-changing, way. It is not just their competence to deal with the subject matter that counts, but the extent to which the subject personally matters to them! What we are talking about here is *passion,* though the expression of this will vary from one person to the next. Whatever form it takes, the extent to which the subject comes to matter to students will significantly depend upon this.

2. As well as doing justice to their particular subject areas, teachers should be able to situate this for learners within the overall picture of God's purposes and dealings. They must provide some account of the "big picture" within which their subject finds its place, as well as trace connections between some of the details they are focusing on and other parts of that wider picture. This helps learners understand more of the full divine drama, and enables them to relate both to the ongoing human drama in which they, and those they are seeking to serve, are participants. What we are talking about here is providing a broader *vision* of what is being taught. However that is done, it affects substantially the extent to which students develop an integrated understanding of what they are learning.

3. Apart from explaining the substance of what they are conveying, teachers should find ways of demonstrating the practical outcome of this and how it contributes to God's ongoing purposes. This is more than a question of relevance, which is all too often defined by the world's trendy agenda rather than God's broader and deeper prophetic purposes. Bridging the gap that often exists between the world of the subject matter and the world around us can take place in various ways. But all involve something more than instruction. What we are talking about here is *action* of some kind that addresses a concrete situation. This may itself be predominantly verbal or even instructional in character, but will also be teaching *into,* not just *about,* whatever is at issue.

So, then, passion, vision, and action are all involved. Teaching involves our feelings, imaginations, and wills as much as our cognitive faculties. For a missional model of teaching, the last is particularly important.

## 2. Some Particular Suggestions

There are currently two main ways that we can attempt to bridge the gap between instruction and action.

1. At the simplest level, we can illustrate how the subject matter links up with current realities, singling out certain dimensions of life as matters for regular discussion throughout the course. This would give learners the opportunity to connect a current experience in their home, congregation, or mission setting with the course content. This is fine as far as it goes but still tends to operate within the boundaries of a theory-to-practice approach that applies some part of the tradition — biblical, historical, theological, or practical — to contemporary life.

2. At a more substantive level, we can encourage learners to undertake an assignment or project that confronts a current concern. We can invite a practical theologian into the classroom to show how to apply what is taught. We can develop a curriculum around student-related and more general concerns, holding classes in an on-site ministry setting and addressing local concerns with the help of a reflective practitioner. All these connect theology and life more closely than the methods already mentioned, but they still do not confront issues in an existential way.[62] Interaction is still largely at the level of ideas, with the teacher more of a commentator than participant.

Though both of these have their place, we can go further. Doing so is easier with the kinds of people who are increasingly coming to seminaries. A majority of these are married with families; they work at least part time in a regular occupation, and also serve in a congregation, parachurch organization, or mission setting. Their greater experience of life has prepared and equipped them to learn in ways that fit a more holistic, integrated, and missional model. In what follows I move

62. Under George W. Webber, New York Theological Seminary set up a premier model of education that took many theological courses into the streets, on which see Robert W. Pazmino, *The Seminary in the City: A Study of New York Theological Seminary* (New York: University Press of America, 1988). Despite moves back towards a more traditional model, this is still a significant feature of the school's life and other aspects of its program continue to develop.

from the less to the more difficult possibilities, from small steps to large strides, towards a missional model of theological education.

i. Integrative courses that take place in the professor's own setting. Though this is easiest for courses focusing on spiritual and communal formation, other types of courses also open themselves up to it. For example:

- A course on a book of the Bible, held partly in a professor's office and partly in a local church, a course that combines exegesis with designing, teaching, and evaluating a class or study group.
- A course on developing the church in the city, involving the professor and built around visits to the sites, records, and people who are key participants in what happens.
- A course in vocational or social ethics, held partly on campus and partly in a workplace setting, based on live case studies involving members of the instructor's congregation.
- A basic course on spiritual formation, meeting in the professor's own home and focusing on family life, theological study, and small-group involvement as spiritual disciplines.[63]

ii. Cross-divisional courses, taught by a professor with interdisciplinary qualifications, could focus on an area of practical theological concern but could draw on biblical, historical, systematic, ethical, and practical resources relevant to it.

- A course on individualism and community that analyzes their roots, examines the biblical interplay between the two and — drawing on the professor's own experience — explores how best to embody these in our relationships, congregations, and neighborhoods.
- A course focusing on the city that includes a study of cities in the Bible, their historical contributions, a theological and ethical critique of contemporary urban life, and a strategy for some aspect of urban ministry, all filtered through the teacher's own experience of and ministry in the city.

63. Three possibilities for courses on Christian education, becoming more and more centered on action, are provided by Ronald H. Cram, "Globalization and Christian Religious Education," *Theological Education* 30 (1) (1993): 177-81.

- A course on the "new age" movement, based on reading about and conversations with people involved in it. The course would include an exploration of its historical roots and the working out of a biblical-theological assessment of its precepts and practices.
- A course on the ministry of the laity that begins with learners' experience of what hinders and catalyzes this ministry, and then examines the biblical role of the *laos,* its historical outworking and immersion in current models of lay-centered ministry in the world and church.

iii. Collaborative courses between a teacher in any of the main theological fields and a practical theologian or reflective practitioner serving in a specific local setting. These would work best over semester-length courses where there was more time for feedback. For example:

- A course on the prophets involving an OT professor and someone involved in urban ministry, in which teacher and students work directly with people in the neighborhood on issues raised by their study.
- An exegetical course involving a NT scholar and instructor in preaching, a course that has as its main assignment preparing, giving, and evaluating a relevant sermon in the students' home church.
- A course on the early expansion of Christianity in the early centuries led by a church history professor and a person founding a church, where the material studied throws light on the development of the congregation.
- A course on the person and work of Christ, co-taught by a systematic theologian and a professor of evangelism, in conjunction with a mission involving both them and their students.

iv. "Live-action" courses held where a professor undertakes mission outside the local congregation, so that the class can both observe how course content is shaped by and translated into action, as well as engage in joint ministry with the professor.

- In biblical studies, an instructor could apply various OT wisdom writings to administrative aspects of a Christian organization she assists or look at how certain NT letters could give direction to the congregation she attends.

- In church history, a class studying heretical movements could involve the teacher modeling to learners how to relate to similar people today, or a course surveying major theological movements could include dialogue with people who have different theological convictions.

- In theology, courses in apologetics or philosophy of religion could include or take their rise from encounters with seekers or unbelievers, or courses in ethics could encourage students to deal with some of their own concrete, everyday issues, such as busyness, mobility, and consumerism in modern society.

- In practical theology — evangelism, homiletics, counseling, Christian education, or pastoral ministry — this is relatively straightforward, though since these areas should be viewed as complementary *dimensions* of ministry rather than professional *areas* of ministry, it would be helpful to find ways of demonstrating their interconnection.

Other possibilities include action-reflection ways of helping students develop a Christian approach to work, popular culture, and the environment, many of which already exist. In the following chapter I shall say more about how some of these might affect the shape of the overall curriculum at an advanced as well as graduate level. All of these suggestions and possibilities are open to being taught in a way that takes account of the multicultural character of an increasing number of churches and local contexts. Where possible, professors or practitioners coming from one or more different cultural backgrounds could co-teach courses, or draw in resource people working in multicultural settings. Experiments along these lines, crossing disciplinary as well as cultural boundaries, are already under way in a number of places.[64]

In all these settings the shift from a presentational to a conversa-

64. On this see the account of what is taking place at New York Theological Seminary by Dale T. Irvin, "Open-Ended Pedagogy in a Multicultural Classroom: The Case for Theological Education," *Spotlight on Teaching* 4 (1) (1996): 3-4, 7. Also courses at other institutions, especially linking church, seminary, and city, noted in W. Dennis, K. Day, and R. Peters, "Urban Theological Education: A Conversation about Curriculum," *Theological Education* 34 (1) (1997): 46.

tional model of teaching and learning is paramount. While there is a place for lengthier, more formal instruction, it is ultimately secondary. Over the last twenty years there has been serious investigation into and evaluation of lectures in education. This suggests that while they have their place, they need to be kept in their place. They are only one way of contributing to others' learning, and should serve that wider process rather than dominate it. While lectures can have a personal stamp, cater to a wide range of needs, and have a practical cast, they are not always the most appropriate or effective form of communication. We can learn much here from the ways in which teaching takes place in the Bible, in the teaching of Jesus as much as elsewhere; and I have already set out how varied, circumstantial, and creative this was. In the area of teaching, "all things are ours" (1 Cor 3:21), and we should have no hesitation in drawing on any one of the multiple ways we can use — plenary discussion, small groups, informed panels, formal debate, one-on-one tutorials, field trips, journaling exercises, simulations, video or film, and others. While teaching larger numbers partly restricts our options here, it by no means abolishes them.[65]

In particular we need to reclaim the role of conversation in this whole process. There is certainly biblical and historical precedent. For example, we often find Jesus talking with his disciples as they ate a meal together or journeyed from place to place. Sometimes it is outsiders who generate a discussion between them (e.g., Matt 19:1-12), sometimes one or more of the disciples (e.g., Matt 20:20-27), sometimes Jesus himself (e.g., Matt 16:13-28). On the road to Emmaus, after his death, Jesus converses with two "disciples" about the meaning of the events of the past week and opens the scriptures to them (Luke 24:13-32). Paul also trained people such as Timothy, Titus, Aquila, and Priscilla for missionary service largely through working and talking with them on his various journeys. This pattern continued alongside more structured discussion in the teaching of Clement of Alexandria. Augustine emphasizes the importance of conversation not only

65. On the value, proper use, and limits of lectures see Donald A. Bligh, *What's the Use of Lectures?* (Harmondsworth, Middlesex: Penguin, 1974); Alasdair MacIntyre, "Reconceiving the University as an Institution and the Lecture as a Genre," in *Three Rival Versions of Moral Enquiry: Encyclopedia, Genealogy and Tradition* (Notre Dame: University of Notre Dame Press, 1990), pp. 216-36, and Erving Goffmann, "The Lecture," in *Forms of Talk* (Philadelphia: University of Pennsylvania Press, 1981), pp. 162-95.

for nurturing Christians but for community effective education.[66] Martin Luther's collected "Table Talk" shows how he supplemented his formal lectures with conversations over meals about ethical and theological matters. This was also part of the life of the underground seminary Dietrich Bonhoeffer set up during World War II. The role of conversation is now coming back into discussion — as a metaphor for interaction with and writing of texts, a function distinguishable from debate, polemic, chatter, or gossip. Conversation in this sense is a model and metaphor for dealing inclusively with theological diversity, and a concrete way of doing ministry and theological education.[67]

The more theological education opens itself up to flexible approaches to learning and participatory discourse such as conversation, the more it develops what we might term a "charismatic" dimension. This does not mean that it has to become predominantly situational and ex tempore. It should, in the broader sense, be an exercise in contextualizing the truth, and it should always have room for the unexpected to occur. But it does not at all exclude the importance of bodies of knowledge or thoughtful planning or structuring of the learning experience. A lively view of the Spirit, one that is appreciative of both content and tradition as well as creativity and versatility, should undergird any such pedagogical approach. This is precisely what informs Paul's profound approach to edification in 1 Corinthians 12–14. Indeed, as noted earlier, a missional model stresses the importance of the upbuilding and practice-forming nature of all genuine theological education.

66. There is an extended discussion of the role conversation played in Augustine's approach to teaching in G. Howie, *Educational Theory and Practice in St. Augustine* (London: Routledge and Kegan Paul, 1969), pp. 163-79.

67. See respectively David Tracy, *The Analogical Imagination: Christian Thought and the Culture of Pluralism* (New York: Crossroad, 1981), who is followed here by Rebecca Chopp, *Saving Work: Feminist Practices of Theological Education* (Louisville: Westminster/John Knox, 1995), p. 108; Philip S. Keane and Melanie A. May, "What Is the Character of Teaching, Learning, and the Scholarly Task in the Good Theological School?" *Theological Education* 30 (2) (1994): 42-43; and Robert Banks, "Conversation," in Robert Banks and R. Paul Stevens, eds., *The Complete Handbook of Everyday Christianity* (Downers Grove: InterVarsity Press, 1998), pp. 231-35.

# Conclusion

In concluding this section, I wish to look at some past approaches to theological education to see if they can suggest any practical possibilities that will move it in a more holistic, missional direction. In other words, do they contain any practices that we might be able to reclaim and refurbish for own time and place?

In the early centuries, changes were partly a function of more general shifts in church and mission. From the middle of the second to the fifth century, there was an increasing focus on the internal affairs of the church at the expense of mission, with the result that "the praxis of the Spirit became subordinate to the ecclesial office and teaching."[68] As we have seen, the first organized efforts in theological education focused attention on the intellectual and moral formation of students rather than on "active service" instruction and learning. Yet insofar as seekers were sometimes present, these schools involved some hands-on apologetic work. Also, they did not operate by means of a fixed curriculum based on lectures but on a dynamic life-based dialogue between teacher and students. They were schools for training in virtue of the "whole person," where the teacher was a model as well as instructor. It was here that the idea of

68. Ray S. Anderson, *Ministry on the Fireline: Revisioning the Church's Life and Mission* (Downers Grove: InterVarsity Press, 1993), p. 200. Compare also on this E. Brunner, *The Misunderstanding of the Church* (London: Lutterworth, 1952), pp. 84ff.

182

imitation as well as spiritual formation first became central in theological education.[69]

This model remained in force until the Middle Ages when, through figures like Thomas Aquinas, it began to include a more discursive analysis, comparison, and synthesis of beliefs. At this stage theological education became university education, and though this prepared people for various professions, all the education that took place was essentially theological. Though the formation of character and wisdom was still paramount, education was now directed to nurturing leadership for a broader range of important institutions in society.[70] Efforts at the renewal of training for ministry by Protestants during the Reformation preserved much of this, but gave it a more biblical base and a more everyday cast. Though subsequent doctrinal conflicts among Protestants themselves, as well as between Protestants and Catholics, resulted in more emphasis being placed on the content of right belief, among Protestants the study of doctrine was primarily to produce preachers and teachers who could build up the Christian community; and for Catholics, the earliest seminaries were primarily to train priests for overseas mission. Meanwhile, influential Puritans in England argued strongly for the formational and pastoral orientation of theological study. Though early Protestant colleges in North America maintained this emphasis, as well as the preparation of leaders for other institutions in society, there was an increasing preoccupation with students' learning right doctrine.[71] In the initial separation of theological education into seminaries, as at

69. See the illuminating article by Robert L. Wilken, "Alexandria: A School for Training in Virtue," in Patrick Henry, ed., *Schools of Thought in the Christian Tradition* (Philadelphia: Fortress, 1984), pp. 15-30.

70. See further E. Farley, "Theology and Practice Outside the Clerical Paradigm," in Don S. Browning, ed., *Practical Theology: The Emerging Field in Theology, Church and World* (San Francisco: Harper & Row, 1983), pp. 21-41, though in what follows I modify his account to place in sharper relief the focus on right belief, or the content of faith, in post-Reformation theological education.

71. For the situation in the earlier Colonial period, see further Melvin B. Endy, Jr., "Theology and Learning in Early America," in *Schools of Thought in the Christian Tradition*, pp. 125-41; James W. Fraser, *Schooling the Preachers: The Development of Protestant Theological Education in the United States, 1740-1875* (Lanham, Md.: University Press of America, 1988); Glenn T. Miller, *Piety and Intellect: The Aims and Purposes of Ante-bellum Theological Education* (Atlanta: Scholars Press, 1990).

Andover Newton and Princeton, for example, there was a strong missionary orientation. During the following century, however, this increasingly took on a more exclusively academic, and later professionalized, character.

These variations in theological education down through the centuries suggest the adoption of some interim measures where there is a desire to revitalize dormant or marginal aspects of the missional model. Drawing on what took place in the early "schools" in Alexandria there is the possibility of:

- utilizing some learners' ignorance of the Christian tradition to demonstrate in class how to apply the tradition to people who are typical of so many churchgoers,
- focusing in class on students' own doubts and uncertainties about the faith, and showing how apologetics and theology can overcome these,
- giving time in a class for issues of spirituality, community, or vocation — with respect to the actual questions, practices, situations, and longings of its members.

Drawing on the way in which theological education took place in some Reformation or early Colonial settings there is the possibility of:

- meeting over meals with learners for "table-talk" about anything they wish to discuss, including course content, practical application, and spiritual life,
- taking one or two students into your local church or on speaking engagements so they can see how you translate your ideas into action,
- inviting one or more such people to live in your home to see how you live out the things you teach.

While these interim steps are being taken, some faculty could have more exposure to certain ministry or mission situations. Although there is a definite place in a seminary for people whose primary orientation is academic, such people could also direct their efforts towards an intellectual mission to the wider academy or culture. For the remainder, alongside the internal "half-way houses" I have mentioned, we need external "way-stations" that could help faculty gain greater

184

ministry or mission experience. This is already happening in some places as faculty are temporarily freed from their regular duties in order to immerse themselves in some mission context.

Drawing on his own experience, R. Paul Stevens suggests ways in which faculty could develop their skills as reflective practitioners by:[72]

- becoming part of a pastoral or ministry team in a local church,
- working on a practical project with a parachurch organization,
- living for a time among the poor, marginal, or disadvantaged in one's own city,
- teaching as well as researching in a Third World college,
- becoming a Christian consultant to a business or other market-place institution.

From my own experience, or that of others I know, we could expand this list to include:

- working with a community-oriented group in an urban setting,
- helping to plant and nurture a church in a new area or among a new population group,
- joining a mission team or order in a cross-cultural setting,
- acting as a consultant to a particular vocational or occupational group,
- taking a team of students into a Third-World setting to gain experience and undertake ministry.

In the long term, there is need for more than an immersion or short-term experience of mission. This has most force when it is an enduring and integral dimension of a person's teaching, and is valued and regarded by their institution as much as research — indeed, when it is demanded as part of their *intellectual* contribution. Such involvement broadens and deepens our understanding of our culture, raises issues that require serious reflection, and forces us to find new resources from the Christian tradition. It should also become an essential part of theological institutions' wider *social* and *cultural* mission. As R. Paul Stevens points out: "For systematic integration of academy, marketplace, and congregations to take place in Western institutions, the fac-

72. R. Paul Stevens, "Marketing the Faith — A Reflection on the Importing and Exporting of Theological Education," *Crux* 28 (2) (1992): 15.

ulty must lead the way by experiencing that integration within themselves individually and among themselves communally."[73]

For all this to happen, relationships between faculty must become less purely professional and more based on friendship. According to Mark Schwehn, academic vocation flourishes best when educational institutions "become communities where the pleasures of friendship and the rigors of work are united."[74] Augustine was a great exemplar of this; he nurtured intellectual and social friendship, and wrote eloquently of its delights.[75] Without this, academic life tends to become primarily a professional affair, and the possibility of vital intellectual and educational growth is genuinely circumscribed. All this underlines the importance of drawing in new faculty who can most enter into and forward these kinds of relationships. It is probably also through new faculty that we can best address the fragmentation in theological education. We must look for faculty ". . . who, regardless of their discipline, are able to think theologically, and to think of their own disciplines within a larger theological frame. Faculty of this kind are uncommon."[76] Indeed, recruiting the right kind of faculty is probably the most important contribution we can make at present to the future renewal of seminaries.[77] As James Burtchaell comments: "If formation for the student is most important when he or she is actually in our harness, then it's important for us to realize that formation will probably take place only when the right people come into our company."[78] Of course, even this is not enough. Unless the structures in theological institutions can remold themselves around the approach to theological education such faculty bring with them, we will still not see a missional model coming to fruition. It is the kinds of changes required in those structures, as well as in the culture and curriculum of such institutions, that will be discussed in the next part of this investigation.

73. R. Paul Stevens, "Marketing the Faith," p. 15.

74. Mark R. Schwehn, *Exiles from Eden,* p. 61.

75. See further Peter Brown, *Augustine of Hippo: A Biography* (London: Faber & Faber, 1969), p. 61.

76. David F. Wells, "Educating for a Countercultural Spirituality," in D. G. Hart and R. A. Mohler, eds., *The Future of Evangelical Theological Education* (Grand Rapids: Baker, 1997), pp. 297-98.

77. James Gustafson, "Priorities in Theological Education," *Theological Education* 23, Supplement (1987): 67.

78. James T. Burtchaell in *Theological Education and Moral Formation,* p. 220.

PART FOUR

# BRINGING ABOUT
# SYSTEMIC CHANGE:
# SOME GUIDEPOSTS TO REFORM

Crucial here is the issue of power, for whoever has this or is willing to distribute it among the various stakeholders in theological education, will largely determine the fate of any of the proposals in the debate, at least within existing theological institutions. The crucial question here is not so much: "What should theological education be?" as "Who determines what theological education should be?"

LYNN N. RHODES AND NANCY D. RICHARDSON[1]

1. Lynn N. Rhodes and Nancy D. Richardson, *Mending Severed Connections: Theological Education for Communal Transformation* (San Francisco: San Francisco Network Ministries, 1991), p. 43.

# 1. Reconfiguring the Student Profile

It is not easy to broaden the discussion of changes needed in seminaries beyond those related to teaching. This involves covering the whole constituency, culture, and curriculum, as well as the wider world of academy and the church with which they are so intimately related. The problem is partly due to the diversity between, and partly to the diversity within, theological schools. I hardly need give examples. Groups of faculty or students may have different views on theological education. Parts of the curriculum may embody approaches that are at odds with others. Various aspects of corporate life may send mixed or different signals. The traditions or even mission statement of a school may be in tension with its present self-understanding or practice. The presence of this diversity within and between seminaries makes it difficult to develop concrete proposals that are generally applicable to individual institutions. As Francis Schussler Fiorenza has reminded us, many of the problems that surface in the debate over the aims and purposes of theological education "arise from the particular tasks, specific constituencies, [and] specific institutional settings of theological education."[2]

Mindful of this, I would still like to suggest some practical steps for consideration. These have the character of concrete *possibilities* for some institutions more than others, *general kinds* of things that may be considered by various institutions, or *thought experiments* that may

2. Francis Schüssler Fiorenza, "Thinking Theologically About Theological Education," *Theological Education* 24, Supplement 2 (1988): 111.

prompt those for whom they are not relevant to further reflection. While in most cases implementing such suggestions would not be easy, all are ultimately operational. If some of them create difficult challenges, we should not forget the role of vision that has already come up within the debate. If some of them sound impractical, we should remember Jacques Ellul's insistence that it is the seemingly "impossible" rather than the merely "calculable," that alone contains hope for the future.

With regard to offering practical guideposts for action, at present the debate seems midway between diagnosis and prescription. To move it forward we need not only more conceptual breakthroughs but more concrete recommendations that open up our options. Contributors to the debate have already suggested and tested some possibilities. Others are still in the probationary stage. It is important here to look not only at what is happening on the edges of mainstream theological education, whether in seminaries, Bible institutes, or lay programs, but also at what is happening outside seminaries altogether on the margins of Christian experiment. That is the place from which most innovative change comes. The future, as someone I know often says, is already on the margins. I begin, however, closer to the center, by looking at the challenges raised by the kinds of students involved in theological education today, especially at how a missional model of theological education would help address these. Then we consider the organizational cultures of theological institutions, professional guilds, and the wider church, asking what changes need to take place if seminaries are to move in a more missional direction. Finally we focus on what often comes first in such discussion, namely, curriculum reform, at the graduate and postgraduate level, evaluating how this new model would handle some of the key issues around which the present debate has revolved.

As one contributor has recently pointed out: "The recent works on theological education largely ignore the dramatic change in the student body of theological education."[3] In the discussion up to this point, I have sought to avoid that mistake. But here it is pertinent to look more closely at the changing student profiles, and see what challenges they raise and what contribution they could make to a missional approach. While theological institutions do not all operate

---

3. Rebecca Chopp, *Saving Work: Feminist Practices of Theological Education* (Louisville: Westminster/John Knox, 1995), p. 12.

with the same criteria in recruiting or accepting students, they do have much in common. Few students are rejected, and when this happens it is generally on academic, occasionally psychological, grounds. With the exception of some smaller places, with a strong devotional and communal ethos, most theological institutions have an open-door policy. There are many reasons for this, chiefly the cost of running theological institutions and the desire to be as inclusive as possible. Consequently, there is a greater range of people in these at present than at any point in their history. Increasing equality for women, greater pluralism in society, and higher levels of education among minorities have all affected this. The kinds of diversity fall into three main types.

## A. Differences in the Students' Maturity and Experience

Students in theological institutions possess varying degrees of personal, intellectual, or vocational maturity. An increasing number come from unstable or broken homes, and bring many unresolved issues into their theological training. While God can certainly transform such experiences, today more students struggle with identity issues than in the past, and become distracted by all that is involved in this. Students' marriages are also under greater tension today than in the past, and more couples break up during their time in theological institutions, especially seminaries. Greater time and financial pressures certainly contribute to this. A further problem is that more incoming students these days are "burned out" as a consequence of trying to meet too many unrealistic demands and expectations in their previous position.

In addition, as already noted, many students know little about their Christian tradition. According to Edward Farley, who is thinking primarily of seminaries and divinity schools:

> almost no theological school can presuppose anything about an admitted student's educational background except the bare fact of the B.A. degree. . . . Except for the ability to read English and write sentences, the school cannot with confidence suppose any specific body of knowledge or skill. It cannot assume or build on a classical education, any specific language, European history, philosophy, psychology or sociology. . . . Most students will have a smattering (introductory course-level) of most of these things, but not enough

to serve as a base for further education. . . . In short, there is some question as to whether seminary-level work can presuppose the liberal arts education which theological studies have always required.[4]

Also, for whatever reason, theological schools are attracting less of the intellectually gifted, though the growing number of mid-life people entering them does bring people with greater life experience.

While these older students have often had more ministry involvement, students now mostly have a wider range of vocational choices before them. Though some begin formal theological education with a clear idea of what they wish to do, others come with little sense of direction. The proportion of students on the pastoral track, looking towards ordination, may be as few as one-third of the total body. A growing number of lay persons are attending seminaries, some heading towards church or parachurch work, others wishing to remain in the marketplace. Some surveys indicate that around two-fifths or more of those initially on the pastoral track ultimately end up in the same position. Other students come into such schools to sort themselves out spiritually, to deepen their new-found faith, or even to engage in a search for God.

How does the model I am proposing deal with this complex situation? Positively, I would suggest, despite what might at first sight appear to be the case. The reason for this is in part straightforward and in part paradoxical. Straightforward in that such people bring with them genuine strengths as well as weaknesses, and paradoxical in that it is out of weakness that the greatest strength comes.

1. When we consider the disciples that Jesus called around him, the presence of *weakness* is not a decisive factor. The disciples had weaknesses enough: their in-fighting and jostling for status, their lack of spiritual or staying power in certain situations, and their endemic lack of understanding. Paul, too, had people around him, such as Mark and Demas, who either did not rise to the occasion at the crucial moment or could not resist the attractions of a less demanding life. While people may struggle with different weaknesses today and are perhaps more dysfunctional than in earlier times, it is accepting Jesus'

---

4. Edward Farley, *Theologia: The Fragmentation and Unity of Theological Education* (Philadelphia: Fortress, 1983), pp. 14-15.

call and its consequences that is the issue, not the presence or absence of certain weaknesses. In any case, as we see with Peter, a person's gravest weakness is generally only the reverse of their actual or potential strength. Though, as in Acts 6:1-4, these are sometimes a handicap to learning or prevent important things happening, they are the very metal from which people's most positive contribution is forged.

It is precisely the church- or work-based experience of life and ministry that such people bring with them as a *strength* into their theological training. This gives them a decided advantage over the previous generation of students who were predominantly young, mostly unmarried, and often came straight from college. This does not put a person in a strong position to become part of the inner core around a teacher engaged in active ministry. It is clear among Paul's group that, however young one or two of his colleagues may have been, they already possessed significant ministry experience, enough to receive a commendation from their church of origin (Acts 16:1-3). This was necessary for those who formed the inner circle of a key role model's constituency. But, apart from faithfulness in their family, workplace, and community, there was no such expectation for those in the outer circle. We could anticipate something between these two for those who made up what I called earlier the intermediate ring of learner-doers around a teacher. Since that is often precisely the position of many people enrolling in extension courses, once again the missional model seems quite at home in this situation.

2. At first sight, the additional demands of a missional approach might seem to exacerbate the problems raised by many students' *weaknesses*. Let me answer this by first backing up a little. Such students might well benefit from belonging to a recovery group outside the institution. Members of such groups help each other towards greater wholeness without the benefit of expert help, simply by sharing their weaknesses and struggles to overcome them. This demonstrates what Paul himself discovered, and Jesus exhibited on the cross: that it is in and through human weakness that God's strength is displayed (2 Cor 12:10; 1 Cor 1:23-25). As well as the personal benefits this brings, it develops students' capacity to minister to others as a fellow struggler rather than as an expert. They can also read off from this whole experience a great deal about the capacity of ordinary people to deal with and grow through significant problems. If we assist learners to see this as an example of what lay ministry can achieve, and as a

parable of how the church can operate, they have received greater theological insight into and a deeper vision of the church than most people do in their entire theological education.

The reverse side of all this is once again obvious: the *strength* such people bring into their formal theological training because of their greater life and ministry experience. The reigning models of theological education, and some proposals to reform it, do not build on this strength. We need to encourage more participatory approaches to learning, in which students become more like junior partners in the learning-doing enterprise, rather than just pupils. While they will continue to look to teachers for the "big picture," for knowledge and experience in particular areas, and as personal and vocational models of learning in action, they learn more when they are able to discuss and help shape what they are studying, when they process what they are learning in small groups, and when their learning interacts with their home, work, and neighborhood involvements.[5] Along with leading their group into deeper understanding, teachers become more like theological consultants and educational facilitators. As a result, those around them move beyond an unhealthy dependence on experts and individualistic approaches to learning, and learn to integrate their knowledge more fully with the rest of their lives. While all the contemporary proposals move partially in this direction, and the feminist theologians come closest to it, a missional model opens up a more comprehensive and profound way for this to happen.

What would all this mean for admission to theological institutions, and does it have anything to say about our present policy of making academic ability the major consideration? It means that where learners suffer from a real pathology rather than just dysfunction, or where they lack sufficient ministry experience in the church or world, they should begin in the outer circle of theological education before going further. Where they are lacking academically but in other respects seem satisfactory, they should have a trial run to see how they manage. But we also need to consider the possibility of providing varied — or appropriate — levels of theological education, depending on

5. R. H. Cram and S. P. Saunders, "Feet Partly of Iron and Partly of Clay: Pedagogy and the Curriculum in Theological Education," *Theological Education* 28 (2) (1992): 28-32. On different kinds of expectations a diverse student body brings to theological education, see Lyle E. Shaller, *Confessions of a Contrarian: Second Thoughts on the Pastoral Ministry* (Nashville: Abingdon, 1989), pp. 174-76.

the people and contexts in which they will be working. With so many graduates in the general population, focusing on this group does seem sensible; but in some contexts they are not always the most appropriate people, and God does not only call graduates to undertake a particular ministry. One difficulty here is the ongoing assumption that the goal is generally pastoral work in a congregation, whereas there are all kinds of other ministries available that do not require, indeed may even benefit from not having, a "learned" minister in the academic sense. Besides legitimizing *concentric levels* of theological education, we must also make room for a range of *educational levels,* from pre-undergraduate to postgraduate, each with its own integrity.

## B. Variety in the Kinds and Vocations of Students

Alongside these differences there is considerable variety in the kinds of students undertaking theological education and the directions in which they are heading. This variety tends to increase in relation to an institution's size and inclusiveness. Think of a grid consisting of six items both down and across. The items designate students' age, ethnic group, class, nationality, theological tradition, and ministry experience. We could add a further three items where there would be some variety: namely, gender, primary language, and politics. Though in certain settings some combinations would appear more frequently than others, the range of possibilities is enormous. This makes the group around Jesus — and even the sexually, socially, racially mixed group around Paul — look relatively homogeneous. The problems of teaching a group containing such a wide range of people are considerable. Of course, in some respects we could do with even more variety. While the proportion of female and ethnic candidates continues to rise, overall they are still underrepresented among students and faculty. One advantage of this situation is that it provides a ready-made opportunity for seminaries and their members to learn the difficult art of doing justice through affirmative action. Because of their greater diversity, seminaries have a better chance than most congregations for setting new standards of inclusiveness, modeling — as Paul's "mobile seminary" did — a radical unity across gender, class, and race lines.

Among students there is also a wide range of vocational directions. Some of this stems from external factors. In rural areas, full-time

195

appointments in churches are increasingly giving way to part-time ones. In some cases, lay pastors act in a volunteer ministry capacity while employed full-time in some occupation. In these and other settings, the ministry of all God's people is increasingly coming to the fore.[6] In any case, those students who unexpectedly end up in the marketplace rather than the church require practical theological equipping to minister in that setting. Apart from these external factors, for personal reasons students now consider a wider range of vocational possibilities. These include lay pastoring, counseling, family life education, coordinating lay ministry; joining a parachurch, ecumenical, or Christian organization; working as a psychologist, community worker, overseas "tent-maker"; or becoming a marketplace Christian. How can theological education do justice to so much vocational diversity?

What does a missional model have to offer here that is not already available in other proposals?

1. Meeting together in small groups around a common bond or interest is one way of meeting the challenge of a diverse student body. These might gather around common gender, ethnic, and national links; spiritual, theological, and denominational traditions; or peace, social justice, and mission concerns. Such groups enable students to articulate, analyze, celebrate, and work through some of their shared issues. This is good as far as it goes, but we also need more heterogeneous groups, in which people learn from, provide a challenge to, and deeply influence one another. These could take the form of long-term formational groups, basic communities, or community houses. These would provide the opportunity of experiencing aspects of the more holistic theological education that a missional model takes seriously. Unless it serves only one constituency, one of the major contributions of any theological institution is the way it can bring people together from different "tribes" so that they can begin to overcome the barriers that separate them from one another and develop the relationships that will enrich them. In my previous seminary, the opportunity students have of mixing with people from around seventy-five countries is consistently rated by students as the main benefit of their time there.

---

6. J. Borgeson and L. Wilson, eds., *Reshaping Ministry: Essays in Memory of Wesley Frensdorff* (Arvada, Colo.: Jethro Publications, 1990), pp. 223-24. In some seminaries now, the number of lay people studying for various purposes is actually greater than those people who are moving towards ordination.

2. Drawing students into active mission in groups with a faculty person only heightens the degree of learning, challenging, and shaping that goes on among a diverse student body. The forming of mission groups with a diverse membership, living together as well as engaging in a common enterprise, takes this a step further. What devotional, support, and study groups all have in common is a concern for various kinds of personal development. Mission groups are other-directed, yet at the same time they bring indirect personal benefits. Operative here is the gospel principle of finding ourselves through setting aside our own interests. Those who band together in the work of the kingdom will also grow individually and jointly. As they undertake active mission, other issues connected with diversity will begin to fall into place. Members can begin to test out their understanding of their vocation and receive feedback on their performance. This will help them more than any personality or vocational test, or any inventory of spiritual gifts and abilities, however helpful these may be. The whole group will also develop a greater appreciation of the need for diverse team ministry, thus overcoming the tendency towards individual or homogeneous leadership.

## C. Some Additional Comments

Within institutions of theological education, the number of denominations represented continues to grow. When I was in seminary more than thirty years ago, we were almost all attached to the same denomination and had only three approaches to spirituality available to us — evangelical, holiness, or Anglo-Catholic. These days, even in denominational seminaries, students come from a wider range of church backgrounds. For example, at Fuller Seminary, students come from more than 125 denominations, Presbyterians and nondenominationals forming the two largest groups. Newer forms of church life — megachurches, community churches, and house churches — often exhibit a postdenominational identity. This range of church allegiances raises many questions, not only for teaching polity courses but for engaging in corporate worship.

The range of student-church allegiances poses a particular challenge for corporate worship in settings where formal theological education takes place. The larger and more ecumenical or interdenominational the institution, the greater the challenge. How does an institution tackle this, and in what ways might a missional model help? In the area of corporate worship, we need to develop more creative and inclusive forms of service that draw on a variety of ecclesiastical traditions and develop new ones that encompass as many people as possible. One could also imagine other types of special events, such as a day-long or weekend-long festival of spirituality, involving students from a wide range of spiritual backgrounds, and regular retreats where students might forge disparate approaches to spirituality into a new whole. To prepare the way for what faculty and students might do by way of mission, retreats could take place in urban or suburban contexts where mission is happening. The spontaneous celebration of God and one another as the group engages in missional work generates new ways in which corporate worship can express unity-in-diversity. Designing corporate worship to make it as inclusive as possible is one challenge; what can happen as a by-product of joint service for the kingdom is quite another. This is precisely the setting in which God delights to bring something new into being.

These are some of the challenges that await us. At stake is nothing less than the development of a genuinely ecumenical or pluralistic, perhaps genuinely postmodern, corporate worship that has its roots deep in biblical wells but encompasses all that is valuable in the different expressions of Christian commitment. All such gatherings will exhibit both the profound diversity and unity of the Spirit. Ultimately, the answer to the problem posed to corporate worship in theological institutions by an increasingly diverse student body and pluralistic environment lies in a sufficiently broad vision and experience of the Holy Spirit. This will come to full expression only if it includes the possibility of actively working and learning in missional ways.

# 2. Rethinking Personal and Communal Formation

## A. The Role of Personal Formation

In what follows, I use the word *personal* rather than *spiritual* in talking about formation to avoid giving the impression that this is not an aspect of academic work and professional development. Both the content and discipline of study involve spiritual formation, as do the challenges and demands of ministry. Indeed, I have been arguing that it is precisely undertaking mission alongside someone rather than simply imitating them in the abstract that provides the strongest stimulus to spiritual formation. In other words, spiritual formation is as much a dimension of every aspect of theological education as a specific focus of concern. As a concern in its own right, it has already come before us in discussing the nature and contribution of both teachers and learners to theological education. But there is still more to be said about how theological institutions can enhance the personal as well as academic and vocational development of those who attend them.

There are at least two important issues here. First, nowadays there is a broader range of models of spirituality available to students than in previous generations. Alongside older evangelical, holiness, mainline, and Catholic approaches, during the last generation three developments have taken place: (i) traditional forms of spirituality, for example, Catholic, have been renovated and taken up by others; (ii) newer forms of spirituality, for example, charismatic and that associated with radical discipleship, have grown out of older ones and had a wide impact;

(iii) previously marginal forms of spirituality, for example, Quaker and Celtic, have become more mainstream; (iv) elements of non-Christian forms of spirituality, for example, from eastern religions or New Age philosophies, have been adopted by some Christians. This plethora of spiritualities, some of which exist in several forms, has had two contrary effects. On the one hand, charismatic and Catholic spiritualities have had a wide influence and created some common ground for people from different spiritual traditions. On the other, the combined effect of these varieties of spirituality has increased the difficulty of various sized groups to find sufficient common ground.

Second, as the 1992 survey of seminaries quoted earlier indicated, in those institutions less than 40 percent of students felt that their experience helped them grow spiritually. For some, as a mature, older graduate said to me once, "My time in seminary was, spiritually speaking, the driest time in my life." Even when making allowances for the fact that — like Jesus' sojourn in the wilderness or Paul's stay in Arabia before they launched into their particular ministry — time in seminary often involves severe spiritual testing, the figure mentioned is still a cause for serious concern.[7] Although seminaries in particular are increasingly giving more attention to personal formation, too much that happens there is still reactive rather than proactive, piecemeal rather than coordinated, marginal rather than central. Although it is one of the three major goals of training for ministry, personal formation continues to have a lower priority than academic excellence and professional development. This is true even in the new standards for its member institutions being developed by the Association of Theological Schools. Many faculty continue to feel inadequate in this area, sometimes because of time pressures, sometimes because they lack ability, and sometimes because they are not convinced it is their institution's responsibility. Moreover, though students increasingly call for spirituality to have a higher profile in seminaries, they are often juggling too many commitments — to church, job, and family as well as seminary — to make it a priority. More likely than not, they are trying to get through their programs as quickly and inexpensively as possible, and are often burdened with other Christian involvements.

7. See also the survey contained in the recently published book by V. S. Cetuk, *What to Expect from Seminary: Theological Education as Spiritual Formation* (Nashville: Abingdon, 1998).

Apart from suggestions made in connection with particular aspects of personal formation, can we say any more about this — not so much about implementing specific programs in spirituality as about wider factors affecting and encouraging it? Personal formation does not develop primarily through specific programs, or even through regular chapel worship; it takes place mostly as a result of the leavening effect of the personal example of teachers and other key figures (including chief administrators and student leaders), with the broader culture and mission of the seminary, and with a whole range of co-curricular groups and available activities. Curricular offerings and programs in personal formation have a role to play in this. But they will be most effective when they allow participants to engage in formative practices as well as learn about them.

The differences between institutions of theological education make any fixed recommendations problematic, and the following should be seen as part of a general approach to spiritual formation. According to Walter Liefeld and Linda Cannell this is what seminaries particularly need to do:

- Determine the existing need from a biblical perspective on spirituality, a realistic assessment of the student body, and the outcomes expected from their education.
- Distill from the above what kinds of personal formation will most enhance students' experience.
- Construct a map to visualize the kinds of learning and experience that will facilitate personal growth, e.g., reading devotional classics, a sequence of scriptural study, various corporate experiences, and spiritual direction, together with an itinerary to chart routes to that end.
- Provide a spiritual orientation for incoming students that explains both the map and itinerary.
- Encourage faculty to determine what subjects in their courses most fruitfully stress personal formation.
- Create room for faculty and others to discuss together the implications of their being models of spiritual maturity, and include the latter in qualifications for appointments.
- Connect personal formation on every possible occasion, whether inside or outside curricular activities, with ethical behavior and social responsibility.

201

- Make available opportunities for corporate experiences so that students develop relational skills in this area.[8]

In his helpful book on a spirituality of education, Parker Palmer makes some general suggestions relating to the classroom. In contrast to those that do not feel the classroom is the proper setting for personal formation, Palmer suggests that what teachers need to do is:

- View the classroom as a context for creating a particular culture, a culture of teaching and learning that encourages personal as well as academic formation.
- Make the classroom a safe place that encourages the fullest participation of students in the learning process.
- Encourage the expression of feelings, doubts, and dilemmas as well as ideas relating to life and service.
- Allow our passion for and response to the truth to inform the way we teach and relate to students.
- Cultivate the possibility of students practicing obedience to the truth inside as well as outside the classroom.[9]

There are other ways in which personal formation can become a dimension of what goes on in the classroom. I am not thinking here primarily of having more or longer devotional introductions to classes, though drawing students into leading these will result in a greater diversity of approach. Also, at any point it is also proper to incorporate praise, song, testimony, or prayer (as, for example, Paul does in many parts of his writings) in what takes place in the classroom. There may be something unacademic about doing this, but there is certainly noth-

8. Walter L. Liefeld and Linda M. Cannell, "Spiritual Formation and Theological Education," in *Alive to God: Studies in Spirituality Presented to James Houston* (Downers Grove, Ill.: InterVarsity Press, 1992), pp. 259-60. See further the recommendations in V. S. Cetuk, *What to Expect in Seminary,* pp. 93-129. From a Catholic perspective see also Austin C. Doran, "The Integration of Theology and Spiritualities: A View from the Seminary," in P. W. Carey and E. C. Muller, eds., *Theological Education in the Catholic Tradition: Contemporary Challenges* (New York: Crossroad, 1997), pp. 308-19.

9. Parker J. Palmer explores these in the latter half of his book, *To Know As We Are Known: A Spirituality of Education* (San Francisco: Harper & Row, 1982). See also T. Smith, "Spiritual Formation in the Academy: A Unifying Model," *Theological Education* 33 (1) (1996): 88-89.

ing untheological! We can go further, not just by expanding the range of courses or developing a program focusing on personal formation, but by ensuring that it is a dimension of the most rigorous and systematic theological instruction or reflection. In even the most traditional disciplines not only can such instruction or reflection, rightly understood, contribute to someone's personal as well as intellectual formation, but there are ways of engaging in it that enhance the possibility of this happening. The writings of some of the great theologians, both past and present, contain fine models of this: witness Anselm's *Proslogium*, many of Luther's writings, Calvin's *Institutes* and commentaries, Kierkegaard's *Edifying Discourses* and other works, and Bonhoeffer's *Life Together* or *Letters and Papers from Prison*.

Adding more artistic or visual expressions of faith in the classroom would enhance this further. Too much personal formation has a predominantly cognitive or affective orientation. It does not draw sufficiently or profoundly enough on people's imaginative and creative abilities. Once again, this is not primarily a matter of introducing more courses or programs in the arts into the curriculum. There is a need for this, though for reasons of wider cultural understanding and creative ministry as well as personal formation. Whatever happens in this area should include folk and popular as well high culture, distinctions that in any case have become questionable. Like personal formation itself, the visual and artistic should be part of a whole range of subjects. The arts and popular culture should have a more integral role than the supplementary one they currently have. In all their forms — painting, sculpture, music, song, novel, drama, poetry, film, video, craft, dance — they should find expression within teaching and learning.[10]

All these suggestions about personal formation in the seminary, classroom atmosphere and culture, the teaching of traditional theological disciplines, and the role of the creative arts in pedagogy, are valuable in their own right. But their impact strengthens when they are form part of a missional model of theological education. This is easy enough to understand, for the practical challenges and opportunities associated with engaging in mission stretch both teachers and learners to the utmost of

10. On this issue see especially Wilson Yates, *The Arts in Theological Education: New Possibilities for Integration* (Atlanta: Scholars Press, 1987), and the edition of "Sacred Imagination: The Arts and Theological Education," *Theological Education* 31 (1) (1994).

their abilities. Here is the answer to a deficiency in other proposals for reform, providing new ways to help students grow — to help them move beyond the inclination to become more Christ-like and to realize it in practice. What we need is a more dynamic context for personal formation, a more vibrant interaction between teachers and learners, and a more urgent need to communicate the faith to others. Working together in mission makes a significant difference.

## B. The Scope for Community Building

From personal formation, we turn to the complementary but interdependent issue of *communal* formation. This is not only important in itself, and an important dimension of a missional approach to theological education, but imperative if the prime need in church and world today is for community builders.

A good starting point here is the work of James Poling and Donald Miller, which lays out the basis for a practical theology of ministry.[11] They suggest that though seminaries are not churches, they are undergirded by covenantal relationships and they possess ecclesial significance. This makes them more than a community of learning; they are not primarily an academy but a community of faith. Theological education rightly takes place within community, and to do this properly it must reflect on its own processes. In this respect the seminary is an analogue of the church in the world: its primary resource for study and reflection is the lives and relationships of its members; its secondary resource is its wider set of relationships with congregations and other institutions. This means that every part of its own institutional culture can have a communal dimension.

> Every class can become an enrichment of the formation of community. Biblical study, theology, and pastoral care have immediate relevance to all the people at hand. Worship, student affairs, and faculty selection have direct and fundamental impact upon the relationships within the community.[12]

11. James N. Poling and Donald E. Miller, *Foundations for a Practical Theology of Ministry* (Nashville: Abingdon, 1985), especially the closing chapter.
12. James N. Poling and Donald E. Miller, *Foundations for a Practical Theology of Ministry*, p. 150.

In this way, theory and practice become united, and a shared praxis develops. If a seminary's members learn to think theologically about their life together, they should be able to think concretely about community in the congregation, and so partially overcome the dichotomy between theory and practice about which their churches so often complain.

The dilution of community is one of the problems facing many theological institutions today, and this increasingly includes Bible colleges and schools of mission as well as seminaries. The increase in commuters on campus, in work and family obligations, and in general time pressures, have all taken their toll. Resisting these forces cannot take place unless there is an institutional as well as individual commitment to encouraging community. Ways of doing this include:

- reserving or reintroducing common lunch hours;
- creating convivial spaces where students, staff, faculty, and administrators can eat and relax together;
- building community in classes through discussion, small groups, and joint presentations;
- incorporating coffee times, even meals, into classes — or extending classes into them;
- cooperative development and evaluation of courses;
- faculty-student reflection and denominational groups;
- celebrating the history of the institution as well as key events in its life;
- marking the major Christian festivals of the church year in some corporate way.

Reminders of the significant role community has played in past forms of theological education can spur action along these lines. Augustine in his community, Luther in his house where students lived, and Bonhoeffer in his small underground seminary are prime examples of this at different points in the history of the church. Among those contributing to the current debate, it is feminist writers who have most to offer here. For example, the Cornwall Collective placed community high on its list of institutional values, and tested out more participatory forms of decision-making and leadership. Helpful structures and procedures included working with open agendas; rotating tasks and representative roles; distributing routine tasks as equally as possible;

agreeing on ground rules for communication; stressing accurate reporting of and open discussion of financial matters; diffusing information to all members; allocating tasks according to ability, interest, and responsibility; developing procedures for sorting out priorities and reaching consensus; assigning tasks to small teams and limited-term task forces; and encouraging individuals to develop new skills.[13]

In this general area, it is not only the dilution of community that is a problem. Given the many differences among students outlined in the last section — to which we can add their wide range of church allegiances — a further question arises: How can we build community among so diverse a constituency? In particular, how can we bring groups together who normally spend little time together or have little understanding of one another? Particularly important here is the role that small groups can play in theological institutions. We need more imagination and versatility in such groups as they seek to worship God together and have fellowship with one another. While, as mentioned above, there is a real place for relatively homogeneous groups made up of women or men, ethnic or racial groups, and people from particular nations or denominations, heterogeneous groups have unique things to offer. As each person contributes according to who they are, where they come from, what they believe, and how they function in Christ, like an orchestra made up of many different sounds — some in counterpoint or even discordant — a common melody emerges.

An ecclesial group creates the best opportunity for this. This is what Paul and his coworkers developed wherever they went, and to which they belonged whenever they were in the vicinity. A basic Christian community or house church does not allow an exclusive approach to membership. It is open to all who come, and it will seek to be as inclusive as possible, extending a welcome to children, the aged, and all those suffering from some disadvantage. Such a group also encourages its members to integrate their spirituality more fully with what goes on in the varied life-settings in which they find themselves — in the family, in off-campus employment, and in their neighborhoods. What develops out of this is a common life that is a unique blend of the form the Spirit is taking in each member, a composite spirituality that breaks down and overcomes the old walls of division. Sharing the

13. The Cornwall Collective, *Your Daughters Shall Prophesy: Feminist Alternatives in Theological Education* (New York: Pilgrim Press, 1980), pp. 58-64.

Lord's Supper regularly together models to such a group the inclusiveness of Christ, and provokes it to reproduce the same in its own life and outreach. We need more of these ecclesial groups on and off campus, cutting across faculty, staff, and student lines and including spouses and children.

One last area where the relational dimension of theological life is sometimes weak, is at the level of administrative structures and procedures. Since Christians do not have a substantial theology of institutions, this is a defect in most Christian organizations. As well as giving attention to this, there should be opportunities for staff and administrators to have common meals, jointly as well as separately, and to meet in small work-station or generic groups for discussion and prayer. This could include theological reflection on their work and work environment. There should also be opportunities for theologically qualified staff to become involved in mentoring students, or joining teachers and learners "on location" when they engage in some common ministry. Community will develop most vitally when faculty, students, and staff form such ministry teams and participate in the same ecclesial groups, whether on campus or off campus, or in communal living arrangements. Where this occurs, theological institutions will have more to share with congregations and neighborhoods on the matter of community. Indeed, it would position them to become directly involved in reinventing congregations so that they become vibrant centers of community in their neighborhoods.

# 3. Refashioning Key Institutional Cultures

Theological institutions have a complex organizational culture. It is a mosaic of traditions, values, practices, relationships, structures, and styles. Understanding the importance of this is not yet as strong as it is within the business community. One point at which there does tend to be more awareness in seminaries is the link between its own culture and that of the academy and the church. Though the nature of this link — and consequently of the degree of overlap or demarcation between them — is interpreted differently, every so often it does become a matter for discussion. Except in seminaries that place a strong reliance on maintaining a strong devotional and communal ethos — as in Orthodox, Catholic, and some Evangelical schools — there is less appreciation of the fact that reform only takes root if the organizational culture also undergoes change. Even less appreciated is the fact that change in seminaries can only take place if this is also happening in the cultures of the academy and church. As for Bible institutes, they tend to have a more suspicious, sometimes even negative, attitude towards the academy, but retain stronger connections with the church and with mission agencies. Lay centers, on the other hand, tend to view the academy more positively. But in all theological institutions, changes will not fully take place without change in the culture of all the interlocking institutions.

The prior question is: What is the proper "sphere" of theological institutions? We start with the seminary. Is it a dimension of the church? Is it a part of the academy? Is it an amalgam of both? Or is it, whatever elements it has in common with the others, a distinct entity in itself? This is not only a matter of identity or self-understanding. It is also a matter of accountability. Theological institutions have given various answers to this question. For example, divinity schools have mostly seen themselves as an extension of the academy, and regarded overt religious activities as a matter of individual preference or on the edge of their institutional concerns. On the other hand, Bible institutes have tended to see themselves as an expression of the church, as communities of spiritual formation, corporate worship, and Christian witness, within which learning takes place. Missionary colleges have also generally seen themselves as an arm of particular denominations. Seminaries have varied in their approach, often depending on how much there has been a struggle for control of their affairs by denominational bodies, and how much they have understood their mission to include influencing the wider world of scholarship. Mostly they have made more of their connection with the church. Influential here was H. Richard Niebuhr's view that the seminary was the intellectual dimension, the center or form of the church's life.[14] In the debate, the one who has given most space to the issue is David Kelsey, who describes the seminary less as a dimension of the church than as a church agency responsible for helping its members grow in true knowledge of God.[15] On the other hand, Richard Mouw has tended to emphasize the connection of the seminary with the academy.[16]

In part this debate misses the point. It is right in considering whether elements of the academy or the church are present in the seminary or other theological institutions, but wrong to assume that these are the only two categories relevant to it. The proper role of a seminary is not reducible to that of an academy, or church, or some combi-

---

14. H. Richard Niebuhr, *The Purpose of the Church and Its Ministry: Reflections on the Aims of Theological Education* (New York: Harper, 1956), pp. 23, 107-8, and, with Daniel D. Williams and James H. Gustafson, *The Advancement of Theological Education* (New York: Harper, 1957), p. 174.

15. David Kelsey, *To Understand God Truly: What's Theological about a Theological School?* (Louisville: Westminster/John Knox, 1992), pp. 55f.

16. Richard Mouw discusses this issue in a paper (presented at a Consultation on the Aims and Purposes of Theological Education at Fuller Theological Seminary, Pasadena) titled, "Seminary and Church: Probings of a Reformed Evangelical," whose findings are shortly to be published. Divinity schools in general tend to view themselves as being more connected to the academy than to the church.

nation of the two. It is not a manifestation or agency of either, but comes under another sphere.

To use a biblical analogy, the work of groups such as the prophetic bands, Jesus and the disciples, or Paul and his colleagues was not primarily intellectual or ecclesial. Certainly Paul spoke in such academic contexts as Mars Hill and the School of Tyrannus, and there was a decidedly intellectual dimension to his activities. Just as certainly, Paul often taught in, and operated in close collaboration with, the churches he founded. But his work was neither a religious parallel to what happened in the philosophical schools nor an academic subsidiary of what was taking place in the churches. It shared something with the first and arose out of the life of the second: it engaged in public debate with the first and regularly gave account of its doings to the second. But it was a separate operation, engaged in activities that overlapped with, rather than were imitative of, the academies; and these activities were interdependent with, rather than dependent on, the churches.

Its proper sphere, as we have already seen, was mission, not primarily education on the one hand or fellowship on the other, even though it contained strong elements of both. In an analogous way, the seminary turns itself into an academy, often but not only in the classroom, and at times it turns itself into a church, certainly but not only in the chapel. Therefore it should be no more ashamed of saying it has an ecclesial dimension than of saying it has an academic one, and vice versa. We can rightly speak of any institution for formal theological education as containing some academic element and as a parachurch nonprofit organization, but neither term nor the combining of these terms fully comprehends its character. It is more than either and more than both. Therefore institutions of theological education must be able to develop their own distinctive culture. This will vary according to the kind of theological institution in view, and neither the academy nor the church should expect them to simply reflect their own priorities and activities. Because of the overlap with these other two organizations, and the way a seminary shapes those who teach and learn within it — and the tangible connections among such people and the academy and the church — it can only completely fulfill its role if these institutions are operating in their own spheres in the way they should. I will now look more closely at each of these spheres in turn.

## A. The Culture of the Educational Institution

A theological institution's organizational culture is influential:

> Teaching, even when it occurs behind the closed doors of a tradi-
> tional classroom, involves not only the relation of student and
> teacher, but the entire organizational life of an institution of
> learning, which overtly and covertly shapes patterns of behavior
> between persons, and between itself and the rest of the
> world. . . . [T]he "teachers" within the curriculum include not
> only the faculty who formally lead classroom instruction and im-
> part the content of courses, but also the administrative practices
> of the institution; not only the audio-visual resources but life to-
> gether in the forms . . . not only the techniques of teaching in the
> classroom, but also the definition of proper "chapel" services;
> not only gender and racial diversity, but also the ways in which
> human relations are conceived within a given economic frame-
> work. A theological institution teaches far more than it is aware,
> and often most powerfully in ways of which it is scarcely
> aware.[17]

All this is part of the "hidden curriculum" of theological institutions,
and this either supplements, limits, or compensates for their educational practice. What people tend to learn most is what the culture of
an institution cultivates rather than what teachers teach. If this is
true, then, as the historian Glenn Miller points out, "To redefine
theological education is first to reconceive the institutions that teach
theology."[18]

Thinking of seminaries, in what ways would their organizational
culture undergo change if the institution moved in the direction of a
missional model of theological education? We can also put this ques-

---

17. R. H. Cram and S. P. Saunders, "Feet Partly of Iron," p. 24 (see also pp.
22-23). In regard to education more generally, see also (among others) A. P. Fiske,
*Structures of Social Life: The Four Elementary Forms of Human Religions* (New
York: Free Press, 1991), and Henry A. Giroux, *Ideology, Culture and the Process
of Schooling* (Philadelphia: Temple University Press, 1981).

18. Glenn T. Miller, "The Virtuous Leader: Teaching Leadership in Theological Schools," *Faith and Mission* 9 (1991): 31-32. He proposes that seminaries become more like liberal arts colleges, but at best this goes only part of the way towards what is necessary.

tion to Bible colleges or even lay centers, for while they are more oriented to mission or to a person's profession, they might still approach this at one remove from actual practice. Here are some steps such institutions could take:

1. They should give more missional content to their existing mission statement. It would then reflect the institution's commitment to the personal formation, theological reflection, and practical development taking place primarily *in* the pursuit of ministry alongside core figures inside and outside the seminary.

2. They should bring future recruiting procedures for both teachers and learners into line with this statement so that the institution's priorities are clear to all concerned. While this leaves room for some faculty to focus primarily on research and supervising, most would have to reconfigure courses and teaching methods in line with a missional approach.

3. They should build this new set of priorities into the work and teaching of top faculty-administrators in the seminary who can model these new priorities from the top. Trustees involved in teaching churches attached to it, or in other associated institutions, should also take a lead in this matter.

4. They should provide more personal and professional development for faculty or chief administrators who have difficulty implementing this. A further possibility is teaming such people with others who are capable of moving in this direction.

5. They should encourage some faculty to be involved in short-term, mobile teams engaging in theologically informed and personally formative mission. Alternatively, as my wife and I have done, some could move into a communal living situation with a group of students, a setting in which learning and growing together is grounded in a common life.

6. They should ensure that all aspects of the seminary are informed, formed, and ultimately transformed by a missional orientation to its surrounding community. This would leaven what takes place in classes and programs, in small groups and corporate worship, in publications and special events.

7. They should consider changes in the location and design of the seminary, for a mission-oriented enterprise has a different attitude about the kind of learning spaces it needs. Some institutions isolate themselves too much from the urban and suburban contexts in which

faculty and students minister, and some buildings have too academic a character to encourage a more holistic learning experience.[19]

8. They should encourage campus-based courses to engage directly with current worldviews, beliefs, values, situations, and practices; and to contain an apologetic, evangelistic, social, or pastoral element. Meanwhile, learning that takes place primarily outside the seminary should exhibit the same spirit of serious learning.[20]

Along with introducing these changes, the whole institution — not just its educational activities — should intentionally inculcate and reinforce a missional approach. Recent writings stressing the need to develop "learning organizations" could help here.[21] Peter Senge complains that though organizations communicate a range of things to their employees, they rarely work at this in an intentional way so that people learn what is most vital to know. Improving the flow of information or communication in an organization is only a part of this. Enhancing people's capacity to know what their work amounts to, and to produce results that really matter to them, is also important. This involves tapping their commitment and capacity to learn at all levels of the organization, helping them to master a certain discipline rather than be led from the top. It means enabling them to reconstrue the world and their relationship to it, and encour-

19. A way of building on this insight is to reexamine the christological foundations of our rationale for theological education. For example, an institution's understanding of the nature of Christ's work will influence the way it relates — or fails to relate — to its immediate environment. Its view of Christ and culture will affect the extent to which its curriculum engages in mission and helps its members integrate tradition and life. It could even implicitly or explicitly affect its choice of a physical location. See further J. A. Ban, *Christological Foundations of Theological Education* (Macon, Ga.: Mercer University Press, 1988).

20. Where, as in a few places, a seminary has a School of Mission, this and its School of Theology should be integrated so that theology becomes a truly missiological enterprise and missiology genuinely theological in character. Some of what happens in a School of Mission tends to cross over into territory occupied by a School of Theology — for example, biblical, historical, and theological courses with a missiological focus — and these would be better as part of the theological core, sometimes co-taught by faculty from both schools. Other distinctives will remain within whatever joint arrangements are developed.

21. Peter Senge, *The Fifth Discipline: The Art and Practice of the Learning Organization* (New York: Doubleday, 1990). A brief, and personal, introduction to his approach can be found in "Peter Senge: Making Better Organizations, Making a Better World," *Business Ethics* (March/April 1993): 17-20.

aging them to act in fresh and creative ways. Basic to this is institutional vision and clear, wide-ranging, systemic social mission that everyone in the institution understands and supports. Leadership in such an organization has more to do with designing, teaching, and modeling the way forward than with typical management functions and top-down decisions. It is not hard to see the relevance of Senge's approach to theological institutions.[22]

## B. The Culture of the Professional Guild

Here again, seminaries, and where they exist within or separate from seminaries, institutions for training Christian professionals, are particularly in view. In so far as Bible institutes and colleges seek to raise their academic credentials to the same level, what follows is also relevant to them. This is not the case for organizations where nonformal learning is the norm.

Through their status as accredited institutions and faculty involvement in academic associations, many theological institutions are part of an influential academic culture. In comparison with the situation before seminaries became common, this has brought obvious benefits at the level of personal and professional networking, setting and maintaining intellectual standards, and connecting with the broader academy. But the strong emphasis on academic respectability and accreditation also brings certain dangers. At this point theological institutions, especially those linked with universities, are vulnerable to criticism. Consider, for example, Karl Barth's farewell lecture in Basel during the winter semester of 1962-63. In too many theological institutions, he said,

> Everything is in order, but everything is also in the greatest disorder. The mill is turning, but it is empty as it turns. All the sails are hoisted, but no wind fills them to drive the ship. The fountain adorned with many spouts is there, but no water comes. Science there is, but no knowledge illuminated by the power of its object. There is no doubt piety, but not the faith which, kindled by God, catches fire. What appears to take place there does not really take

22. On this see especially Neely Dixon McCarter, *The President as Educator: A Study of the Seminary Presidency* (Atlanta: Scholars Press, 1996).

place. For what happens is that God, who is supposedly involved in all theological work, maintains silence about what is thought and said in theology *about* him (rather than *of* him as its source and basis). It does happen that the real relation of God to theology and theologians must be described by a variation of the famous passage in Amos 5: "I hate, I despise your lectures and seminars, your sermons, addresses, and Bible studies, and I take no delight in your discussions, meetings and conventions. For when you display your hermeneutic, dogmatic, ethical, and pastoral bits of wisdom before one another and before me, I have no pleasure in them: I disdain these offerings of your fatted calves. Take away from me the hue and cry that you old men raise with your thick books and you young men with your dissertations! I will not listen to the melody of your reviews that you compose in your theological magazines, monthlies, and quarterlies."[23]

This is a prophetic challenge to the theological guild, even if it requires two qualifications. First, we should not lay all the blame on the academy, for too often the church has been an accomplice in this arrangement. Intimidated by the guild, it has largely surrendered its theological agenda to it, and has allowed its best potential theological practitioners to become mainly academic theologians. Second, we should recognize that, despite the dominance of the prevailing academic model, some individuals and institutions have sought to resist its excesses. As well, through revising its standards for accreditation the theological guild itself is now opening itself up to a more holistic approach to theological education. At the level of teaching and learning this allows more room for personal formation. At the level of research and publication it opens up the possibility of imaginative integration of disparate theological fields and practical application of theology to contemporary issues. Even teaching itself is being considered as a scholarly activity.[24] Attention is also being given to broadening faculty development and evaluation.[25] It is not yet clear how far

23. Quoted in H. G. D. Wolff, *Joel and Amos* (Philadelphia: Fortress, 1977), pp. 267-68. This is Barth's paraphrase of Amos 5.

24. Philip S. Keane and Melanie A. May, "What Is the Character of Teaching, Learning, and the Scholarly Task in the Good Theological School?" *Theological Education* 30 (2) (1994): 40-41.

25. On this see the issue on "Faculty Development, Evaluation, and Advancement," *Theological Education* 31 (2) (1995).

these moves will go, or how much they will enable seminaries to avoid Barth's strictures, but at least they are heading in a healthier direction.

What shape would the ethos and expectations of the guild possess if it began to redefine its mission in terms of the model I am advocating?

1. Faculty in the classical theological disciplines would begin to perceive themselves and meet together in ways that had more in common with associations of practical theologians or of practicing professionals. This is simply an extension of Browning's proposal that all theological disciplines see themselves as aspects of a more fundamental practical theology, and of Sullivan's recommendation that the future training of professionals take place mostly in the context of their work. Following this through would open up discussion of teaching as well as research, as well as on how theological disciplines could advance personal and ministry development. Within this, faculty could design collaborative ministry projects with students, and explore the new issues these raise for theological research. Broadening of current approaches to mentoring of doctoral students could also take place. In other words, every aspect of the faculty's vocation as teachers, not just the academic component, would come up for reconsideration.[26]

2. Faculty would seek to develop a *theological understanding* of professional associations and publications. How much do theologians think theologically about the purpose, dynamics, and structures of professional organizations and meetings, apart from the content of their own presentations? Are we sure that we fully understand from God's point of view the purpose of such groups and meetings or what they could potentially achieve? All of us develop at least an implicit theology of professional conferences. We know they are not just about addresses, seminars, and workshops: they are about socializing and networking, job-hunting and recruiting, soliciting publishers and book buying. Is this all or even chiefly what they

26. There is a welcome move in this direction in Donald Senior and Timothy Weber, "What Is the Character of Curriculum Formation, and Cultivation of Ministerial Leadership in the Good Theological School?" *Theological Education* 30 (2) (1994): 32, where the importance of recruiting faculty with the formational as well as academic needs of students is kept in mind. While there is reference to faculty having close links with and ministering in churches, the idea of their modeling ministry and mission in some way alongside their students is not mentioned, except insofar as this happens in the classroom.

should be about? What would happen, for example, if participants in an annual theological conference committed themselves to a variety of collaborative ministry efforts during part of their stay in the city where they were meeting? In his book *The Trouble with the Church,* Helmut Thielicke advocates the holding of ecumenical gatherings only if their members contribute more than their dollars to the life of the place in which they gather.[27] As a small move in this direction, each year a People's Theology Group I helped coordinate prior to the annual AAR/SBL conference tried to draw in people from the host city in order to hear and address some of their specific concerns. If conference members sought some way of "seeking the welfare of the city" (Jer 29:7) — through accessing congregations, Christian organizations, marketplace spokespeople, voluntary associations, or civic bodies — it would provide a unique academic witness to the wider church and world.

3. Faculty research and publication could further extend this outward focus. Too much research and writing focuses on in-house concerns, and too much of this is purely technical, epistemological, and methodological. In other words, much of what passes for theological scholarship is merely a linguistic, historical, or philosophical exercise. While these disciplines, and others such as psychology, sociology, and anthropology, contribute much to theological reflection, they do not exhaust it. In particular, too much theology today lacks a vital prophetic edge: much of what passes as "prophetic" is secular social and political indignation in theological dress. Going further, more faculty should break out of their in-house disciplinary or ecclesiastical concerns and develop an intellectual mission to the wider culture. This is a special responsibility of Christian professionals teaching in seminaries or in other institutions seeking to integrate Christianity with a particular profession or professions. While Christian thinkers in universities sometimes undertake this, theologians in general rarely do so. The more theological faculty involve their postgraduate students in such work, both in joint writing projects and joint sorties into the main institutions in society, the more they would be modeling to them the importance of high-level missional scholarly work.

27. Helmut Thielicke, *The Trouble with the Church: A Call for Renewal* (Grand Rapids: Baker, 1965), p. 83.

## C. The Culture of the Wider Church

Theological institutions also overlap with congregations and denominations, and with parachurch and mission organizations. These structures significantly shape incoming students and are the main settings to which they return. For all the complaints about too great a separation between these and some theological institutions, their influence is still strong. This is legitimate. Problems arise only when such institutions are subject to the wrong kinds of expectations and pressures, or when confusion or misunderstanding occurs about the nature and role of the church. In the fifties, H. Richard Niebuhr argued that some of the uncertainty in theological schools stemmed from lack of clarity about the form, matter, relations, and composition of the church.[28] Almost all contributors to the debate on theological education, among them Farley, Hough and Cobb, Kelsey, and Chopp, make reference to the importance of the church and ecclesiology for theological education, and occasionally the reciprocal role of theological institutions in revisioning and reforming these.[29] This is not the place to investigate the purpose and role of the church, or of other Christian organizations; I have addressed these issues in other writings.[30] But unless fundamental changes take place in these settings also, any proposal for change in theological education will be severely limited.

There is a great need for a more relational form of congregational life and for redefining leadership primarily in terms of community building. The main images of the church and ministry today come from the traditional marketplace, or are strongly influenced by it. Though regular mention is made of other images of the church that have a more biblical ring, these tend to have little impact on the life of a congregation or are domesticated by it. For all their talk about being

28. H. Richard Niebuhr, *The Purpose of the Church and Its Ministry,* pp. 17-18.

29. See especially Chopp's chapter on "Places of Grace: The Practice of Ekklesia," in *Saving Work,* pp. 45-71.

30. See further Robert Banks, *Paul's Idea of Community: The Early House Churches in Their Historical and Social Setting* (Peabody, Mass.: Hendrickson, rev. 1994), and Robert and Julia Banks, *The Church Comes Home: Reshaping the Congregation for Community and Mission* (Peabody, Mass.: Hendrickson, 1997).

a "body" or "family," many churches have more in common with clubs, societies, businesses, and corporations. On the whole they are religious collectives rather than communities; they are retreats from the world rather than vanguards of the kingdom. Leaders in churches are "managers" and "directors," "counselors" or "therapists," "orators" or "lecturers," more than "leading servants" in the household of God or "community builders" among the people. While recent discussions of the "professional" model of ministry refer to facilitating community as an important element in pastoral work, they do not define community primarily in terms of relationships, and they continue to view leadership individualistically.[31] For all the complaints in seminaries about the quality of congregational life, or about the superficiality of sermons and programs, they offer little *theological* critique of these, despite the existence of significant biblical and theological resources for doing so.

Even from mainline denominational circles we are beginning to hear calls for a paradigm shift in understanding the church,[32] and for "reinventing the congregation."[33] Only if this happens can the church reclaim its proper responsibility for the theological agenda. Otherwise the theological education it calls for will remain too preoccupied with institutional and professional concerns, and will mute its calling to be a kingdom community whose prime task is to undergird its people's vocation in the world. One glimpse of what reinventing the congregation entails forms part of the well-known "dream" of the late Episcopalian Bishop Wesley Frensdorff:

> Instead of a community gathered around a minister, a ministering community: instead of a community gathered around a learning person (parson), a learned and reflecting community . . . a theolog-

31. On the professional model of ministry see J. W. Carroll, "The Professional Model of Ministry: Is It Worth Saving?" *Theological Education* 21 (2) (1985): 10-44.

32. It is this need for change that should qualify the suggestion in the report mentioned earlier by Donald Senior and Timothy Weber, *Theological Education* 30 (2) (1994): 29-30, that it may be time to give less attention to prophetic critique of the church and more to building up confidence in its capacity to actually make a difference.

33. On the first see Loren B. Mead, *The Once and Future Church: Reinventing the Congregation for a New Mission Frontier* (Washington, D.C.: The Alban Institute, 1991).

ically reflective community, knowledgeable in its basic traditions.[34]

Building communities — not only of understanding or faith, but of love and hope, is the basic responsibility of those at the core of the church. This, according to biblical scholars, is central to scriptural understanding,[35] and according to social critics, what contemporary culture most urgently needs.[36] But for this to happen, we must understand community primarily in relational rather than organic or mechanical terms.[37] Modeling this within the congregation is impossible as long as unbiblical ideas of the solo pastor and the clergy/laity distinction continue.[38] Ministry is the responsibility of the whole *laos* or people of God, with a group of core *laos* authorized to facilitate, equip, and commission them for their work in the world and church.[39]

In the early church, education took place primarily through the dynamics of communal life, as well as through ongoing family, workplace, and city involvements. In these basic communities, or house churches, there was creative interaction between the stuff of daily life, the traditions concerning Israel, Jesus and the apostles, and the dynamic presence of the Holy Spirit.

For the early Christians there was no fundamental distinction between learning (especially theological learning) and everyday life,

---

34. J. Borgeson and L. Wilson, eds., *Reshaping Ministry*, p. 226.

35. See, primarily for the Old Testament here, Paul D. Hanson, *The People Called: The Growth of Community in the Bible* (San Francisco: Harper & Row, 1986), and for the New Testament, Gerhard Lohfink, *Jesus and Community: The Social Dimension of Christian Faith* (Philadelphia: Fortress/New York: Paulist, 1984).

36. So Robert Bellah et al., *Habits of the Heart* (San Francisco: Harper & Row, 1985) and *The Good Society* (New York: Knopf, 1991).

37. See further the typology developed by F. F. Kirkpatrick, *Community: A Trinity of Models* (Washington, D.C.: Georgetown University Press, 1986).

38. See most recently and cogently the significant work, cited earlier, by the Catholic historian A. Faivre, *The Emergence of the Laity in the Early Church* (Mahwah, N.J.: Paulist, 1990), chapter 1.

39. Multiple staffs do not basically break this pattern, partly because they generally appear in large churches where the ratio of pastors to people remains roughly the same, and partly because in such a group there is always still a *primus inter pares*, the senior pastor.

[and] worship provided not only a setting for education, but was itself the expression of educational praxis in concrete actions.[40]

It was this common life together, oriented around participatory worship and fellowship, and directed towards obedience and mission, that constituted both the setting and the essential content of their theological education. Meetings became voyages of exploration, understanding, and encouragement within the more general adventure of life with God. It was in these meetings that people's dreams and hopes, stories and dilemmas, opportunities and disappointments, were expressed and weighed. The central focus of corporate worship was neither a sermon nor a cultic meal, but mutual bonding and instruction, with a view to living a counter-cultural lifestyle and seeking to bring God's justifying grace and concern for justice into daily life.[41] This took place through listening and praying, through singing and hearing, in the context of a full, and fully sacramental, sit-down meal, in which conversation was a vital factor.[42]

Where, in terms of further theological education, might this lead? Building on Wesley Frensdorff's dream, we would find people in these churches

> awakening to a sense of vocation with all the abundant energy and zeal which so often accompanies this discovery, [who] would not automatically be whisked away to seminary to be "formed and trained." Instead they would exercise their baptismal ministry in the community of the faithful in which the vocation was heard.

40. Cram and Saunders, "Feet Partly of Iron," pp. 44-45.

41. Rebecca Chopp, *Saving Work*, pp. 62-70, draws attention to the early Christians as a community of friends, in a counter-public sphere of justice, and refers to images of round table connection, kitchen table solidarity and welcome table partnership in the work of Letty Russell, *Household of Freedom: Authority in Feminist Theology* (Philadelphia: Westminster, 1987).

42. In the following centuries theological education was still for all members but became centered on formal catechetical instruction by a member of the priestly hierarchy, often prior to baptism. The loss of this dimension in the elitism fostered by the monasteries and universities was significantly reduced by the churches of the Reformation, which based their understanding of Christian education on the priesthood of all believers. Here too, however, a new clericalism developed which partly reintroduced the earlier divorce between expert and amateur, and an initial concern for the whole of life was replaced by a preoccupation with church-related concerns.

Those whom with the help of the Spirit the community identified as having the required giftedness, experience, and servant disposition, would be encouraged to find their place in one or other of a seminary's concentric circles of in-ministry learning, so that they could grow in their excellence in, understanding of, and personal resources for it. It would be understood that distinctions in role are not distinctions in rank but in function, so placing the issue of leadership in its proper context, for prior to questions about it are questions of community and it is from these that our models of leadership should devolve. They should not mainly come from outside, certainly not be imposed or self-appointed, but rather identified and affirmed in and for service which should model to the world what leadership-in-community or a community-of-leaders is all about.[43]

In small ecclesial groups, these people would continue their education, and teachers would visit these groups to learn and enter into dialogue. As all this took place we would find "ministering communities" rather than individual ministers engaged in theologizing, as well as interaction between the more grassroots theology in the churches and the more professional theology in the seminaries.

43. J. Borgeson and L. Wilson, eds., *Reshaping Ministry,* pp. 231-39.

# 4. Reshaping the Theological Curriculum

As contributors to the volume on The Good Theological School agreed, a curriculum is not basically "an accumulation of courses and other sorts of academic experiences but . . . an overall process of critical reflection and integration. The curriculum itself, understood in this holistic manner, is 'formative' in the full sense of the term."[44] Fundamentally, we are in the business of teaching people, not just courses, and of transforming their understanding in ways that will enhance them personally and vocationally, not just passing on knowledge. As indicated earlier, spiritual formation is a dimension of this. In the broadest sense, then, without confusing the two, the curriculum is formational and formation is curricular. But for this to happen, the course of study should have coherence stemming from the mission of the seminary; it should be flexibile enough to cover students' varied vocational goals, and to reflect the distinctive ethos of each school.

I have already made a number of suggestions about the form and content teaching might take if it had a more missional character. I will now focus on the primary goals and outcomes of a course of study, on some of its distinctive or representative components, and on its overall organization or shape. In the course of this I will also address the issue of what to do with the fourfold theological encyclopedia. Before launching into this, it is appropriate to take account of the general

44. Donald Senior and Timothy Weber, "What Is the Character of Curriculum Formation?" p. 22.

problems that can arise with the curriculum. The Third World theologian Emilio Nuñez has summarized these well. Sometimes the curriculum is too rigid or fashionable, sometimes too much an import from elsewhere or too pragmatic in character. In terms of its basic approach, it is sometimes biblicist or unfocused, sometimes reductionist or ideological, sometimes too theoretical or idealistic.[45]

## A. Curriculum Goals and Outcomes

To see the curriculum issue in proper perspective, we should begin by asking about the ends the curriculum serves. For many over the last two decades it has meant producing the best type of *servant leaders*. For such leaders, ministry is about service not status, authority is a consequence of function rather than position, and the main task is the eliciting, equipping, and empowering of others' gifts.[46] In a survey of several seminaries that sought to determine how well they prepared people for servant leadership in the church, Robert Ferris concluded soberly that the results were "not encouraging." Although some faculty modeled the desired characteristics, he found that "no consensus was observed related to curriculum elements intended to develop qualities of a servant minister" and that "demonstration of servant minister qualities in present seminary curricula, furthermore, exists primarily in unstructured, informal elements. Whatever the stated purpose of the seminary regarding training people for ministry, in practice other objectives dominated, especially those relating to specific course subjects or disciplines or to ecclesiastical traditions."[47]

At the least this suggests we have to reevaluate our estimate of curriculum and pedagogy; according to Ferris, these make only a secondary contribution to forming servant leaders. To overcome this deficiency, he argues:

45. E. A. Nuñez, "The Problem of Curriculum," *New Alternatives in Theological Education* (1988): 73-87, especially 74-80.

46. There is an overview of the discussion of this image in Donald E. Messer, *Contemporary Images of Christian Ministry* (Nashville: Abingdon, 1989), pp. 97-115.

47. Robert W. Ferris, *The Emphasis on Leadership as Servanthood* (Ann Arbor, Mich.: University Microfilms International, 1982), p. 159.

i. Theological schools should specifically state their commitment to training for servant leadership and adopt that as the integrating focus of courses, functions, and activities.

ii. Admissions officers should give special preference to persons whose applications evidence higher levels of a servant minister.

iii. The curriculum should undergo revision in light of the institution's clearly stated commitment to training for leadership as servanthood.

iv. The administration should explore means of developing the faculty's repertoire of teaching methods, with special attention to those which have demonstrated value in training for helping professions.[48]

A related way of approaching this issue of goals or outcomes is through the report of a two-year task force in my own seminary, involving both pastors of local churches and leaders in Christian organizations, one of which was in a marketplace setting. All of these had developed some creative approaches to ministry. The group was reflecting on the character of their ministry, and how well their seminary experience had prepared them for it. For all the differences between their stories, there were a number of common features. From these we can read off some of the key elements in creative ministry, and how best to help develop people for it.[49] For this particular group, the most desired outcomes of training for ministry were an ability to listen, to build community, to articulate vision, and to create flexible structures, long-term perspective, and a sense of timing. The character traits on which their ministry had most depended were a hunger for reality, recognizing their humanness, struggling with and surviving failure, exhibiting humility, operating relationally, and spiritual growth. They also emphasized patience, perseverance, and a willingness to take risks, pleasing God rather than the denomination.

Looking back over their seminary program in light of their ministry, what they valued most was, first, the proximity of good role models and, second, course content and methods that pertained to real life

48. Robert W. Ferris, *The Emphasis on Leadership as Servanthood*, pp. 169-76.

49. For a fuller account of this exercise, which was very much in the spirit of Hopewell's approach, see Robert Banks, "The Challenge of Tomorrow's Church to Today's Seminary," *Theology, News and Notes* (October 1993): 17-23.

— for example, the tensions in theology that helped them confront tensions in the real world. On the co-curricular side, they valued an emphasis on prayer and worship and the way certain people embodied these, the breaking down of fixed denominational and theological attitudes, the sharing between peers and the peer mentoring. What, from their point of view, were the changes most needed in seminaries to equip people better for creative and life-giving forms of ministry inside or outside the church? They suggested that there be (i) more time for genuine reflection, (ii) closer integration of main subject areas, (iii) more interest in understanding the wider culture, (iv) better help in balancing home and work responsibilities, (v) a stronger emphasis on personal formation, (vi) joint mentoring by faculty, pastors, and lay people, and (vii) greater assistance in dealing with the struggles and failures of ministry.

What this report underlines is the need to induct those undertaking formal theological education, whether heading into religious organizations or the general marketplace, into a set of *practices* — intellectual, personal, and vocational — that will stand them in good stead for whatever God calls them to do and help them to do this creatively and appropriately. This becomes especially important given the changing character of any kind of work today — including pastoral or other church or parachurch work — where it is difficult to predict exactly what will be involved. Along with a set of practices, students should also be forming a set of *attitudes,* at the center of which is a hunger for reality in their relationship with God, self, and others, as well as in their ongoing work, and an ability to build community inside and outside the church. For these practices and attitudes to develop, a genuine *understanding* of the Christian tradition — biblical, historical, and theological — is required, otherwise there is no base on which to build them. This understanding should also include awareness of what is happening more generally in the culture so that there can be a relevant and discerning contact with it. These attitudes, understandings, and practices — which is just another way of talking about personal formation, theological reflection, and ministry development — form an inseparable threefold cord that requires knitting together in the most effective way.

They will be most tightly woven together through *learning-in-ministry* rather than *learning-for-ministry* or *learning-alongside-ministry.* A missional approach to theological education gives to all three the sharpest focus, and brings them into contact with one another in the most vital way. It is like the difference between merely studying a play, reading it together as an exercise, and actually rehearsing and presenting it on stage. While the first two both have their part to play, participants gain most from them when they are working towards an actual production. It is then that the studying and reading come most to life and become most integrated in people's experience. In order for basic attitudes, understandings, and practices to be most strongly linked in the overall curriculum and in individual courses, we need to ask ourselves how we can (i) best set up the conditions for these attitudes, understandings, and practices to appear; (ii) most embody these three in our lives as well as our courses; (iii) teach in ways that model how these can impact most forcefully on others. Asking such questions is preferable to asking primarily what theological content our students will end up knowing, what personal experiences they will have undergone, or what specific competencies we want them to have. It is also preferable to asking primarily whether those working and learning with us are developing a true theology of God, gaining a certain theological *habitus*, or becoming practical theologians who will engage in relevant ministry. All three will come into their own, and find their proper place, if in fact they are not the main point of focus.

## B. Experiments in Curriculum Change

According to informal surveys, what most people coming into theological institutions desire is the opportunity to get to know their teachers personally, and learn from them in ways that will help them grow spiritually and minister effectively. The desire to know teachers in more than a classroom setting stems from students' interest in how their teachers live out their beliefs, what spiritual and communal resources they draw on, and whether they are engaged in ministry outside the institution, what theological knowledge they have, and why they have the views they do. While as teachers we regard academic concerns as the most important, students are equally or more interested in the personal and practical implications of what they are learning. This is no different to what brought most of the people into close contact with a prophet, the disciples around Jesus, or the group that ended up accompanying Paul. It is a natural and legitimate desire, and we should seek to satisfy it as best we can. We know the difficulties in even thinking about this. We are too busy already; there are too many students; it is not where our abilities lie. The following three experiments suggest ways we can respond to these student hopes. These are more holistic in character than reigning approaches and contain some missional elements. The first approach is a pilot Master of Divinity program in an extension center of a major seminary, the second a quasi-decentralized approach to ministry training for all students in a small-scale denominational seminary, and the third an alternative noncampus model of theological education for students in a minor denomination. There are some interesting similarities and differences among them. After outlining these approaches I will highlight their strengths and suggest ways they could move further in a missional direction.

1. A significant reshaping of students' experience, of theological education based in part on a cohort approach, is now in place in an extension center in the Northwest. This admits into the Master of Divinity program only twenty-five to thirty students each year, and these students take all their ministry courses together in sequence over the next three years. These ministry courses are taught by a mixture of extension-center faculty, visiting faculty from the main campus, and adjunct faculty from churches in the vicinity. Other courses in the biblical, historical, and theological areas are provided in the traditional way, though there are occasional colloquia attached to them to help students integrate their content with personal and vocational issues. Each year they also take part in a week-long summer intensive course in one of the classical subjects, held in a retreat setting with a faculty person teaching the course, and sometimes with his or her family in residence.

The courses students take as cohorts include regular worship experiences, exposing them to a variety of ecclesial traditions. Throughout their time in seminary students maintain existing or take up new part-time positions in local churches, sometimes voluntary and sometimes paid, under the supervision of a pastoral and a lay mentor. Sometimes they also continue to work part-time in secular employment. Monthly support groups for each student help develop annual growth-learning covenants for them. To help with evaluation, each student compiles a ministry portfolio, involving self-assessment and feedback from mentors and fellow students. There are also complementary assessments of various aspects of students' performance by individuals and peers, by faculty involved in the program, by learning support groups, by pastors and lay people in teaching churches, and by relevant denominational or congregational bodies. In similar ways there is a regular monitoring of the whole program's value.

2. A second approach is presently under way in a small denominational seminary in my home country. One of my earlier writings, I discovered, played a part in this development. In redesigning the program that all students undertake, the seminary wished to break away from the clerical paradigm of training, to integrate personal formation and practical ministry concerns with academic learning, and to bring the seminary into a closer working relationship with local churches. At its heart is "an instruction-action-reflection model, as exemplified in the lives of Jesus and Paul."[50] This involves:

i. relating instruction more closely to field work. This takes place through including reflection on field-based application in written assignments. Also by setting assignments in various departments that are essentially field-based, such as delivering sermons (communications), undertaking specific counseling activities (pastoral ministry), leading group scripture studies (biblical studies), and applying theology to pastoral encounters (for systematic theology). Another approach is to give teaching faculty responsibilities in the field.

ii. structuring field work more carefully as training. This takes place by orienting theoretical sessions in the curriculum to desired ministry outcomes and orienting field-based learning to theological reflection. The interaction between these two is cumulative. Coupled with this is contact with appropriate supervisors and ministry situations, together with campus-based analysis and synthesis of field experience.

iii. reorganizing placement of students in the field. After several introductory and survey courses, students are formed into six-member field teams for three semesters, followed by three semesters of individual field placement. In their three years in seminary, students spend twenty-five hours a week in the field, involving ten hours of supervision and fifteen hours of ministry, some of which directly

50. From an unpublished paper by Keith R. Farmer, "Integrating Academy and Field" (Sydney: Churches of Christ, 1991), p. 2.

relates to course work. The final semester involves an internship with a final two-week debriefing on campus.

iv. enhancing the role of the pastoral supervisor. Throughout this process, supervisors spend time with students individually and in teams, following careful guidelines and requirements that are available for public scrutiny. In these ways careful evaluation and accountability are built into the whole operation.[51]

3. The third field-based approach is a product of the Baptist-based Seminary of the East. Drawing on what it sees as New Testament precedent, this stresses the seminal role of the congregation in theological education, especially by house groups within it. Instead of a central campus, there are meeting spaces in churches scattered throughout the region. Here students train *in* ministry rather than *for* it. Ownership of the operation is in the hands of the local churches. Drawing fully on the best adult education principles, and the problem-positing approach to education developed by Paolo Freire, the program keeps classes small and focuses on students' learning rather than professors' teaching. At the heart of this model is a vision of personal discipleship, involving the development of "head, heart, and hands" for ministry. Since mentoring of students by professors is crucial to this, faculty must have spent at least five years in effective ministry and be spiritually mature.

Some of the main features of this approach are:

i. Every student has a supervisory team consisting of a faculty advisor, a pastor, and a member of a congregation. The latter two meet weekly with the student, and attend a monthly workshop arranged by the seminary containing relevant minicourses and discussion of faculty research and writing. The weekly supervisory conference with the student — attended once a term by the faculty advisor — focuses on the theological implications of what is being learned in the church or in courses, and a monthly log is kept. At the end of each term, in consultation with the student, the two church-based supervisors write separate reports on the general progress in ministry skills, character development, and other specific work. All three supervisors conduct an annual

51. Keith R. Farmer, "Integrating Academy and Field," pp. 2-3.

evaluation with a view to improving the quality of what is taking place the following year.

ii. Spiritual and character formation is encouraged through students determining, with faculty help, what they most need to work on during a year and how this can best be assessed. Each week students and faculty meet for an hour in discipleship cells to study scripture and pray about practical issues. The weekly supervisory conference already includes spiritual direction and mentoring. Alongside this there is the student's own personal experience of and growth in ministry.

iii. One day each week, courses take place at a central church location in different regions. These begin with an introduction to theological education, followed by study of the doctrine of the church. The general contours of a threefold theological encyclopedia are discernible in the subjects that follow, though there is less church history than normally. Teachers see themselves as educational facilitators rather than knowledge-brokers, and make considerable use of panel discussions, debates, small groups, forums, case studies, simulations, field trips, and general discussions. Their goal is to help students design personal educational projects that will meet their lifelong learning requirements. There is also a practical course on new church development that includes spouses of students, a small team from a local church, a faculty member, and a skilled church planter.

iv. Assessment by the lay and ordained supervisory team is primarily to establish how far the student has developed relevant competencies and what he or she needs to learn next. Students are not graded but placed on a scale according to whether they have merely learned some information, can make genuine personal observations about what they have studied, have properly internalized whatever they are focusing on, can take independent action on it, or have gained real proficiency. All this revolves around a series of individual learning contracts covering personal, academic, and ministry development. Students are held accountable to these, and contracts are renegotiated along the way according to their changing needs.[52]

52. There are similarities between this approach and the model proposed by Ted Ward, as recounted in Richard Carnes Neese, "The Road Less Traveled: Theo-

All these approaches move in the right direction. In light of what I have said about the strengths of my previous seminary's introductory course the ways in which they do this should be quite obvious. They place a greater emphasis on doing theological reflection as well as gaining theological knowledge, on the importance of personal and communal formation, on strengthening the link between the theology and ministry, and on cooperation between seminary and church, faculty and students. All of them seek to carry through these priorities in assessing students and all, in various degrees, individualize training to each student's needs, objectives, and circumstances. The third approach also hires faculty on the basis of these priorities, by looking for greater personal maturity and ministry experience than seminaries generally require.

Each of these approaches, however, still operates within certain

---

logical Education and the Quest to Fashion the Seminary of the Twenty-First Century," *Faculty Dialogue* 20 (1993-1994): 27-64. A further example of mission-oriented, field-based theological education comes from that part of my own country which is part of the Third World, that is, theological training of Aborigines for various kinds of ministry.

1. Students come to a central campus from different parts of the country, initially for a nine-month series of courses. Given the separation of Aboriginal tribes from one another, this forms an important part of their overcoming tribal suspicions and divisions.
2. After this nine-month exposure to basic Christian teaching, as well as enhancement of English language and community development skills, students return to their communities where they had been ministering.
3. During the following nine months study continues through a theological education-by-extension approach, with audio and written materials provided by the college and nearby graduates of the center assisting as tutors, together with occasional visits from the campus-based faculty.
4. They come back for an intensive seasonal program, before returning again to their field of ministry, where the same education-by-extension pattern continues.
5. Finally they return for another intensive time of study to complete their training.

Though this, and similar approaches, would require considerable adaptation to Western educational and cultural conditions, the risk in drawing on such models for inspiration is that seminaries will cry that academic standards are being lowered and these new models will be discredited, or these new models will be distorted to fit the preexistent knowledge package of seminary training.

limits. (i) Although the second speaks of trying to break through the clerical paradigm of theological education, it still focuses on training people for church-related ministries. Only in a supplementary way in external and extension courses does this takes place. Parachurch work, Christian organizations, nonprofit institutions, community work, public life, and marketplace ministry do not come into view in any of these approaches. The first and third in particular orient themselves exclusively to pastoral ministry. (ii) The degree to which they successfully integrate learning the biblical, historical, and theological tradition with personal, communal, and vocational formation varies. In the first approach, teaching the classical disciplines still takes place along traditional lines, and in the third approach practical ministry subjects tend to edge out some of these. (iii) With regard to supervision, in the second approach, which has only tutors in the field, this remains too campus-based, though this is not the case with the other two. In all three there are moves to bring faculty and students into a closer relationship, but even in the third approach, which maximizes this, they meet together only an hour a week. In the second and third approaches there is an attempt to involve faculty and students together in missional work, but this is only optional for faculty in the small denominational seminary; at the Seminary of the East it happens only once during the entire time in seminary, and in any case has been the hardest to get off the ground.

## C. Reframing the Curriculum

Earlier I looked at arguments for moving the theological encyclopedia, whether in its threefold or fourfold form, away from its dominant place in the curriculum. Some contributors to the debate believe that this structure should continue to exist as a general theological rather than as a specialized disciplinary framework. Despite its theological inadequacy, others view it as so entrenched institutionally that they are willing to tolerate it. A few conclude that, historical discipline apart, other areas can now continue only as "heuristic devices" to help us understand the connection between what we are doing and what earlier theologians have done.[53] What I would like to do here is step back for

53. So, for example, Cornel West, *Prophetic Fragments* (Grand Rapids: Eerdmans, 1988), p. 248.

a moment from this discussion and look at some attempts to structure theological education differently, returning later to the role of the theological encyclopedia. Extending the examples I gave in the last chapter of collaborative and integrative ways of teaching courses, I begin with the possibility, mentioned earlier in passing, of having a central theme for a year that could bring more cohesion to curricular and co-curricular activities.

One year at Fuller Seminary we decided to make "reconciliation" the theme, partly because of its overall theological centrality, and partly because it is a pressing issue in racially torn and economically divided Los Angeles. Where this was a major feature of a course, professors were urged to look for ways of relating it to issues inside and outside the campus. This took place across the three schools in the seminary — Theology, Psychology, and World Mission. Where other courses touched on the theme, professors were encouraged to highlight it in some way. The seminary president made it the focus of his first address to students in the new academic year, and weekly chapel services included it in sermons. It was also the chosen theme of an annual film festival in the city cosponsored by the seminary, and an annual festival of the arts in the seminary. The theme also appeared during a month devoted to African-American history and concerns, and was the subject of several student-organized brown-bag lunches, and several issues of the weekly student publication. Any number of other themes would lend themselves to being taken up in this way.[54]

A more thoroughgoing proposal suggests making "community" a major focus of theological studies. This could involve a series of courses examining students' calling, relationships, and common life. It could also draw in administrative aspects of the seminary's life and its relationship to other institutions. Attention could focus on the intersection of students' vocation and the seminary's mission, as well

54. As Calian argues, in *Where Is the Passion for Excellence in the Church?* pp. 29-39, forgiveness could form the centerpiece of a three-year core curriculum across the theological encyclopedia; a few integrative studies could be specially designed around such a theme; so could a field-based course integrating into this a history, ethics, and spirituality of forgiveness with an emphasis on helping local churches to become forgiveness centers. There could also be small group seminars under faculty leadership that probed enemies of forgiveness such as pride, power, property, and pluralism, by means of a case-study approach.

as on practical issues of community formation. Biblical exegesis, church and denominational history, theological and ethical study, and the practical disciplines relating to ministry, would all have a role here. Making "such a theme central would lead to a gradual change in the content and style of traditional courses, and would result in a new role for the traditional divisions within theological education. It could even lead to joint faculty-student publications and so to a new approach to research and writing."[55] In the course of time, the seminary as a whole might not only become a model of community life for congregations, but invite church leaders to return to the campus for ongoing discussion of this area. In this way the seminary "would operate on the time of the community, rather than on the time of lecture units."[56]

In all these examples, the traditional divisions of the curriculum remain in place, even if they serve a wider goal. A missional approach would take this a stage further. While at a secondary level it would preserve the general contours of the fourfold theological encyclopedia as a secondary organizing principle, it would refashion this to place the Bible in the center and then encircle it with history and tradition (study of the Christian movement, systematic theology, ethics), church and mission (apologetics, practical ministry, mission studies), experience and culture (personal formation, cultural studies, and other religions).[57] Two basic courses encompassing all the main disciplines could act as a preface, the first giving students access to theological resources for reflecting on everyday life, and the second assisting them to develop capacities to solve problems and implement ways of furthering discipleship and mission. In the examples of integrative courses mentioned above, what is also absent is again direct missional experience. If the focus on reconciliation, forgiveness, or community included their active pursuit outside the seminary, a greater degree of integration would take

55. This proposal is made by James N. Poling and Donald E. Miller, *Foundations for a Practical Theology of Ministry*, pp. 153-58.

56. R. H. Cram and S. P. Saunders, "Feet Partly of Iron," pp. 45-46.

57. This is close to, but a variation on, the revision of the Wesleyan quadrilateral suggested by Robert K. Johnston, "Becoming Theologically Mature: The Task of Theological Education," *Ministerial Formation* 73 (1996): 41-49. Johnston separates out experience and culture, and does not mention mission alongside church, though he includes it along with formation as a general dimension of the whole.

place.[58] But this is true for the whole program of theological study. Throughout, beginning with the two basic courses I have just mentioned, there would be dynamic movement between the actual challenges of everyday life for personal formation and ministry experience and reflection on these from a theological perspective. The curriculum would not have to follow a linear progression, but would possess a spiral structure that developed and drew into itself themes across courses. Courses would then represent stages on the way from reflection to practice, into reflection again, and back into practice; and they would move between a biblical center and a real-life circumference.[59]

Refashioning the structure of studies in the way I have just suggested brings courses in missiology — and, where they exist, departments or schools of mission — within the framework of theological studies instead of existing separately as they sometimes do. This would not lessen the importance or centrality of missiology for theology, so much as allow it to become the integrating center and operational framework for all theological study. If this is done, as Ray Anderson suggests:

> The variety of degrees granted by a theological seminary or college can each be defined in terms of ministry or vocational outcomes as appropriate, drawing upon a faculty which is rich in the interdisciplinary fields relating to the total mission of God in the world through his people. Where the content of the Bible is taught, there should be faculty who are experts in teaching the Bible, preaching from the Bible, using the Bible in addressing social and spiritual needs of persons, as well as those who are experts in the critical

58. Martin Thornton, *The Function of Theology* (New York: Seabury, 1968), argued many years ago that the training of reflective pastoral practitioners focusing on issues in the church and world required a more integrative approach to these with the help of all the theological disciplines as well as relevant field experience. He only had to generalize from this for all theological education, and go beyond field education alongside study to undertaking study in the context of active ministry, to articulate a fully developed missional model.

59. I am drawing some of this from an unpublished paper, mentioned earlier, on theological education by Tim Dakin prepared in the early nineties for Church Army Training Colleges. For a more recent alternative, see the proposed reframing of the curriculum along missiological lines by J. Andrew Kirk, *The Mission of Theology and Theology as Mission* (Valley Forge, Penn.: Trinity Press International, 1997), pp. 53-61.

study of the text and its sources. . . . In a similar way, where formal academic theology is taught, there should be faculty who are experts in evangelism and church growth, equipping members of the church for ministry, leading and managing the church organization, pastoral care and counseling, as well as experts in the history of the church's life and theology. Though this would lead to the displacement of systematic and historical theology as the theological core, and create a multiplex faculty with mission theology as the integrating force, systematic and historical theology would remain of critical, but instrumental importance.[60]

All that this needs to fit the model I am proposing is extending it to include engaging in mission as well as studying it, and drawing into the evaluation of students reflective practitioners and actual receivers of ministry.

## D. Integrative Postgraduate Study

Where does postgraduate study fit into a missional model, and what are its implications for faculty called to academic research and mentoring? There is a place for both, but only if their work is viewed differently to the way it is at present. On the one hand we need to recognize that such work is itself a form of action, not its antithesis. On the other hand, such work should have the character of "a thoroughly practical task in which a concern for application drives it from the beginning."[61] Schner concurs, arguing that we should assess theological scholarship by the way it contributes to various practical areas, including teaching and theological education.[62] For this to happen, there must be a move away from the "publish or perish" mentality that still pervades too many institutions. High-level research certainly has its place, but it has to be *put in its place*, alongside other essential components of the intellectual and educational task. The focus of such re-

60. R. S. Anderson, *Ministry on the Fireline: Revisioning the Church's Life and Mission* (Downers Grove: InterVarsity Press, 1993), p. 207.

61. Don S. Browning, "The Nature and Criteria of Theological Scholarship," *Theological Education* 22 (1) (1986): 8.

62. George P. Schner, "Theological Scholarship as a Form of Church Service," *Theological Education* 32 (1) (1995): 13-26.

search should primarily or mostly serve not *the academy* but the *church or world* in some intentional way. This does not mean it always has to have immediate, tangible relevance; but the pursuit of knowledge for its own sake by Christian intellectuals should primarily take place in universities rather than seminaries. It can take place in a seminary setting as a form of intellectual play or leisure, but this should not occupy center stage in a research and writing program.

Far from dissuading postgraduate students from pushing back the frontiers of knowledge, this simply means that they should attempt this in a way that deepens or extends ministry in the church and world. There are three basic questions here:

i. What existential questions have already surfaced for me out of my personal, church, or vocational life?
ii. How will my work edify the people of God or benefit a needy world?
iii. In what form can I best make my research available so that it will have a broader influence?

Asking these questions would also help these students identify the issues that would intellectually most advance the work of the kingdom. It would also lead to changes in postgraduate study programs. Instead of searching for a topic suggested by past, present, or emerging research, students should consider issues arising out of congregational life, everyday situations, vocational dilemmas, and community projects, that await academic investigation. James Hopewell and others have already opened up ways of studying congregational life, though this should move beyond analysis to include biblical, theological, and ethical critique as well as experiential, field-tested, practical theological recommendations. Such study and research can proceed from any disciplinary standpoint; it can draw on the social sciences, on practically oriented biblical, theological, or ethical evaluation; and it can include field-tested, practical theological recommendations.[63] Out of my own involvement with Christians in the marketplace, I know of several occupational groups that would welcome a postgraduate student to help them identify and work through some of their major pressures

---

63. Once again reference can be made here to James Hopewell, *Congregation: Stories and Structure* (Philadelphia: Fortress, 1987).

and dilemmas. At the broader cultural level, there are many problematic aspects of contemporary life that cry out for serious practical theological attention. In other words, at the postgraduate level there is much missionary work to be done!

There is another dimension of advanced theological study that needs attention. Those undertaking it who gain academic positions have to operate in more than an academic way. This is as true of those who end up teaching in Christian colleges. Unless they grow at the personal and relational level, as well as in their capacity to teach and administer, they will not be able to fulfill their faculty responsibilities properly. Farley touches on this when he notes how the recovery of *theologia* in postgraduate education requires teachers to transcend their guild loyalties and specializations so that they develop a genuine *paideia* and their mentoring serves the aims of church leadership.[64] We need only add to this the importance of leadership in the marketplace as well. Barbara Brown Zikmund has taken this further. We should be training people for the full range of responsibilities in theological institutions, not just for academic research or even teaching. We expect faculty to develop good relationships with their colleagues, help build a scholarly community, and perhaps initiate or engage in common theological research. We also expect them to care for and fulfill administrative responsibilities in the institution, and become active members in the guild and other scholarly or vocational networks.[65] If these are the kinds of people we would like to recruit, we need to nurture all these aspects of postgraduate life. In other words, we need to prepare them for their future ministry as *faculty*, not just as *academics*. As an example of what can be done here I include guidelines I helped develop for advanced studies in practical theology in my own seminary.

These define mentoring as:

- including a concern for the spiritual and communal, as well as academic, development of learners, to be worked out individually by faculty and through structured discussion;
- involving learners where possible as teaching assistants, co-

64. Edward Farley, *Theologia*, p. 199.
65. In an address at the Association of Theological Schools Bi-Annual Meeting in June 1993.

teachers, or adjuncts, so that through helping to plan, lead, and evaluate courses they can gain practical teaching experience;

- incorporating learners where feasible into occasional off-campus teaching activities, so that they can learn better how to relate their area of study to the wider Christian community;
- establishing a seminar where students and visitors can share and debate their work, and encouraging them to attend annual meetings of relevant professional societies;
- advising learners to link up with other networks revolving around particular vocational, gender, ethnic, or denominational concerns relevant to their study or ministry;
- providing opportunity to take on some small administrative responsibility, if possible alongside a mentor, so that students can gain experience of institutional responsibilities.[66]

---

66. A fully fledged missional model would extend this further, by looking for additional ways of engaging in co-ministry with students in various contexts outside the seminary or in other educational settings.

# Conclusion

Let me return to my earlier discussion of the three concentric circles of theological education. This three-tiered approach both supports and challenges our current practice of campus-based, extended education, and distance learning. A residential seminary or center experiences some overlap with what I have termed the first circle around a core figure. Extension-center theological education, which generally involves some time in residence on the main campus, possesses some parallels to the intermediate circle. Distance learning has some similarities with the outer circle, involving only a remote link to a teacher. So while all three have some warrant from the biblical writings, what we require is their reshaping in a missional direction, blending them in a way that fits the particular calling and life stage of each student.[67] This raises some important logistical questions.

1. It means that the whole idea of living in residence has to undergo some change. Increases in commuter students, extension courses, and distance learners have affected this, often in ways that have more to do with students' convenience than divine calling. There is still a place for it in most theological institutions, but we should reserve it more for those called to work closely with a faculty person. The mechanisms for doing this require careful attention. As mentioned earlier, these should involve prior testing of students in a distance-learning or extension-

---

67. This is already becoming a feature of certain proposals being put forward, and developments taking place, in Anglican circles in England.

center context, and through faculty contacts or recognized people in local churches, Christian organizations, and marketplace contexts. If there is a will to do this properly, the means will gradually emerge. The principle of residence will need to undergo a further change: apart from improving the quality of faculty contact for campus-based students, it must expand to include both groups' working together in ministry off campus. The language of residency is not adequate to this, and should be replaced with something more fitting.

Certain elements of what is still valuable in residency have ongoing value in extension-center and distance-learning settings. These include: engaging in regular corporate worship as a cornerstone of spiritual growth; learning corporately how to handle conflict and diversity creatively; enhancing the analysis and communication of others' ideas, insights, and experience; and developing appreciation of collaborative ministry through reflecting on life in the home, work, and church as well as school. Any future "mixed-mode" approach to training for ministry should retain these elements in some form or other.[68] But with more people undertaking theological education away from the main campus, and those on campus having more of their courses off campus, there will be less need for as much plant and facilities as are presently available. The relationship between the physical resources of the school and the nature of theological training that occurs there needs to be reconceptualized, and old assumptions about what is absolutely necessary reexamined. This will lead to an enlarging of the technological infrastructure of theological schools, and a reconfiguring and down-scaling of physical resources and support services to match new requirements and circumstances.

2. If we are to increase the quality of extension and individualized distance-learning programs, we need to significantly improve the way this happens. More and better resources have to go to our intermediate and outer circles. But supplying these is not the responsibility of institutions of formal theological education alone. Other stakeholders such as churches, parachurch groups, mission agencies, and lay centers have a unique contribution here, as they also do for the in-

68. See further the excellent analysis of individualized distance learning provided by Elizabeth Patterson, "The Question of Distance Education," *Theological Education* 33 (1) (1996): 59-74. See also *Residence: An Education* (ACCM Occasional Paper No. 38, 1990).

nermost circle of learner-doers. We should move towards *greater ownership* of training-in-ministry by all these groups, combined with *functional diversity* in the way they contribute. If seminaries and Bible colleges have most to offer the inner circle, churches and other Christian organizations have most to offer the outermost one. Working out the most effective ways of collaborating across all the circles will not necessarily be easy, but here and there we see the beginnings of this. Cooperation with churches could take several forms, for example, with an individual megachurch, a cluster of mid-sized churches, and a network of house churches. But we need to develop wide-ranging regional partnerships with parachurches and nonprofit organizations, with lay centers and organizations, and with Christian business and professional networks.

Decentralizing and diversifying theological education may help deal with two problems seminaries in particular are facing. First, at both the megachurch and house-church ends of the spectrum, they are the object of some suspicion. Practitioners view them as too academic, and as giving too little attention to spiritual and ministry formation. It is better to educate and equip leadership within the church or parachurch itself, cultivating those who have proven themselves in some form of ministry. Though megachurches and house churches have genuine grounds for complaint about seminaries, in going it alone they run the risk of excluding their own models of church and ministry from theological scrutiny, and their own students from contact with a more diverse range of people, traditions, and cultures. Past efforts at creating alternative theological institutions suggest that gradually they come to resemble the very model they sought to avoid. A win-win situation for such churches and seminaries would be a collaborative arrangement, where each has the possibility of contributing what they do best. This could significantly lower the cost of much theological education and open up the possibility of joint positions for some faculty with churches or other religious, nonprofit, and even marketplace organizations.

3. The approach I am suggesting would make theological education more accessible to a growing number of interested lay people. This is partly a problem of content, for most seminary programs focus on preparing people for church- or mission-related positions. Only in a few places have they rethought content from the vantage point of Christians who operate in the wider community, and only a few teach-

ers can relate their courses to lay issues and settings. A collaboration between institutions with a stake in resourcing lay people could make a real difference here. Connected with this problem is the relative inaccessibility of lay theological education. Experience shows that "a full-time residential program will have its greatest appeal to people who are preparing for a Christian service career. They gain a marketable skill and a valuable career credential; lay persons doing graduate theological education lose one or two years career advancement while they pursue what their employers regard as an unprofitable 'diversion.'"[69] It is not just residency or admission requirements that need overhauling, but the availability of courses. While some lay people who are undergoing a vocational transition may be open to taking part in a residential program, and others are occasionally willing to travel for intensive courses, for most such people theological education should take place in their *normal settings*.

Another group that is often disadvantaged by the cost and remoteness of theological training could also benefit here. I am thinking of students from other countries, especially poorer Third World students. The cost of theological education in the West is far too high for most students outside a few industrially and technologically advanced Asian nations. Unless there are a number of such people from various countries studying together, or some faculty have spent substantial time in such places, it is also difficult to contextualize what they are learning. These students can best apply what they learn in their own settings: the danger in spending too much time elsewhere is that they become so assimilated into Western culture that they lose their ability to relate effectively to their own, often staying in the West at the end of their studies. Many Western students would also benefit from spending time in a different environment. One way of funding this would be for Western students to continue paying for an overseas experience what it would cost them in their own country. The surplus could subsidize overseas students coming for a time to the West. If we developed greater collaboration between theological institutions in different countries, some overseas students could do most of their training in

69. R. Paul Stevens, "Marketing the Faith — A Reflection on the Importing and Exporting of Theological Education," *Crux* 28 (2) (1992): 11. He has in mind here institutions such as his own Regent College, Vancouver, but this also applies to others like New College, Berkeley, and the London Institute for Contemporary Christianity.

their own countries, yet also spend time in the West. A good model of this at the postgraduate level is the arrangement between some Third World seminaries, the Oxford Center for Mission Studies, and the Council for Higher Education in England.[70]

70. On the variety of possibilities, see further Ken R. Ganakan, "The Training of Missiologists for Asian Contexts," and Viggo Søgaard, "Missiological Education Through Decentralized Partnerships," in L. D. Woodberry, C. Van Engen, and E. J. Ellison, eds., *Missiological Education for the 21st Century: The Book, the Circle, and the Sandals* (Maryknoll, N.Y.: Orbis, 1996), pp. 114-15 and pp. 200-201, respectively.

# CONCLUSION

> I suppose I am asking for nothing less than the conversion of
> seminaries.
>
> ALAN JONES[1]

The suggestions I have made in the previous section all have the present system of theological education in view. They demonstrate that though movement towards a missional model is practicable, there will only be substantial progress if changes take place at all the levels discussed. Fully embracing this paradigm, however, requires institutional reform on a wide scale. But so far I have said little about the financial implications of such a move. These cannot be ignored. For example, while many students express their longing for more spiritual formation and on-the-job training, are they willing to pay for this rather than the usual kind of educational qualification? Also, while I have outlined the changes in outlook and approach most faculty will need to undergo, how realistic is it to believe that these will take place? Will not the combined weight of these factors and the usual institutional inertia effectively vitiate any hope of my proposal being taken seriously?

---

1. Alan Jones, "Are We Lovers Anymore: Spiritual Formation in the Seminaries," *Theological Education* 24 (1) (1987): 11.

# 1. Further Barriers to Institutional Reform

## A. Financial and Personal Constraints

As noted earlier, many theological institutions, especially some older mainline seminaries and some newer lay centers, are either living off a depleted financial base or existing on a razor-sharp financial edge. Apart from the small number of heavily endowed or rapidly growing institutions, most have to keep a close watch on their monetary resources and are involved in cost-cutting or downsizing. Given this state of affairs, and the probability that it will only get worse, how likely is it that the kinds of changes I have mentioned will find a welcome? Since such exigencies normally place institutions on the defensive, the odds do appear to be against what I would like to see happening. But two factors give pause for hope.

First, in times of pressure there is always the possibility that some institutions will not close their ranks around present practice but instead open themselves up to more radical change. It all depends on the sense of threat they feel about their future or the kind of vision they see for new opportunities. It is generally when things are going well that institutions alter least; for the most part it is the appearance of some unexpected possibility or setback that lays the foundations for some change of course. Second, many of the suggestions I have made will actually *lower* the cost of theological education. For example, drawing on the expertise of more reflective practitioners is less costly than always hiring full-time, academically qualified faculty; moving courses partly or wholly off-site reduces the need to maintain or acquire as much physical plant; creating room for more extension or distance-learning courses lessens the cost of theological education for both students and the institution. These are only some of the areas where savings may take place. Where this entails reducing the number of regular faculty, in most cases these could develop links with congregations, parachurch groups, nonprofit organizations, or lay centers as theologians-in-residence and partly supported by them.

What about the personal hopes or expectations of students and faculty? Are students prepared for the paradigm shift involved in a missional model of theological education? Some may feel that this will not be as prestigious as the more "ivy league" education they can presently obtain. Others may wonder whether the qualifications they receive will carry as much weight with the judicatories and organizations to whom they will be applying for jobs. These responses are all too likely. On the other hand, the more holistic approach to theological education embodied in a missional model will also attract other people who presently keep their distance. In any case, helping students to see that their view of education and qualifications is inadequate is surely part of the educational task of theological institutions. Indeed, we should tackle head on the elitist and at times materialistic values embedded in so much thinking about status and qualifications with respect to ministry, as is already happening in the best institutions.

Undoubtedly, many faculty will resist the shift away from an academic model. Yet, as the new ATS Standards indicate, such a shift is gradually taking place, and some faculty are welcoming this shift with open arms. What I am proposing goes further and is more threatening, not only to many trained in the classical theological disciplines but in practical theology as well. Some consider that academic standards have already fallen too far, and would see my suggestions as further evidence of decline. We have to help such faculty see beyond the criteria for excellence that have predominated since the Enlightenment, to earlier, more holistic ways of assessing the value of theological education. This takes time and will not always succeed. Only astute and patient institutional encouragement of faculty has much chance of easing them through the transition.

## B. Space and Time Considerations

Quite apart from these financial and personal obstacles, there are two other major constraints. One has to do with the issue of space, the other with the pressure of time.

Some institutions' link with their campuses is so strong, and so much history is embedded in them, that they have become almost sacred sites. Who will be willing to consider partly or perhaps wholly moving from these locations to enable a more vital working partnership between those teaching theology and others who are thoughtfully living it out in the field? Although on occasions campuses do close down, merge, or move, it is basically on economic grounds over which they feel they have no choice. Lacking desperate financial circumstances, how many institutions are open to moving in the direction I am proposing? Being realistic, probably just a few. Yet perhaps this is all we need. If even only a few took this step, especially if they contained one or two widely respected institutions, this would open up the possibility of others considering such a move and in some cases ultimately making it.

The pressures of time and busyness are so endemic in most theological institutions today that it is almost impossible for people in them to really think through the basic issues confronting theological education, let alone embrace a new model for it and work out its practical implications. It is partly because of the weight of their existing responsibilities that faculty have had such little discussion of any proposals put forward in the debate, let alone one involving as far-reaching changes as the missional model.[2] Only an easing of their teaching and administrative load would provide much hope of anything substantial happening. In a cost-cutting climate, where faculty loads tend to be increasing rather than decreasing, this is not easy. But more use of students with skills and experience in the classroom, and a legitimate downsizing of committee work, would begin to make a difference. Even if only a few faculty made time to think through these issues and move forward on them, unexpected possibilities could open up. As more than one expert in change dynamics has said, it takes only 5 percent of a group to begin serious discussion of the need for change, and once 15 percent of a constituency commits itself to this, it is only a matter of time before what they are seeking largely becomes a reality.

Among contributors to the debate, some do see the possibility for

2. James Fowler, in Richard Neuhaus, ed., *Theological Education and Moral Formation* (Grand Rapids: Eerdmans, 1992), p. 217, argues that this is a problem just for developing a more formational emphasis in seminaries. As he says: "I see the problem in terms of our seminary regime building no leisure into life . . . our manner of ordering life is, on the one hand, individualistic, and on the other, exceedingly full."

change as limited. Some of them do not press for much change in the fourfold theological encyclopedia, even though ideally this is what they prefer. On the whole, though, they seem to assume that in time schools could make many of the changes they are proposing, though whether this view is too naive is a good question. Is there anything we can learn here from students and theorists of change? These generally distinguish between two types of change: one that modifies only an institution, and one that changes the system. While both have their place, where circumstances require more substantial change, incremental adjustments tend to compromise new endeavors so much that they never realize their potential. Also, substantial change happens more in private enterprise than in professional bureaucracies like theological schools.

Yet some contributors to the debate envisage the possibility of some radical alterations, at least in the effects of technological innovation.[3] "Some institutions may be forced to adopt, and others may choose, a very different model. Teaching and learning may be so reconfigured that traditional classrooms are no longer necessary, or the physical site of a school may be a technological center with teaching and learning taking place in a variety of other sites."[4] Could this take place around an approach to theological education driven more by a conceptual than technological change? If the recent debate about seminary education is anything to go by, "rarely does any fundamental question regarding the existence of a theological seminary arise." An alternative vision raises the question: "Which of the traditional, mainline theological institutions will be willing to risk a different way?"[5] As the historian George Marsden concludes: "Reformation isn't going to come from seminaries, even reformed seminaries. If there's going to be a reformation, which I think is needed, it will have to come from institutions other than seminaries."[6]

3. P. Watzlawick, J. Weakland, R. Fisch, *Change: Principles of Problem Formation and Problem Resolution* (London: W. W. Norton, 1974), p. 10.

4. James H. Evans, Jr., and Jane I. Smith, "What Is the Character of the Institutional Resources Needed for the Good Theological School?" *Theological Education* 30 (2) (1994): 50.

5. R. H. Cram and S. P. Saunders, "Feet Partly of Iron and Partly of Clay: Pedagogy and the Curriculum in Theological Education," *Theological Education* 28 (2) (1992): 41, 46.

6. George Marsden, in Richard Neuhaus, ed., *Theological Education and Moral Formation,* p. 153.

If this scenario is correct, where does it leave faculty who wish to head more fully and quickly in a missional direction? Must they resign themselves to this situation and seek ways to nurture a more missional approach informally in churches and other settings alongside their official responsibilities? Could they have more room to experiment within the existing structures? Or should they move outside their seminaries and begin to develop a more thoroughgoing missional model? Alternatively, do we as Marsden tends to suggest need new types of institutions for theological education? And if so, where and how are these beginning to appear? In addition, are there any resources or networks that might guide those who are ready to take up the challenge? These are the questions I would like to address in what follows.

# 2. Other Avenues for Change

## A. Informal Opportunities

There are a number of good examples today of faculty supplementing their regular teaching with missional activities in settings that involve students. These take many forms. In the seminary where I did my basic training, all faculty and students went out in teams for two weeks each year on evangelistic missions in parishes. In my previous seminary, some faculty involve students periodically in a range of largely informal missional activities. These include:

- a ministry group, headed by a faculty person, that spends time with local congregations and models pastoral and other skills;
- immersion experiences in which faculty develop students' contextual awareness and sharpen their vocational calling;
- involvement in counseling, healing, and apologetics that demonstrates how a faculty person practices what he or she teaches;
- using part of a sabbatical to spend time involved in creative ministry as a theological advisor, coworker, and recorder;
- leading a mission team made up of students in an ethnically, culturally, or nationally different context.

Apart from seminaries, Bible institutes and training colleges tend to institutionalize these kinds of learning experiences and build them more into the curriculum. Other faculty in all types of theological education could follow their example. The form these missional activities take can vary as much as a faculty's ministry concerns, thus creating room for variety. Becoming involved in such joint ministry activities can bring greater challenge into a faculty person's life, as well as provide new material for teaching and open up new avenues of scholarly inquiry. In seminaries where little movement in the direction of a missional model is taking place, these opportunities become all the more important. Such ventures between faculty and students give rise to what we may call a little "seminary within the seminary," that prophetically points the way for the seminary as a whole.

In time, engaging in this kind of activity might help seminaries and other theological institutions to consider new kinds of learning experiences or courses that are as inventive in approach as in content. In a sense, all that these informal opportunities require is a more intentional theological dimension. Providing more theological preparation for, reflection on, and evaluation of, such activities opens up the possibility of taking them for credit and of building them into the regular educational program. If faculty-led archaeological trips to Palestine, or tours of Turkey following in Paul's footsteps, can gain academic credit, why not other thoughtfully designed and taught faculty-student excursions? This would move us on from informal co-curricular missional activities to formal curricular ones open to a wider range of students.

## B. Institutional Openings

In some seminaries such institutional opportunities already exist. These mostly occur in the field of urban ministry. Here the challenges and complexities are so great, the need for a genuinely contextualized theology so critical, the discovery of practical ways forward so pressing, the ethnic and cultural mix of students so striking, their financial situation so slender, and the time left over from part-time jobs and churches so limited, that only a different kind of ministry formation has much appeal or integrity. In most theological institutions, urban ministry programs tend to have more flexibility than other parts of the curriculum. Accrediting agencies also realize that standards and criteria for evaluation should be more flexible. In a few places, mostly through the appointment of a creative director and the openness of the top administration, faculty can take full advantage of these openings to set up an urban ministry program with a strongly missional character.

Consider, for example, the urban ministries program developed under Eldin Villafañe at Gordon-Conwell Theological Seminary, which has influenced what takes place in a number of other institutions.[7] Villafañe argues that theological institutions with such a program ought to indicate their seriousness by including reference to urban theological education in their mission statement, by making a long-term commitment to it, by incorporating its concerns into their co-curricular activities and upper administrative operations, and by granting it a serious stewardship in their financial, intellectual, and personnel resources. The program developed out of a partnership between the seminary — located in a wooded area northeast of Boston — and churches and parachurch organizations in the city. Prior to this, all were grappling with the need for renewal and reform in the church, and for justice and human development in the community. The program matches its structure and dynamics to the specific social, economic, and political needs of its context. All parties are committed to helping their members reflect and act on this in a participatory, liberating, creative, and effective way.

Organizationally this involves:

- situating the urban program, both administratively and operationally, in the specific contexts where ministry in the city is taking place, for little that is worthwhile can be done at a distance;
- appointing as key administrators and as some of the faculty in the program credible representatives of the main constituencies served;
- developing a nonhierarchical and nonbureaucratic, face-to-face, and communal administrative style and ethos that reflects the sociocultural realities and needs of the groups it is serving;
- shifting the location of classes into church and parachurch facilities, and holding classes at times most convenient for church leaders and others who wish to take part.

7. See especially Eldin Villafañe, "Elements for Effective Seminary-Based Urban Theological Education," in Rodney L. Petersen, ed., *Christianity and Civil Society: Theological Education for Public Life* (Maryknoll, N.Y.: Orbis/Cambridge: BTI, 1995), pp. 121-36, and Efrain Agusto, "The Gifts of Urban Theological Education: A Personal and Professional Reflection," *Theological Education* 33 (1) (1996): 93-105. Agusto highlights the way urban theological education also gives a voice to disadvantaged groups in society. On other approaches to education for urban ministry, see now R. V. Kemper, "Theological Education for Urban Ministry," *Theological Education* 34 (1) (1997): 51-72.

Educationally it involves:

- combining theological reflection, ministry practice, and personal formation in the context of understanding the complexities of the city and the diversity of ministries within it;
- embracing the whole range of ethnic minorities, blue collar groups, middle-class employees, and upwardly mobile professionals in its concerns and language;
- developing an integrated action-reflection and reflective-action approach that includes the classical disciplines but dialectically relates them to the practice of ministry;
- creating different levels of programs from certificate to postgraduate levels to fit people's varying educational qualifications and ministry experience;
- designing and reviewing the curriculum as a joint effort between faculty, administrators, and students, the latter often being church or community leaders;
- establishing colloquia, reflection groups, and mentorships that are credit-bearing, and so integrating classroom content, in-ministry experience, and personal formation.

As well, there are a number of one-off educational events set up according to need, changes, and opportunity. These range from special forums through city-wide conferences to short-term seminars.

Central to this program is that those who lead and teach it all live in the context of ministry, exercising their gifts both in churches and in the community. In this way they become role models to students of what to do as well as what to think, of practice as well as understanding. They incarnate their teaching in concrete service. Though the program does not draw as specific a link between the active ministry of such people and the particular classes they teach, the possibility of doing this lies open and would further enhance what takes place. Here, then, is one setting at least in which members of a seminary, whether faculty or students, who have a commitment to a missional approach to theological education, might find a place to develop some of their particular interests. In so doing, they have an opportunity both to develop a more holistic form of theological education and to actively seek the welfare of the city around them. This missional model within the more traditional model of theological education could assist the whole seminary to move more in this direction.

## C. Innovative Organizations

Whether or not theological institutions move in the direction of a missional model, for the time being there is also a need for institutional experiments in theological education for the coming century. In the past, significant change has often come from groups operating on the margins of institutional Christian life, whose insights and practices only later influenced the mainstream. Over the last thirty years, we have seen several experiments in new forms of theological education. Some of these lasted for a while and then scaled down their aspirations, either because they could not find support, or because unknowingly they disadvantaged themselves by imitating too much of the reigning model of theological education. Others are still in progress and going well, partly because they are an extension of proven innovative approaches, and partly because they involve people who have gained respect for modeling what they are attempting.

I can think of two such endeavors that moved part of the way toward this missional model. Though neither — given its particular constituency — felt compelled to go all the way in this direction, in both cases they could have gone further. The first of these experiments developed out of the globally recognized ministry of a church statesman.

1. Beginning in a disused church building in the center of a major world metropolis, surrounded by businesses, shops, and commercial enterprises, in its initial phase it ran three two-month residential courses annually for local and international graduate students. It also developed evening courses for people who work in the city and summer schools for attendees from all over the country, with occasional extension centers in various provincial cities. Admission to the program did not require qualifications, and participants did not receive qualifications when they concluded it. The main purpose of its lengthier residential programs was to give students a greater awareness of the way the Christian faith should relate to the changing global scene. There were courses in biblical studies, theology and ethics, apologetics and mission. A small number of regular faculty, actively involved in ministry, taught some of these courses, as did a number of reflective

practitioners helping as adjuncts or visitors. Nonresidential courses concentrated more on a theology and ethics of work, neighborhood and city, covering a wide range of moral, social, political, and cultural issues.

2. Another experiment grew out of the needs of a constituency poorly served by most theological institutions, that is, graduate lay people wanting to undertake theological education. The main goal was to help marketplace Christians integrate faith with their family, workplace, civic, church, political, and cultural life. Attendees could take courses at both the diploma and degree level, mostly at times when they were free from their work responsibilities. This meant a large number of evening and weekend classes, as well as summer and winter intensives, with extension programs in several parts of the city. Those who regularly taught in the program sought to relate the classical theological disciplines to the areas and concerns mentioned above, and to exemplify this in their own lives. Students also met weekly with these faculty for a time of sharing, reflection, and prayer, and twice a year went on retreat with them to deepen relationships and build community.

Though both these initiatives changed course after a number of years, they illustrated possibilities for approaches to theological education that reached a wider group of people and covered a wider range of concerns. In both cases, students engaged in missional work, and pursued study with the goal of integrating this with their regular activities. In the first case, their instructors had long-standing and ongoing experience in the areas and issues they were discussing. Though not actively leading their students into field-based ministry, they maintained their own ongoing ministry commitments. In any case, some students had decided to take a short time away from their work to reflect on what they were doing, and others sought to integrate study into their daily routines. In the second case, the majority of students were also folding their studies into their everyday concerns, and were encouraged to regularly connect their studies to other aspects of their lives and complete a final major integrative project. In this institution there were also more adjunct and visiting than regular faculty, most of them reflective practitioners working in the fields in which they were teaching. The handful of regular faculty had extensive ministry experience, participated in ministry projects of various kinds, and in one case, lived in a mission-oriented community with a number of present and past students.

Other continuing experiments take a further step in the direction of a missional model. I mention three that indicate something of the range of possibilities.

1. Consider an adaptation of the Pauline approach to ministry formation under a Chinese-Canadian church planter. The latter, who has high theological qualifications, has developed a practically based, spiritually formative, theologically engaged form of training for successive groups of around twelve students and their spouses over a three-year period. This begins with a lengthy study of the Sermon on the Mount. The focus here is as much on learning obedience as gaining understanding. Study of other biblical, theological, and ministry areas follows. Learning is communal, with classes taking place mostly in the church planter's home — where a number of the students also live — and in various ministry settings. Throughout the program students are frequently observing the way their mentor planter lives out his faith as he works in evangelistic, church-founding, and pastoral settings. There is also regular praying and worshiping together, and reflection on personal and relational growth. Students only graduate when, after completing their studies and apprenticeship, they have demonstrated their capacity to evangelize seekers and plant a church themselves.

2. Next consider the work of a well-known church in the national capital. Its year-long so-called "school for servant leadership" is a hands-on learning experience in an economically disadvantaged, racially volatile part of the city. Alongside courses focusing on personal formation, biblical and theological understanding, ministry skills, and cultural interpretation, students learn to undertake ministry to and with the urban poor. Classes are taught by long-term members of the mission communities or house churches within the congregation. All of them embody what they are teaching on a daily basis. Participants in the program live in one of these ecclesial mission groups and join in their weekly corporate worship. They also belong to reflection groups where they have opportunity to discuss the connections between what they are learning, doing, and experiencing.

3. Finally, here is a glimpse into the new venture in theological education I have just joined. An interdenominational group in Australia is developing a lay theological education program in collaboration with a major university in a capital city. This group has founded a learning company that has been granted permission by the university to develop courses and programs it will accredit. These include:

(i) several courses in Christian studies that undergraduate students could fold into their Bachelor degrees;

(ii) a quarter or more of the courses in undergraduate or graduate programs of schools within the university in which Christians are training for various professions and occupations, for example, education, health care, business, the media, law, etc.;

(iii) the possibility of developing a new degree at the master's and doctoral level for lay people wishing to integrate their work and their faith, or desiring to develop an operational Christian worldview or understanding of servant leadership.

Where does the missional component enter directly into this venture? All these programs will be led by vocationally oriented teachers who are themselves engaged in active service in the world and church, in collaboration with highly regarded reflective practitioners with extensive experience in the marketplace. Participants in the programs will be teamed with individual and group mentors who can encourage them on their vocational path. Learning will take place in a communal way, and assignments will have a practical reference. Some courses, or parts of courses, will take place in workplace or everyday life settings and involve experience of these as part of the learning process.

These are just a few examples of what a missional model of theological education might involve. They are suggestive only, not prescriptive, but they at least point the way to some of the newer forms theological institutions may take in the future. As I reach the end of this book, I would like to return to its beginning. I began my investigation of the debate by considering the work of Edward Farley. As the one who largely initiated the ensuing discussion and continues to play a major role within it, it seems only fair to give him the last word before I conclude. In one of his most interesting statements he expressed the view that our time is "a situation parallel to other times in the history of Christendom — the early Middle Ages, Europe prior to the rise of universities, the United States prior to the coming of the seminaries — when a whole new institutionality was called for."[8] It will be clear from what I have proposed that I am very much in agreement with him here. As in earlier times, both the challenges before us and the prece-

8. Edward Farley, *Theologia: The Fragmentation and Unity of Theological Education* (Philadelphia: Fortress, 1983), p. 16.

CONCLUSION

dents behind us call for a new form of ministry formation that pre-
serves all that is valuable in our present model but also goes beyond it.
We must do this not only because the past encourages it and the future
demands it, but because we have the presence of our ever inventive
God to aid us in our work.

# Index

American Association of Bible Colleges, 7
Anderson, Ray, 236
Anselm, Saint, 166, 203
*Apologia,* 75, 146; Stackhouse on, 40-41, 148-49
Apprenticeship model. *See* Missiological education
Aquinas, Saint Thomas, 64, 65, 68, 183
Association of Theological Schools (ATS), 4, 5, 63, 200, 248
Aston Training Scheme, 154-55
Augustine, Saint, 180-81, 186, 205

Barth, Karl, 214-15
Basic Christian community. *See* House church
Betz, H. D., 112
Bible Institutes. *See* Theological institutions
Boman, Thorlief, 151
Bonhoeffer, Dietrich, 121, 203, 205
Browning, Don, 160, 216; on four movements in practical theology, 160
Brueggemann, Walter, 77, 81
Burtchaell, James, 186

Calvin, John, 65, 203
Cannell, Linda, 201
Catholic approach to theological education. *See* Confessional model
Chesterton, G. K., 42
Chopp, Rebecca, 54-56, 60, 218; on doing theology, 55-56; on feminist theology, 55; on idea-forming practices, 54-56, 61. *See also* Dialectical model
Church leadership: as community building, 218-20, 222; professionalizing of, 35-36; as servant leadership, 224-25; and theological education, 1-2, 53, 59. *See also* Communal formation; Cobb, John B., Jr.
Classical model, 17-33, 70, 143; criticisms of, 31-33; divine wisdom in, 19; personal formation in, 24-27; social transformation in, 28-31. *See also* Personal formation
Clement of Alexandria, 145, 180
Cobb, John B., Jr., 34-36, 38, 43-44, 61-62, 133; on professional church leadership, 35-36, 44, 53; on sociopolitical realities in theo-

263

264